Fictions of Old Age in Early Modern Literature and Culture

Routledge Studies in Renaissance Literature and Culture

Fictions of Old Age in Early Modern Literature and Culture

Nina Taunton

Routledge
Taylor & Francis Group
New York London

Routledge
Taylor & Francis Group
270 Madison Avenue
New York, NY 10016

Routledge
Taylor & Francis Group
2 Park Square
Milton Park, Abingdon
Oxon OX14 4RN

© 2007 by Taylor & Francis Group, LLC
Routledge is an imprint of Taylor & Francis Group, an Informa business

International Standard Book Number-10: 0-415-32473-4 (Hardcover)
International Standard Book Number-13: 978-0-415-32473-1 (Hardcover)

Library of Congress Cataloging-in-Publication Data

Taunton, Nina.
    Fictions of old age in early modern literature and culture / Nina Taunton.
        p. cm. -- (Routledge studies in Renaissance literature and culture ; 8)
    Includes bibliographical references and index.
    ISBN 978-0-415-32473-1 (alk. paper)
    1. English literature--Early modern, 1500-1700--History and criticism. 2. Old age in literature. 3. Aging in literature. 4. Intergenerational relations in literature. 5. Old age--History. 6. Shakespeare, William, 1564-1616--Characters--Older people. I. Title.

PR428.O43T38 2007
820.9'354--dc22   2006037343

Visit the Taylor & Francis Web site at
http://www.taylorandfrancis.com

and the Routledge Web site at
http://www.routledge-ny.com

To the memory of
my brother, my mother and my father
as always

Contents

Illustrations

Acknowledgments

I want to express my gratitude to Brunel University and the School of Arts for twice providing relief from teaching and administrative duties in order to research and complete the writing of this book. My thanks go also to Tala and Thomas Birch, proofreaders extraordinaire, to Max Novick for his accessibility, help and guidance, and to the two anonymous readers for their faith in and support of the project in its initial stages. My most heartfelt thanks go to the three friends and colleagues who gave up their time to wade through drafts of this work; Lawrence Normand for his expert advice, his perceptive and careful reading of the chapter on old witches, Tony Bromham, a Middleton specialist, for his forbearance, patience, expertise, detailed and insightful comments on the three chapters which feature *The Old Law,* and above all to Kathryn Perry, who undertook to read the entire manuscript. Nothing escaped her gimlet eye, and her observations were invaluable in the final stages of preparation. All three were generous and committed readers, and their detailed and astute remarks have pulled this book tightly into shape. I alone am responsible for any residual error or bagginess.

Reworked sections of the prologue and chapter five appear by permission of the publishers from 'Time's Whirligig: Images of Old Age in Coriolanus, Francis Bacon, and Thomas Newton', in *Growing Old in Early Modern Europe: Cultural Representations*, ed. Erin Campbell, Aldershot: Ashgate, 2006, pp. 21–38, and an altered version of the epilogue appears by permission of the *Journal for the Study of British Cultures* Vol. 1312, 2006, 133–145 from 'The Triumph of Age. *All's Well that Ends Well;* Shakespeare and the Dramatization of Transdifference', eds. Doris Feldmann, Ina Habermann and Dunja Mohr.

Prologue

The whirligig of time

At the end of *Twelfth Night*, Feste reveals to the assembled company the story of the gulling of Malvolio. He alone seems indifferent to the cruelty of the plot against Olivia's steward, considering it just recompense for an insult: 'I was one, sir, in this interlude, one Sir Topas, sir, but that's all one.' And then he throws Malvolio's words back in his face: 'But do you remember, 'Madam, why laugh you at such a barren rascal, and you smile not, he is gagged?' And thus the whirligig of time brings in his revenges' (5.1, 375–6). For Malvolio, the whirligig of time brought a short period of intense mental suffering and physical deprivation as punishment for dowsing the wit of the below-stairs revellers and for interrupting their loud and drunken partying. For the old, too, in the prescription and fictional literature of the early modern period, time's revenges meant an end to corporeal indulgence, and its depredations were ushered in via a deluge of printed matter on the need for the old to sublimate the weakening of the physical self by strengthening the mind and spirit. For early modern literature and culture, the Ages of Man schema, inherited from the middle ages and represented in print, painting and woodcut, showed how the whirligig of time finally brought the old back full circle to the helplessness of an infant, 'sans teeth, sans eyes, sans taste, sans everything' (*Works*, 1961, 2. 7, 166). Jacques' famous description of old age in *As You Like It* follows representations of the various stages of life by subdividing old age, alone of all the ages, into three distinct phases. The broad splitting of human life into three categories by Hippocrates, Aristotle and Galen — youth, maturity and age — was subsequently fine-tuned into Ages of Man *topoi* varying from three to twelve. Steven Smith, Mary Dove, Pat Thane and Aki Beam provide useful summaries of renaissance appropriation of ancient and medieval division of human life into seven (or more), four or three ages (Smith, 1976, 128–30; Dove, 1986, 10–19; Thane, 2001, 46–52; Beam, 2006, 98–102). Women were not included in this schema, since it was assumed that their lives followed the same pattern as men's, though speeded up. The onset of old age could thus be anywhere from the late forties to seventy for men but was accelerated by ten years in women. Notably, all of these representations of aging, whatever terminology they employ, create a separate category for old age, which alone of all the ages was regarded as a disease, and which contained its own distinctive regression.

Cultural historians have used a variety of materials including documentary sources, wills, diaries, censuses, records of provision for the elderly, prescription and imaginative literature to build up a picture of how society treated the old, and how the old perceived themselves. Given the relative paucity of documentary evidence, their reach is of necessity broad.[1] Whilst greatly indebted to works such as these, the aim of this book is to bring a variety of texts into relationships of meaning which depend on the use of one text as an interpretative tool which releases meaning in others. The book thus puts into operation a procedure which aims to bring about a textured and nuanced perception of old age in the period by cross-pollinating texts which sometimes belong to different and seemingly unrelated discursive and historical fields. So, for example, chapter 1 brings a range of dietary formulae to bear upon Shakespeare's *Comedy of Errors* as a means of drawing out its subtext on displacements of old age, and in chapter 2 early modern inheritance practices are marshalled as an interpretative key for bringing to light generic relationships of sameness and difference between Middleton and Rowley's tragicomedy *The Old Law* and the tragedy of *King Lear*. The book reappraises these key texts through different prisms. Both plays open up issues to do with the pragmatics of old age, just as ideas and practices open up the plays, and a major part of this book's remit is to tease out ways in which they are alike and unalike. It aims to bring to the fore their cultural significance through their relationship to a substantial body of material on the state's involvement in the process and effects of aging in addition to classically-derived ideologies. In the point and counterpoint of its discursive aim, therefore, the project takes advantage of a methodology favoured by literary scholars whose frame of reference is trans-linear and cross-historical and whose reach extends beyond the confines of new historicism and cultural materialism.

The overwhelming emphasis on stocking the mind did not discourage writers in the sixteenth and seventeenth centuries from attempts to devise extensive prescriptions for old age which would slow down the inexorable imprint of time's revenge upon the body. Though Bacon's treatise on the prolongation of life broke new ground, it was still one of a long line of such works going back to ancient the Greeks and Hebrews (cf. Gruman, 1966, 1–97). The physiologies of old age of Hippocrates, Aristotle and Galen collectively provided a narrative of inevitable decay, yet were at the same time accompanied by recommendations on how to delay the ravages of time. Cicero's *De senectute*, the chief source of inspiration for the compensatory benefits of senescence, relied upon such advice. His moralising of old age was, in turn, invoked wholesale by essayists, dramatists and his sixteenth-century expositors, though not always in the spirit in which the treatise was intended. The implications and outcomes of this fast-flowing stream of re-appropriation form a major strand of this book. In fiction and prescription, the mind–body split when applied to old age reflects a profound ambivalence which is extensively researched, observed and explored in a variety of genres without ever attaining resolution. Representations of the aged condition in early modern literature and culture, till now an area of neglected scholarship because it is presumed not to bear features distinct from medieval concepts of old age, thrive on paradox. The contradictions found in every kind of text that is either centrally or peripherally to do with old age have wide-ranging implications for fictional representations which depended on received wisdom on aging, yet adapted this knowledge as a response to specific social pressures. It is the task of this study to examine unfamiliar examples taken from wills, testaments, meditations, legends, ancient and early modern idealisation, denigration and prescription together with literary re-workings and projections of age and aging, in order to give new readings of familiar texts, and first-time readings of those perhaps unfamiliar even to an informed scholarly readership, but which nonetheless bring into the critical arena preoccupations with and experiences of age. When subjected to intertextual and interdisciplinary analysis, this diverse body of writings, some of which are not normally associated with age at all and which are therefore absent from recent historical analysis, cast new light on themes of senescence which normally depend upon the requirements of genre but which also push generic boundaries to the limit.

Fictions of Old Age is designed to give readers a sense of the variety and depth of early modern thinking about old age. This multiplicity calls for fresh consideration, angled on age, of formulations of youth–age polemic, politics and gender which must also include the ways in which early modern writers in a range of genres shaped their classical sources. What assumptions and aims underwrite these (re)fashionings? What cultural significance may we attribute to ambiguous and contradictory images of old age, and to interest in the processes of aging that are either the primary subject matter or a significant subtext to so many different literatures? To what extent was there a premium on youth, and how was this counterbalanced by images of the authority of age in men? How can we account for the discrepancy between stage and non-fictional representations of the difference between old men and old women in the aging process, and in society's differential treatment of each? How can we evaluate these depictions alongside depictions of old age in genre art, family accounts and wills? These questions have wide-ranging implications for early modern fictional representations of old age, which both adopt and repudiate the stereotypical images handed down from the classics, and which give rise to the main argument of the book.

Simply put, the argument is that though society cast old men as figures of authority and the manuals taught that they should be revered, their manifestation in fiction and sometimes non-fiction is much more complex and fraught with ambiguity. Sometimes they appear as weakened in mind and body, lacking the respect of the younger generation, either humiliatingly dependent on their children or ridiculed for attempting to hide their age and weakness, sometimes as blocking figures (in drama particularly), unbending and formidable bastions of authority who must be challenged by the young. The trajectory for old women, however, is directly in reverse; ignored by society when old, ignored also by the manuals and cast by literature as hags, crones and witches, they nevertheless achieve an astonishing measure of freedom and independence denied to them during their childbearing years. Chapters 1 and 2 show how fictional writing variously re-works in different genres the commonplaces and stock characterisations of old age, while the two central chapters (3 and 4) on disgraceful old age interrogate the ways in which genre confronts gender contradictions.

Cicero's *De senectute* was used by the writers of ancient Rome and by a host of subsequent authors through the ages as an example of the honours and benefits of old age. Cicero wrote it when he was sixty-two; he dedicated it to Atticus, who was sixty-five, and he put it into the mouth of Cato the Elder, who was then eighty-three. Cicero wrote the treatise in exile from office and it is, for this reason, usually dismissed by present day historians of antiquity (in both senses) as a bid for re-employment, in much the same way as the question of continuing or re-employment of people over the retirement age splutters into life in current affairs programmes on BBC Radio 4.[2] The text was widely read from the moment it was written around 44 BC, and continued to be read from the twelfth century onwards. In particular, its wide dissemination in the fifteenth, sixteenth and seventeenth centuries, made possible by the invention of the printing press (and incidentally translated by its inventor, Caxton), informed humanist thought and both Protestant and Jesuit teaching. Erasmus, Luther and Montaigne all drew inspiration from its positive account of old age, and it was translated and published twice by Thomas Newton. Its place at the core of questions about age in politics and the politics of age make it, along with Plutarch's greatly indebted essay, 'Whether an Old Man Should Engage in Public Affairs' (1991, 75–153), a particular focus for the relevance of age-related matters in *Coriolanus* in chapter 5.

Cicero and, later, Plutarch, extol the virtues of elderliness in a bid to improve its status, and to show that men advanced in years continue to direct state affairs. Whatever his political objectives (he was writing just before the Ides of March, in the midst of great upheaval), Cicero's concern is manifestly to enhance the status of *senectus*, and to underscore its continuing importance in counsel. Following Cicero, both Thomas Newton and Francis Bacon are aware of the viability of old age. Yet their own work mutates into medical prescriptions on health and preservation of life which paradoxically imply and deny its value, and they recycle the negative images peddled by Horace, Aristophanes and above all Juvenal. Three-quarters of the way through a treatise that describes the best ways of enhancing and prolonging an old person's life, for example, Bacon inserts a section on some of these negative stereotypes. He reproduces the opinion of 'an ingenious young Gentleman' from Poitiers, France' that if old men's minds were visible, they would be as deformed as their bodies; the mind's defects in age mirrored those of the body; old men's bodies were 'dry skinn'd, impudent, hard bowell'd, and unmercifull: bleare-ey'd, and envious; down-looking, and stooping, and Atheists; Earth, not Heaven, being their constant Object'; they had wobbly knees and trembling limbs, 'wavering, and unconstant;' their fingers were crooked, they were greedy and covetous, they were fearful, wrinkled and crafty (Bacon, 1638, 279–80). Physical imperfections mirror defects of character which to an extent amount to a breach in the decorum of old age itself, and seep into even the most knowledgeable and sympathetic accounts. This context for the Janus face of old age is the staple for chapters 3, 4 and 5.

Indeed, these two conflicting aspects of old age lie at the heart of the contradictions explored in this book. Bacon's *Historie of Life and Death. With Observations Naturall and Experimentall for the Prolonging of Life*[3] presents a useful introduction to tension between positive and negative attitudes towards age and aging. He provides various strategies for halting the body's inevitable decay. He tells his reader that longevity can be achieved 'by safe, convenient, civill, but untryed new waies and meanes.' God willing, 'our shoos and the garments of our frail bodies' can 'be here little worne in our iourney in the worlds wildernesse' (Bacon, 1638, *To the Reader*). Old age is a condition worth preserving, and by knowing how to prevent the body's decay, man is in position to fashion nature so as to slow down the whirligig of time and significantly delay its revenges on the body. In this, it shapes responses to health regimens for the elderly as an instrument for the interpretation of literary and dramatic texts. This 'angling' of one text as a conceptual key to other features operates particularly in chapters 1, 4 and 5. These chapters' aim is to demonstrate that the upbeat messages which culminate in the epilogue on its triumphs are paralleled at every turn by representations of grotesque, disgusting and corrupt old age.

The paradox of old age underpins this project's central tenet, which is that didactic literature's idealisations of masculine elderliness is a defensive strategy, and that the unsettling reality is exposed in works of fiction which undermine such rosy images and which promote an equally unsettling and transgressive image of old women, mostly forgotten in the manuals, as beings with an exuberant and alarming agency and purpose in life which galvanises the plotlines of comedy and tragedy. These contradictions give rise to interesting fictional and non-fictional representations of old age. Bacon, for example, co-mingles two current models of human science, the Galenic and the Paracelsan, with the result that his work on the prolongation of life, along with the works of fiction which this project examines, is shot through with ambiguity. His premise is that decay can be retarded and the body repaired, though unequally, for some parts of the body repair better than others: 'spirits, blood, flesh, and fatnesse are in the declining estate of Age easily repaired; but there is much difficulty and danger in repairing the dry parts, [...] and all of the organicall and instrumentall parts' (Bacon, 1638, 5). This ambivalence manifests itself in a variety of complicating ways and is examined particularly in 1, 3 and 5. In general, Bacon's work on aging mutates into varying positions of ambiguity in textualising the aged body that fall into the humanist trap of simultaneous dependence on classical authority and a desire to valorise the new science of observation and experimentation. This results in morally weighted but contradictory recommendations on how to ease the pains of old age. Shakespeare exposes this same ambivalence in his portrayal of Egeon and Adriana in *The Comedy of Errors* (chapter 1), and the two tribunes and Menenius in *Coriolanus* (chapter 5).

The arguments for the complexity of perceptions of and attitudes to old age in the early modern period are compelling, and undermine the thesis of Georges Minois' *History of Old Age* (Minois, 1989, 249). His claim is that in art and literature, attitudes to old age were simply ones of disgust:

> The Renaissance, like every time of renewal and rebirth, celebrated youth, the fullness of life, beauty, and novelty. It abhorred everything that presaged decline, decrepitude, and death [...] the unprecedented violence of attacks against old age in the sixteenth century was derived from the impotent rage of a generation which worshipped youth and beauty.

He explains its ubiquity in literature as a morbid fascination because 'it formed the great obstacle to the deification of man, rendering it impossible' (249). Yet, by 'flagrant contradiction' (288), the old were everywhere in positions of esteemed authority in society, politics and the arts (288–301). It is true that each age has its own take on the process of aging, and its own culture-specific ideologies of old age. However, writers were interested in old age not only as a bipolar opposite of youth, but in its complex multiplicity which rendered images of old age confusing and until the most recent historical scholarship of, for example, Shulamith Shahar, Pat Thane and Lynn Botelho, only partially understood. The paradoxical nature of old age is taken for granted in most writings of the period, and stems in some part from the humanist impulse towards the text, textuality and its fondness for taxonomies; in other words, the rhetorical nature of experience, and, contradictorily, newly emerging ways of arriving at knowledge of the world direct, unmediated by the written word.

It is not surprising therefore that early modern writers, puzzling over how to prevent time enacting its revenges upon body and mind, drew heavily upon idealisations of old age which gave instructions to the ruling elite on how to ride the whirligig of time by valuing intellectual over physical vigour, and by fostering wisdom and respect as the dues of old age. Thomas Newton's preface to the *Worthye Booke of Old Age*, the first of his two translations of *De senectute*,[4] exploits this connection and helps introduce the process of textual cross-fertilisation that is the methodological linchpin of this book.

The first of Newton's translations, *The Worthye Booke of Old Age,* written when he was twenty-seven, was dedicated to William Paulet (1485–1572), First Marquis of Winchester and Lord Treasurer of England, who still held the reins of office at the age of ninety-three. Newton exploits his model, *De senectute,* by using the substance of the original as a means of advancing his own fortunes. Echoing the final part of Cicero's treatise which describes death at worst as mere oblivion, at best a gateway to eternal happiness, Newton ends his dedication with a hyperbolical flourish spun around a pun on translation and the metaphor of man as player upon the world's stage:

> after the Epilogue and last Pageaunt of this mortal and transitorye lyfe (Wherin your Lordship with much worshippe, more honour, and most authorytie these lxxxxvi yeres hath ben a worthye and honourable Actor) you may be translated into the ioyes celestial, and be made partaker of his glorious kingdome (Newton, 1569, iv verso).

Textualising the aged body and ensuring its life everlasting through transmission of the written word by translation performs several useful functions for Newton. It allows him to accentuate the art and labour of the translator in his bid for patronage, while at the same time minimising the risk of offending with a work from his own pen. Translation, Newton's vehicle for immortalising the extraordinarily prolonged and continuingly active life of William Paulet, also permits, through an elaborate compliment, an identification of his would-be patron with the hero of the original text, Cato. In his dedication, Newton offers Paulet the 'gift' of his translation with an apt quote from Seneca, that a gift should 'haue a diligent eye and respecte' (Dedication, ii recto) for matter and argument to suit the recipient. As 'a fruitful and learned discourse of age' and wisdom in war and policy, it recommends itself particularly to Paulet's advanced years and high calling. He offers it as one 'in whom Old age to the great reioycing of al your welwillers most triumphantly flourisheth' (Dedication, ii verso). Thus Newton's translation ensures that the idealising rhetoric of old age in the original percolates into the politics of aging in his own day. By stressing the continuities of tenure in office and the enduring wisdom and authority of age with which he targets Paulet as a compellingly appropriate patron for a younger man, he forges links between Cicero, the sixty-year-old statesman writing to persuade senate to continue with his services, Cato, still in office at eighty-four-year, and Paulet, aged ninety-three (Newton adds on another three years), 'who is and longtime hath bene the principall husband of this famous Realm,' giving honourable and faithful service in 'manifold and waightye affayres at home and abroad' (Dedication, iii verso). This complex appropriation of text for specific social engineering is examined further in chapter 2 which looks at the relationship of *The Merchant of Venice*, *The Old Law* and *King Lear* to a variety of texts, revealing their participation in the historical realities of inheritance.

In addition to its debt to the classics, the early modern period inherited from the middle ages types of behaviour and outlook expected of the old. Both eras grafted onto biblical example models of old age taken from the writers of antiquity, who treated it as a topic ripe for moral, political, religious and physiological instruction. Simon Goulart's *The Wise Vieillard*, Thomas Sheafe's *Vindiciae Senectutis, or, a plea for old-age* and John Smith's *Pourtract of Old Age*[5] are just three examples of the many who leavened with personal experience the copious advice on morals and health found in ancient, medieval and biblical texts in order to outline and promote the notion of a comfortable old age. Borrowing the weighty sentiments of writings from these texts, early modern treatise writers set out to prepare their readers for the onset of the disease of senescence, and to teach them how to come to terms with its unavoidably terminal consequences. The assumption was that idealisations of masculine elderliness (from Cicero, Plutarch, Plato) and biblical examples of long livers helped those on the frontiers of old age to withstand its anticipated trials. But a hoary head and wrinkled visage were prime signifiers of conflicting messages; they were simultaneously markers of the enduring virtues of the wisdom and experience needed for a healthy politics of family and state, and of the inevitable physical and mental decay caused by loss of heat and 'radicall moisture' in the body (Bacon 1638: 3–4).[6]

The instruction literature on old age in the early modern period hinges on the premise that lapsed humanity cannot revert to the enviable condition of ancient and biblical long livers, yet those who are old have triumphed over time — that is, they have triumphed over life expectancy norms and have in consequence achieved an enviable proximity to the Almighty. Having survived war, illness and calamity, it behoves them to age gracefully. Pierre de la Primaudaye, whose full book title expounds his discursive aim,[7] summarises types of behaviour and outlook expected of the old and favoured by the writers of antiquity. Cato's bequest to subsequent writers was his belief in self-regulation as the passport to a dignified and comfortable old age, despite its inherent 'deformities'. True authority emanates from a life lived in honesty and guided according to 'the best end of our being whereunto everie age is to be referred' (Primaudaye, 1589, 539). The treatise writers, in their desire to change the image of old age, sought to elevate it into a perfect condition achievable only through wisdom. Old age thus became a title and privilege conferred upon intellectual attainment and lifelong moderation in diet and exercise. But important as it was, nourishment of the mind and body was merely an adjunct to nourishment of the soul; intellectual strength counted for nothing if a man neglected or ignored his spiritual self. Both are inseparable, and indispensable as a means of counteracting the damaging effects of time: 'To such olde men as have their soules nourished with heavenly light, old age is not grievous, and in such the desire of contemplation and knowledge increaseth as much as the pleasures of their bodie decrease.' (540). Such conceptualisations form the backdrop to this project's final section. Having explored representations of enfeebled old age, and in the opening chapter having uncovered textual displacements of the infirmities of age onto youth, *Fictions of Old Age* concludes by exploring projections onto the young of the qualities of age in Shakespeare's *All's Well that Ends Well*. In so doing it brings the work itself back round full circle to the image of the movement of time as a whirligig, but with the crucial difference that in some instances at least the changes wrought over time upon the body are not so much vengeful as transformative.

1 Commonplaces and stereotypes

Stereotyping is the identification of a person, situation or condition accord-ing to a pre-conceived, standardized, oversimplified impression of the char-acteristics which typify them. Stereotypes are formed by taking a stance on assumptions about that person, situation or condition, and are con-veyed textually through a *locus communis*; that is, a shared text. This writ-ten vehicle of the commonplace is passed round, quoted from, re-used in other contexts, widely applied, and its acceptance and use is general to the point of platitude. The experience and understanding of old age was formulated and conveyed in this way in the early modern period, where attitudes typifying this final stage of life originated in classical texts, medi-cal tracts based on ancient medical knowledge and the bible. These texts peddled lists of the physical ailments and spiritually damaging personal-ity blueprints of old age, and instructed those approaching its denizens on how best to bear its physical and spiritual burdens. At the same time, contradictorily, they sought to reassure older people that of all the ages of a man's life it was the most rich and fulfilling, if only because it brought with it a wisdom denied the young. It took a lifetime of learning and expe-rience to acquire the wisdom that only the old can possess, and enabled a spirituality all the more enhanced because it belonged exclusively to those about to leave behind the care-torn world and enter into the blessed realm of God their maker. The ubiquitous fictions of age thus turned upon the axis of contradictory positions, which were taken up in complex yet criti-cally neglected ways by a generically diverse body of writers — the poets, the playwrights, the (auto)biographers, diarists and purveyors of the 'new' science such as Francis Bacon — to the extent that, with regard to old age, the years 1500–1700 are marked out by symbiosis between works of fiction and its prescriptive debates. This chapter takes a random sampling of such works in order to identify and analyse diverse textual responses to society's classically derived and medically endorsed stereotypes and commonplaces of this final stage of life.

Thomas More's fictionalised account of his last days, *The Dialogue of Comfort Against Tribulation*[1], and Shakespeare's *Comedy of Errors*[2], pre-suppose a range of shared assumptions about age found in sixteenth–century medical treatises, prolongation of life tracts and translations of 'ideal old age' material. Two enduring yet contradictory commonplaces flourished side by side, the one deriving from Aristotle, which of the various stages of life defined old age alone as akin to a disease; it was a painful, hopeless condition, making the body decrepit and malfunctioning, and of course inevitably led to death. The other, deriving from Cicero and Plutarch, saw it as the richest part of life; cushioned in the bosom of one's family, frugally yet nourishingly fed, the body frequently bathed, oiled and massaged, it was a time of ease, joy and contentment. As a result, old age literature gives plenty of advice on how to make a man's old age as comfortable as possible in the same breath as it lists its pitfalls and sufferings; and these simultaneously thriving features make their appearance on stage.

THE COMEDY OF ERRORS

Age stereotyping proliferates in the Shakespearean canon. Its profound exploration in *King Lear* arises from commonly held viewpoints and many of the comedies and histories use old age as a *topos*, a sub-theme or as a structural device. In *The Merchant of Venice,* the commodification of boys is enabled by the older male characters, who continue to control the fortunes of their children both on and off stage; it is because old Sir Launcelot Gobbo, near-blind and easily confused, continues to hold his son's fortunes in the palm of his hand that Launcelot is impelled to sell himself to the highest bidder. Portia's dead father exerts from the grave a stranglehold on his daughter's fortunes, thereby driving the Belmont narrative, and Shylock (whose forebears are the stock figures of miserly old men inherited from Greek comedy and refined by Plautus) makes Jessica's home life a hell from which Lorenzo fortuitously delivers her. *Pericles*, a story in which happiness and recovery are achieved in old age, is itself framed by the storytelling of the poet Gower as a very old man, capable of exercising only his tongue; age is the condition of reconciliation in *The Winter's Tale*, in which a couple are reunited only in the final stage of their lives, and *The Tempest* draws on yet problematises the idealisations of wisdom and control that the literatures on senescence, from ancient to early modern, invested in old men. But perhaps most unexpectedly and in a very interesting manner *The Comedy of Errors* expands the Plautine stereotypes of hapless age into an interrogation of what it means to be old and powerless, propelling the age theme into a territory remote from the pre-conceived, over-simplified standardisations of its trials and failings into new and unexpected areas of concern and interest that frame and intersect with the main action of the comedy. Though the 'old' framework of the play remains on the periphery of critical attention, I suggest that it shapes the main events all the more effectively for being unimplicated in their laughter-provoking double disguises and fast-paced events. Plautine comedy provides Shakespeare with the stereotype of the wrought-upon old, which he reworks into the Egeon/ Emilia framing device. This transformation of classical material allows him to explore facets of old age that show it to be just as much a state of mind as an inevitable condition defined by chronology, while the age framework performs the structural, narrative, historicist and characterological tasks of the comedic tradition hitherto prioritised by critics (cf. Miola, 1997, 3–28; 55–56; 71–93; 113–54; 183–89; 335–92).

As the prelude to his underlying concern with age, Shakespeare inserts into his main action a personage mentioned only in the Prologue to *Menaechmi* in order to transform commonplace experiences of being old into a probing of painful psychological states which issue from constriction, deprivation, neglect, victimhood and alienation. In his Prologue, omitted in William Warner's 1595 translation of *Menaechmi*, Plautus describes how an old merchant from Syracuse took one twin on a voyage to Tarentum, and how he was stolen by another old merchant, from Epidamnus. In Syracuse the grandfather of the boys, also called Menaechmus, renames the other twin after his lost brother. The merchant from Epidamnus, himself old at the play's opening, has made the stolen boy his heir and has found him a wife. The source of confusion in Plautus is not, as in Shakespeare's play, two masters both named Antipholus and their two servants both named Dromio; it derives from the wife and father-in-law of the stolen Menaechmus who mistake one twin for the other; the young woman and the old man are paired as the victims of mistaken identity (Plautus, *Maenachmi*, 1965). In *Errors*, a transference occurs that may not at first be glaringly apparent. The stock *senex* figure of Roman comedy, Maenachmus the father-in-law[3], is replaced by a young woman, Luciana, who takes over the championing of her brother-in-law's right to freedom, and the parasite and the old merchant/father-in-law is replaced by an estranged elderly couple, Egeon and Emilia.

Shakespeare used two other sources alongside the *Maenachmi*. He borrowed elements from Lawrence Twine's *Pattern of Painful Adventures*, probably published in 1594 (*Errors*, 2002, 29) to sculpt his own (obscured) narrative of age, first using in *Errors* the romance of lost happiness recovered in old age by the reunion of a dispersed family that is essentially the source of *Pericles*. In the main, he takes from Twine's Apollonius story Egeon's lengthy account in the first scene of his long life of loss and mourning, and the events of the final scene, when the family is reunited (31). For 'the brilliant farcical centrepiece' (25) of his play he used another Plautine source, *Amphitruo*. In the original, the Theban general Amphitryon returns triumphantly from the wars only to find himself locked out of the house by the god Mercury, impersonating his servant Sosia in order to guard the door while Jupiter, in Amphitryon's shape, makes love to the general's wife. But even though Shakespeare, who probably read it in Latin, since there was no translation available to him (*Errors*, 2002, 25), compresses the entire action of the source plot into one scene, he transforms the figure of the poor old man struck down by Jupiter (in the original) into one whom the buffetings of fortune throw at last into the arms of his long-lost wife. In addition, Shakespeare concentrates the entire action in Ephesus, an ancient and notional place which Shakespeare reinvented from Acts and Ephesians in the New Testament, and by grafting on to it the reputation of Plautus's Epidamnus, he turns Ephesus into a place of injury, harm and loss for the old man who at the start of the play has just landed on its shores.[4]

Shakespeare gives the stock *senex* figure of Roman comedy new dimensions and a new direction as part of the play's undertow on old age. Plautus makes his old men the authors of the misfortunes of the young. They are present and active, but do not leave the various stereotypical moulds of the *senex* figure. In *Maenachmi* there are two variants; the beleaguered old (the merchant) and the mischief-maker (the thieving merchant), and they function very narrowly within the mechanics of stock situations enacted by stock types, distancing the audience and leaving them emotionally uninvolved. Whereas the old father of the twins dies of grief in *Maenachmi*, in *Errors* he is the victim of life-threatening experiences as a result of the grief and frailty held to accompany advancing years. As Charles Whitworth notes, the removal of some of these stock types — the old man and the parasite, combined with the addition of an invented younger sister for the wife, and the reduced role of the courtesan — have the effect of humanising the harsher aspects of Roman urban domestic satire. This removal also provides a harmonious ending to Shakespeare's changes, so that the play becomes a 'family romance' (*Errors* 2002, 20). But these alterations also result in equally interesting though far less obvious complications. Shakespeare's comedy is shot through with contemporary assumptions about old age which to an attentive reader provide positive and negative formulations of old age commonplaces — and which are, moreover, projected onto the young. These projections, and the play's frame, provide a melancholy reflection on the passage of time and its ravages upon human life, even though the ending is an affirmation of the protective and life-extending role of family and climate. The play merges the stereotypical features of the foolish *senex* in *Maenachmi* and Amphitruo with a third Plautine source, *Aulularia*[5], and intermingles these classical sources with the commonplaces of old age found in the manual literature of the period in both a comical and a tragical way. Even though the restoration of family life reaffirms the 'pleasures' of age, projections onto the young of the experiences and behaviour of the foolish, jealous, impotent old highlight the constrictions suffered by those at the extremes of the gender and generational spectrum. In this play, the sufferings normally associated with masculine old age are endured by Adriana. Thus young women and old men combine to form a third, alternative, category of social constraint.

Though Apollonius is the main source for the Egeon/Emilia story, and Plautine stereotypes of aging the starting point of his own interest in the aged, Shakespeare draws upon a variety of other sources to initiate his

meditation upon the vicissitudes of the aged body. One of the most frequently occurring commonplaces in the manual literature is that the old are
voluble and jealous. Henry Cuffe, for example, states that the reason why
the old are 'talkative and full of words' is because

> nature loues to exercise that part most which is least decaied: or that
> knowledge, the onely thing old age can bragge of, cannot be manifested
> but by vtterance; or that old men, the nigher they are to their end, they
> much more desire to haue their memory not onely by children and
> posterity, but euen by the speeches and deedes fore-vttered and per-
> formed intheir life: or that wisedome (as all good things naturally com-
> municate their good properties) makes them desirous to profit others'
> (Cuffe, 1607, 132; see also Aristotle, 1984, 2: 2214; Bacon, 1638, 282;
> Steele, 1688, 46)

Interestingly, Shakespeare's transposition of volubility and jealousy onto
another stock figure, the shrewish wife, enables one of the youthful characters to dilate, in the idiom of the disabled and disgruntled old, upon the
constraints of time, thereby reserving ideals of honour, dignity and fortitude for the portrayal of Egeon. But displacing the less appealing traits of
old age results, perhaps unexpectedly, in a re-investment of sympathy with
the old, precisely because they are communicated through the sufferings of
a young woman.

Like the old, Adriana's self-image is stripped of allure. She sees herself immured at home in the chill of her husband's neglect, grown dull
and wasted:

> Hath homely age the alluring beauty took
> From my poor cheek? Then hath he wasted it:
> Are my discourses dull? Barren my wit?
> If voluble and sharp discourse be man'd,
> Unkindness blunts it more than marble
> hard. (*Errors*, 2002, 2. 1, 90–96)

Henry Cuffe explains how, even though nourishment shores up moisture, it
cannot prevent the body's decay, because there are impurities in the nourishment ingested by the body which over time 'by degrees tainteth that naturall ingenred humidity', and by continual adulteration, causes the body's
corruption and degeneration. Thus 'the purity of our complexion being by
degrees and by time diminished, at length there followes, euen of necessitie,
an absolute corruption' (Cuffe, 1607, 84). Adriana attributes this speeded-
up inner corruption, manifest in her 'wasted' looks, to her husband's disregard. His neglect starves her spirits and corrodes her youth and beauty.
Adriana, confined to the hearth while her husband is too busy enjoying
himself to remember to return home for the midday meal, imagines herself
growing old indoors, where her conversation is 'dull' and her wit 'barren'.

If the power of eloquence and sharpened wit is an accomplishment which thrives only in male company, then her husband's desertion has blunted hers; as a woman 'grown old' in neglect, volubility is her only weapon, and in her self-projection into old age the only part of her body which can exert influence is her tongue, the member which in the old is 'least decaied' (Cuffe, 1607, 132). Rejected, she has become a shrewish, garrulous wife, losing her femininity and power to attract by adopting the mannish weapons of 'voluble and sharp discourse.' Her husband, by depriving her of his company, denies her the nourishment necessary to protect her from the premature ravages of age; her cheek is 'wasted' and her 'alluring beauty' taken by 'homely age'. In another displacement of the stereotype of the old as jealous, suspicious and grasping (Cuffe, 1607, 131-32; cf. Aristotle, 1984, 2: 214; Bacon, 1638, 280) Adriana ages through jealousy, a damaging emotion known to bring on the symptoms of old age (cf. Wright, 1601, 101–108). The old possess increased knowledge of the world which robs them of their credulity, and the nearness of death makes them want to hold on to life all the more. Adriana, too, strains for life-enhancing activity by wanting her husband to be more involved in domesticity and desires a greater share in his business activities abroad.[6] But lack of the kind of nurture and care that preserves life and prolongs youth causes Adriana to prematurely experience withering and decay. Adriana's lack of mobility and choice resembles the plight of the old. Like them, she is isolated and perceives herself as useless, wasted and dull, identifying in herself the stereotypical images of old age as voluble, jealous, possessive, hidden from sight and unable to move outside its own front door (cf. Montaigne, 1894, 427–30). The vigour, freedom of movement and choice which define young masculinity are missing from the confined world of young women. Denied the freedoms of youth, the experience of young women is here articulated as the constraints imposed upon the old by the inexorable passage of time. For young men time is a liberating force, releasing them from the restraining influence of their fathers by marriage, and empowers them anew as heads of households in their own right. When Adriana accuses the Antipholus she wrongly assumes to be her husband of infidelity, he replies 'In Epheus I am but two hours old' (*Errors*, 2. 2, 151), expressing the idea that time itself is young and on the side of young men.

Time plays an integral part in the play and in manual evaluation of the aging process in other ways, too. George Strode laments the sufferings that age brings to mankind in the well-worn trope of the world grown old through sin: 'the times beginne to waxe old, and we are borne weaker and more feeble than all creatures' (Strode, 1618, 28). In old age

> man receiues many incurable wounds, as baldnesse, bleared eyes, deafe eares, wrinckled browes, stinking breath, trembling hands, faint spirits, leane cheekes, corruption of stomacke, with like miseries innumer-

able, which neuer leaue to wound the bodie, disquiet the minde, and torment the conscience. (18)

Other writers suggest ways of forestalling these damaging effects of time; one is to eat at regular times of the day to prevent 'corruption of stomacke' and to prolong life by avoiding over-rich food; hence proliferating manual debate about the value of meat in the diet of an old man. According to Cuffe, those 'surfetting and ouercharging their stomacks with too much and too riotous vse of meats, vntimely end their daies' (Cuffe, 1607, 99). Too much meat hinders good digestion, engenders 'crudities' and causes overheating, which depletes the body's store of moisture, thereby accelerating the aging process. Those with a choleric complexion (itself an enemy to longevity because it is hot and dry like fire and brings on premature old age by consuming the body's moisture) should avoid certain kinds of meat and drink (98–99). The liver of a choleric man, 'distempered' by heat, causes large and hard veins, thick blood 'by reason of vehement heat consuming the subtle parts of moisture', a hairy belly, an excessively hot body, bitter red choler in youth, and, most damaging of all, black choler in age, as a result of 'adustion of red choler' (Elyot, 1541, 13). Old men who are 'testy, froward, sad, melancholy; especially those who are cholerique' because of their miserable lot should take heed (Goulart, 1621, 53). Choler and anger, 'which commonly keepe possession in old men, by reason that they still feele sharpe goades in their mindes, and grieuous woundes in their bodies' (76), may be controlled and reduced by cutting down on drink, eating less 'meates and sauces too much spiced' and 'by refraining the company of scoffers, quarrell-some, mutinous, and mad-braine-sicke persons' (77). Unfortunately for old men, a surfeit of phlegm accompanies the drying out of their bodies. This results in hair turning white and baldness: 'white hayre com[m]eth of Phlegme and of a humoure cold and moyst' (Newton, 1576, 41), whereas dryness feeds upon and wastes the humours of the body and results in thin hair, 'soone bald'[7] (Newton, 1576, 69). For these reasons, time is figured as an old man with flowing white locks, or as bald, since both are one of the many 'incurable wounds' of old age. In short, time has run out for the old — that is, it has run its course and cannot be retrieved; consequently, there is 'no time for a man to recover his hair that grows bald by nature' (2. 2, 72–73).

The banter between Dromio and his master accumulates around such images of beleaguered old age by playing on time and the effects of aging, two major motifs in manual and play. The trope is not a new one; it is a commonplace going back to Ovid's verse on the four ages of man, and is quoted in Newton's translation of Levinus Lemnius:

Do we not see the year by course in quarters four divided [...]
Old crookebackte Hyems las[t] of all,
with trembling pace appears;

With furrowed face, clean, bald, or else
all white and mylky hairs. (Newton, 1576, 30)

In its proverbial form, time (or occasion) should be taken by the forelock, for she is bald behind (Tilley, 1966, T311), while Cuffe informs his readers that the ancient Egyptians portrayed God as a 'decrepit-old-man' to stress the continuity of time, and as a youth in his prime to represent his 'livelinesse and immunity from all manerdefect and alteration by cancred corrupting time' (Cuffe, 1607, 5–6). Belief in God robs time of its ruinous passage because 'One day with God, is as a thousand yeares, and a thousand yeares as one day' (10), length of time adding nothing to a man's ability and wisdom, any more than 'fewness of daies' detracts in any way from 'the perfection of his workmanship' (10–11). Cuffe endorses his rosy image of the passage of time by reference to the ancient poets, who 'called Saturne, that is Time, Heauens Sonne, because that from their circular mouing, came the distinction of Daies, and Moneths, and Yeeres' which Cuffe prefers as a more encomapassing definition than Aristotle's of the past, present and 'future indurance of things' (41).

Preoccupation with time and its effects dominates the prescriptive literature on old age and finds its way into the comic exchange between Antipholus and Dromio of Syracuse in Act two, Scene two. The episode begins in the midst of confusion; Antipholus of Syracuse mistakes Dromio of Ephesus, who has been instructed to take his master's gold to a safe place, for his own servant. The Ephesan Dromio knows nothing about this; instead, he has his own commission to discharge, which is to make sure his master goes home to lunch with his wife. When Antipholus of Syracuse meets his own servant, and is reassured that the money is indeed safely deposited, he begins to question his Dromio on the 'merry humour' that made him deny any knowledge of the gold he had been entrusted to place in safekeeping and to insist, inexplicably, knowing him to be a bachelor on foreign shores, that his wife requires his presence at the dinner table at home. Of course Dromio has been mistaken for his double, so is bemused, not acting dumb. Then the conversation abruptly changes course:

A. of S. [...] But say, sir, is it dinner-time?
D. of S. No, sir; I think the meat wants that I have
A. of S. In good time, sir; what's that?
D. of S. basting.
A. of S. well, sir, then 'twill be dry.
D. of S   If it be, sir, I pray you, eat none of it.
A. of S. Your reason?
D. of S. Lest it make you choleric and purchase me another dry basting.
A. of S. Well sir learn to jest in good time: there's a time for all things.
D. of S. I durst have denied that, before you were so choleric.

A. of S.	By what rule sir?
D. of S.	Marry, sir, by a rule as plain as the plain bald pate of father Time himself.
A. of S.	Let's hear it.
D. of S.	There's no time for a man to recover his hair that grows bald by nature.
A. of S.	May he not do it by fine and recovery?
D of S.	Yes, to pay a fine for a periwig and recover the lost hair of another man.
A. of S.	why is Time such a niggard of hair, being, as it is, so plentiful an excrement?
D. of S.	Because it is a blessing that he bestows on beasts; and what he hath scanted men in hair he hath given them in wit.
A. of S.	Why there's many a man hath more hair than wit.
D. of S.	Not a man of those but he hath the wit to lose his hair.
A. of S.	Why, thou didst conclude hairy men plain dealers, without wit.
D. of S.	The plainer dealer, the sooner lost. Yet he loseth it in a kind of policy.
A. of S.	For what reason?
D. of S.	For two, and sound ones too [...] The one, to save the money that he spends in tiring; the other, that at dinner they should not drop in his porridge.
A. of S.	You would all this time have proved there is no time for all things.
D. of S.	Marry, and did, sir; namely, no time to recover hair lost by nature.
A. of S.	But your reason was not substantial, why there is no time to recover.
D. of S.	Thus I mend it: Time himself is bald and therefore to the world's end will have bald followers.
A. of S.	I knew 'twould be a bald conclusion. (*Errors*, 2. 2, 53–111)

On the surface, Dromio plays upon warnings about the damaging effects on anger to the digestion; irregular mealtimes and dry meat are prematurely aging, particularly for those old men with a choleric disposition. If a choleric person gives in to anger, he shortens his life and hastens the symptoms of age; in addition to baldness and white hair, time's ravages to the body manifest themselves in bowel trouble. Elyot explains this fully:

Old men, in whom natural heat and strength seems to decay, should use always meats which are of quality hot and moist, and therewith easy to be digested, and abstayne utterly from all meats and drinks which will engender thick juice and slimy [...] Finally, let them beware of all meats that will stop the pores, and make obstructions or oppilations, that is to say, with clammy matter stop the places, where the natural humours are wrought and digested. (Elyot, 1541, 39)

Those who are of a choleric disposition, old or young, need to ensure that their meat is moist. It can happen that nature is kind to some old men, endowing them with stronger digestions, stomachs and livers than 'the said' choleric young (39), but as a general rule, the 'property' of old men, coldness and dryness, requires special dietary measures to counterbalance nature's deficiencies.[8] This particularly applies to old cholerics, who need more moisture in their meats than young men 'of the same complexion' (Elyot, 1541, 39–40).

Elyot's strictures and observations help bring to the surface the motif of age in Act two, Scene two. Dromio is in effect alerting his master to the probable ill effects even to a young person of losing his temper so far as to give his servant a 'basting'. Dromio thus likens what he takes to be his master's distemper to that of an old man, full of anger and swollen with excrement, unable to digest or to evacuate. Dromio's jest is doubly out of time, which plays tricks on young men by robbing them of their wit just as it robs old men of their hair, and it robs both of their ability to stomach tough food. Nor does time discriminate between youth and age. Because of an accident of time, the innocent servant suffers an undeserved 'basting'; comparably, time punishes old men by unmerited baldness. The dialogue displaces once more onto the body of the youthful the disfiguring marks of age. The trope of bald time and the unwholesomeness of dry meat for the delicate digestions of the old, evoked as a warning to what awaits Antipholus when he grows old, serves also to convey the idea of time disjoint for all the characters, with the consequence that the mistaken identities become literally and figuratively unpalatable to all concerned, but especially so to Egeon. Condemned to die simply for being in the wrong place at the wrong time (trade wars between the two countries have resulted in a decree that any Syracusan found on Ephesan soil must either pay a fine or suffer the death penalty), old, frail and resourceless, he experiences alienation, bereavement, and severance; he continues to suffer and doubt the evidence of his senses right up to the last minute. As the final word on the condition of age, Egeon's plaint, delivered in the last act, draws together the strands on bodily infirmity and its effect on the emotions:

> Not know my voice! O time's extremity,
> Hast thou so crack'd and splitted my poor tongue
> In seven short years, that here my only son
> Knows not my feeble key of untuned cares?
> Though now this grained face of mine be hid
> In sap-consuming winter's drizzled snow,
> And all the conduits of my blood froze up,
> Yet hath my night of life some memory,

My wasting lamps some fading glimmer left,
My dull deaf ears a little use to hear;
All these old witnesses — I cannot err —
Tell me thou art my son Antipholus. (*Errors*, 2002, 5.1, 308–19)

Not recognised by his son and his wits doubted by the younger Duke ('I see thy age and dangers make thee dote') he is nevertheless in the right and all the youngsters wrong, and the attentive reader/viewer can now perceive that Dromio of Syracuse's jokes are a way of keeping before the audience Egeon's plight while he is off-stage.

At first glance, then, the Syracusan Antipholus and Dromio engage in a witty exchange elaborated around the first identity mistake. But the references to the damaging effects of time on the body keep alive negative discourses on old age. Dromio reminds the audience that bald time, with its crippling outcomes, is 'a very bankrupt', owing 'more than he's worth, to season' and a thief, too, 'stealing on by night and day' (4. 2, 57–59). But the master and servant's witticisms on time's irrecoverability and their jokes about the consequences of disrupted midday meals upon the digestion place them at a safe distance from the harmful realities of aging. Adriana on the other hand articulates her husband's neglect and its implied threat to her social position as the same feelings of uselessness and decay expressed by the marginalised old. The social and psychological significance of food in the play thus contributes to the subtext which interrogates the commonplaces of aging — not in absolute terms, but according to gender.[9]

The missed midday meal, along with its implied physiological, social and psychological effects, complicates gender and generational commonplaces about the relationship between the external effects of aging and the malfunctions which increase with age. The midday meal is particularly important in settling the delicate state of old men's stomachs in order to avoid the build up of phlegm, as an aid to the maintenance of the digestive organs, and as a means of preserving the body's moisture. A missed midday meal disrupts the humoral balance of the body, and precipitates the onset of age. As Joseph Candido suggests, the Ephesan Antipholus's failure to attend his wife's midday meal repudiates its role in maintaining social and marital relations (Candido, 1997, 208), but it also identifies him as a foolish and incontinent young person well on the road to premature old age.[10] So when Adriana learns that the man she supposes to be her husband has made passes at her sister during the meal that was planned to re-establish marital harmony, it is not surprising that her angry outburst expresses itself in the derogatory terms applied to the old:

He is deformed, crooked, old, and sere,
Ill-fac'd, worse bodied, shapeless every where (4. 2, 19–20)

The missed midday meal, disruptive of harmony to both young and old but for different reasons, underscores the perception that the marital transgressions of Antipholus of Ephesus rest upon assumptions about the prematurely aging consequences of erratic bodily regimes, and they also bring into relief the contrasts between the Antipholus twins. Though both twins dishonour the midday meal, the Syracusan does so unwittingly, not knowing the offence he commits in paying court to Luciana at her sister's table. The other dishonours it knowingly, missing his wife's repast so that he can dine with a whore. The Syracusan is anxious to keep to mealtimes (2. 2, 54) whereas the Ephesan neglects them; he has let the meat grow cold at his wife's meal because he 'has no stomach', and his 'default' deprives her of nourishment in all senses(1. 2, 48–52). But the episode relies also upon a play on stereotypical images of age for its comic effect. Disruptions to the midday meal, expressed as the withering effects of age, serve a narrative and figurative end. Figuratively, they keep alive the plight of Egeon, and narratively, they pave the way for the finale, a family feast organised by the Abbess to celebrate the reunion of aged husband with wife and parents with grown up children.

The play's underlying preoccupation with age fully declares itself in the final scene. It reaches a resolution of sorts by restoring marital harmony within the larger newly re-formed family group when gender roles are realigned and the composition of the household re-balanced by the reunion of the old couple. Candido hints at this:

> at the end of the play we have no actual nuptial rite or even the symbolic evocation of one as we sometimes do in Shakespearean comedy. Instead the emphasis here is on the unification of an old family (even its younger members are old enough to have grown apart) rather than on the earnest hope for beginning a new one. But this is not to say that *The Comedy of Errors* is without its own significant — and characteristic — comic closure. When the multiple confusions are finally resolved, the Abbess invites the assembled company into her dwelling for a dining experience of a very different sort from those we have seen earlier in this play [...] the whole family assembles to welcome with joy a new member into a social and religious community. (Candido, 1997, 219)

It is indeed significant that the social, moral and spiritual values are reaffirmed at the table of the old abbess, and Candido's brief reference to this in his concluding remarks effectively point ups the gathering significance of the aging theme as the action takes its course. After a prolonged bereavement, timely festivity restores Egeon to his wife and sons. The family reassembles under the sheltering roof of an old woman and as the celebratory feast gets under way, the young receive sustenance in a nourishing, caring household, headed by a paterfamilias restored at long last to the rightful dignity and tranquillity of his years. At peace with her husband, Adriana is able to reclaim her youth; and the realignment of domestic positions restores the correct balance of the household. This is the precinct to which the tropes of time are headed. The reclamation and reunion of the old couple, each rescued from isolation and pining, repairs the rupture to domestic peace. In this the play mirrors accounts which show that the family torn asunder is an aberration of the norm.[11]

However, a potential source of conflict declares itself, and remains unresolved. Just before Egeon and Emilia recompose their household, a likely source of friction emerges around the awkward question as to who has the ultimate authority to quell disputes between husband and wife. Can it be left to the young couple themselves, or does the authority of a parent override the claims of a spouse? This question is raised, but other more pressing matters intervene before it can be resolved. Antipholus of Ephesus has taken refuge from his wife in the priory, not knowing that it is his long-lost mother who shelters him. Adriana meets unexpected resistance from the older woman when she arrives 'to fetch my poor distracted husband hence' (*Errors*, 5. 1, 39). She wants him bound securely and born home to recover. The Abbess, however, asserts her right to keep him where he is on the grounds that he was driven to distraction by Adriana's jealousy and shrewishness. She questions Adriana closely on the likely causes of his bout of insanity. Though she identifies the cause of his straying affection as 'a sin prevailing much in youthful men,/Who give their eyes the liberty of gazing' (5. 1, 50–54), strikingly she describes his symptoms as those more readily identified as the symptoms of bodily malfunction suffered by the old:

> It seems his sleeps were hindered by thy railing,
> And thereof comes it that his head is light.
> Thou sayst his meat was sauced with thy upbraidings:
> Unquiet meals make ill digestions.
> [...]
> Sweet recreation barred, what doth ensue
> But moody and dull melancholy,
> Kinsman to grim and comfortless despair,
> And at her heels a huge infectious troop
> Of pale distemperatures and foes to life?
> In food, in sport, and life-preserving rest
> To be disturbed would mad or man or beast. (5. 1. 71–84)

Broken sleep, lack of rest and overspiced meat shorten life; unconsciously the abbess reprises the theme of the comic sparring between the Syracusan Antiphlus and Dromio, projecting onto her Ephesan son the distempers of old age. She also draws attention to her long lost husband's suffering at the beginning of the play, and the manner in which it is evoked by Adriana and turned into an elaborate joke by the twins from Syracuse. Though this particular spin on manual platitudes is resolved, the idea that the old must avoid extremes of emotion (Cuffe, 1607, 98, 103; Bacon, 1638, 181; Elyot, 1541, 39)[12] is not. Shakespeare's refusal to package things up nicely so early on in his career seems to point to a particularly vexed area of generational conflict in early modern households where a young couple share the home of elderly parents. The parents hold the purse strings and continue to manage their children's lives — a theme taken up anew in the chapter which follows.

From this point of view, the breach between the generations is only partially healed. At the play's opening Egeon's doubly life-threatening predicament sets the plot in motion. As an old man already weakened by travel,[13] he finds himself under threat of the death penalty in a foreign and inhospitable land. The full extent of the toll this has taken upon his emotional and psychological condition becomes apparent only at the end, when, on catching sight of his son for the first time in so many years, he doubts his own sanity:

> Unless the fear of death doth make me dote,
> I see my son Antipholus, and Dromio. (*Errors*, 5. 1, 195–96)

Yet this is not to deny the ending its healing the breach between the generations. Egeon starts off as old, frail, isolated, powerless and in danger of losing his life. At the end, he is cocooned by his newly re-formed family, reintegrated in society and given the chance to prolong his lifespan by domestic comfort in a place whose climate is hospitable to prolongevity (cf. Bacon, 1638, 113–16). The movement from the hardships suffered and the hostility encountered to comfort and respect, at first relying on a complex amalgamation of stock characters from Roman comedy and stereotypes of old age, has by the end developed well beyond the requirements of genre. The first scene in which an unbending younger man gives the solitary old stranger only one day's grace to find a ransom, presents a tableau of intractable youth and vulnerable age. Egeon's plight suggests a pitiful image of helpless old age. In a hostile environment, childless, wifeless and without a circle of relatives to call upon for help, his time appears to have run out, and he faces the prospect of a sorrowful and solitary death. Yet by the end his voyage has been one of discovery, by no means inimical to his advanced condition. In this, too, the play rehearses debates about the benefits of travel to the old, so that the ending shows family restored and time reclaimed for both young and old as a result of the epic journey of an old man. The play thus participates in a range of discourses on old age. Comically figured in caricature, the old are nevertheless able to reclaim their dignity as heads of household, and it is through their agency that the young recover the lost harmony of their lives. In its actions, *The Comedy of Errors* relies for much of its comedy and its pathos upon reversals and substitutions of old age stereotypes, tumbled and spun around so that old age, always a significant subtext, assumes centre stage at unexpected places and in unexpected ways . The result is that the young are forced to confront the disabilities of old age while the old suffer alone at its beginning, but at the end luxuriate in the warmth of family reunion. The play thus joins a host of literatures that rely on commonplaces of old age as a condition both beleaguered and blest.

DIALOGUE OF COMFORT

The hardwiring of age into *Errors* is a feature also of two earlier works in differing genres. Leon Battista Alberti's account of the last day of his father's life installs his family, one of the most eminent and powerful in quattrocento Florence, as the theme and target of *I libri della famiglia*.[14] Thomas More's *Dialogue of Comfort against Tribulation*, written while he was imprisoned in the tower, is ostensibly a lightly fictionalised account of how to prepare for death. Both works represent humanist ideals of the *vita activa* conjoined with the *vita contemplativa*, and both revolve round the figure of the dying paterfamilias. Separated by almost a century from each other and from *Errors*, all three works nevertheless share a preoccupation with and reworking of platitudes about age. From the commonplace territory of the superior wisdom of the old and the duty, care and respect the young owe them (cf. *della famiglia*, 40–41; *Dialogue*, 81, 90, 186-87) to the ubiquitous likening of that stage of life as a guttering candle (*Dialogue*, 85; cf. Cicero, 2001, 45; *Richard II*, 1. 3, 220) each work takes as its reference point the temporal urgency of the circumstances leading to its creation (cf. *della famiglia*, 33–35; *Dialogue*, 3–4). Time has run out for both Lorenzo and Anthony, old men immobilised at the centre of the lives of those closest to them. *Della famiglia* is organised around a series of dialogues between male members of the family as they gather round the bedside of the dying Lorenzo, Leon Battista's father, brought together by Leon Battista into a single narrative and published some years after his father's death. The *Dialogue* was written in 1534, the year before More's execution. Old age, imminent death, and the importance of family shapes each of these accounts, just as it underpins *Errors*. All three works rely on society's commonly accepted characterisations of the old — their frailty, their enhanced wisdom, their delicate stomachs, their superior spirituality (they are all well on into their final journey) and their close relationship to a younger relative, and each concerns the last sufferings of the old. Lorenzo Alberti is on his deathbed, and More's *Dialogue* hinges upon the fact that Anthony is a sick old man preparing to die in captivity far from home. This informs his thinking on the different kinds of comfort available to him in his straitened circumstances. He ponders the need for a man of clear conscience who has fallen into the hands of the Turks to remain true to his faith despite torture, so that 'all his hole payne shall tourne all into glorye' (*Dialogue*, 32), and he rejects as false the "unchristian" kind of comfort that encourages the false hope that he may get better and live. Old age necessarily involves suffering, and man must suffer the burden of his years with patience, even though this is the hardest to bear since in each case the old men's movements are constricted, their bodies are subject to frequent pain and discomfort, and they must conquer fear (*della famiglia*, 35; Marius, 1886, 473; *Dialogue*, 62, 124–25. Both of these works 'turn on a fiction' (Marius, 1986, 472) in that they can be read as an auto-biographical account of the peculiar religious and political menace which faced More, and the peculiar financial deprivations facing Leon Battista Alberti, the younger of two (illegitimate) sons born to Lorenzo and Bianca di Carlo Fieschi, upon his father's death (*della famiglia*, 5; Marius, 1986, 472). In more conventional literary terms, each can be read as a medita-tion in dialogue form upon the last stage of a man's life, with youth a respectful and sympathetic witness. The *Dialogue*'s generic hybridity for instance (part dialogue, part comfort literature, part polemic, part 'merry tale') and its autobiographical basis in the hardship suffered by More in his last months on earth, are all underpinned by the characteristics commonly held to typify the winter of men's lives, and as such it contributes to a body of literature whose main subject, or at the very least a significant subtext, is masculine old age.

There are other affiliations. The narrative in all three is woven around the mutual responsibilities of old and young and relies on classical com-monplaces of old age; *Errors* relies on Plautine stereotypes, *della famiglia* and the *Dialogue* on idealisations from Plutarch and Cicero. While redu-plication in *Errors* depends upon farcical doubling up on twins, *della fami-glia* and *Dialogue* in their own way turn on not just one fiction, but two. The characterisation of Vincent, the young interlocutor of More's fiction-alised alter ego, Anthony, draws on and to some extent duplicates the close emotional and intellectual bond between More and his daughter Marga-ret, whereas the organisation of Alberti's family memoir revolves around the 'fictions' of humanism. Alberti frames his discussion of differentiated responsibilities around humanist preoccupations, depicting the speakers as models of humanist morality (*della famiglia*, 16). Book one deals with the role of a father, and the emotional bonds between family members; married love is the subject of book two; book three examines domestic economies, while book four interrogates the quality and function of the relationships of the paterfamilias outside the family. However, the idealisation and repre-sentation of the chief speakers, particularly of Adovardo (Lorenzo's nephew by marriage) in d*ella famiglia* places the work just as much in the fictional domain. Though Lorenzo treated his two illegitimate sons as Albertis, Leon Battista's account is driven to some extent by a sense of grievance at the treatment he suffered at the hands of his cousins, who deprived him of funds to see him through university, yet claimed, as part of a tax swindle, to have spent large sums on his education (*della famiglia*, 5). It is solely on the dying Lorenzo's power to iron out family grievances and restore har-monious relations. Anthony, More's fictional self, performs a similar task, though as a sideline to the work's spiritual centre. In the *Dialogue*, More brings in his family in a clearly recognisable way but always within the protective scope of fiction. Anthony's digression on tertian fevers, for example, allows More to talk about his own family; the young woman trained in Galenic medicine is a reference to his adopted daughter, Margaret Clement (*Dialogue*, 89–90); and some of the Merry Tales have his wife, Dame Alice, in mind (cf. *Dialogue*, 277).

The old age motif is put to work to define structure in all three works. Common assumptions about hardships suffered by the old shape each text, and each turns these platitudes around by using them to control the direction of events. All three span both genre and generation issues by a narrative framework that uses an old man's relationship to a young man, in each case shadowed by a double, as a means of shaping outcomes. In all three a father's responsibilities continue into his children's adult lives, and all three share a dependence on the classical past; the father figure, close to death, embodies in each a stoicism drawn from Cicero, Seneca, Xenophon and Plutarch (cf. *della famiglia*, 35, 37). The *Dialogue* starts by paraphrasing Cicero: 'for as wee well wot that a yong man may dye sone so be we very sure, that an old man cannot lyve long' — and ends the sentence by quoting him directly: 'no man for all that so old but that he hopeth yet that he may lyve one yere more' (*Dialogue*, 4). *Della famiglia* contains personages who share the Plautine antecedents of *Errors* to the extent that they represent a mercantile ethos; Giannozzo, (*della famiglia*, 16) is an old merchant who towards the end of Book 3 propounds an economics grounded in a pre-Marxist perception of commodities (including money) available as a result of labour profitably managed. In *Errors* commodification is burlesqued in the figure of the goldsmith, and provides the means of enabling the final family reunion. All three subscribe to the premise that hard work is admirable and labour retains its value, though in real life, whilst in prison, More lost all the property the king had given him, and all his goods were forfeited (Marius, 1986, 481; More, 1947, 540, 543). For this reason loss of worldly goods in the *Dialogue* is a prelude to heaven.

Even more to the point, the links between *della famiglia* and the *Dialogue* emerge through a reappropriation of the commonplaces of aging. In each the wisdom of elders triumphs; in *della famiglia*, Giannozzo comes to abandon the warlike sports of his youth, and Adovardo praises the kind of pacifism associated with the early humanists who condemned war (cf. Erasmus, 1978, 79–82). His condemnation of suicide, like More's, owes its origins just as much to Platonic and Stoic philosophies as to Christian teachings. Both works derive their animus from classical thought, though each pay tribute to the teachings of the Catholic church. Both authors combined public office with scholarship and contemplation, so that each participated in the *vita activa*, yet each, as a result of hardships suffered, were in their own lifetimes considered examplars of the contemplative life. Renee Watkins, translator of *della famiglia*, describes Alberti's participation in both worlds as 'a curious combination of the success that men admire with the qualities of soul that provide an easy conscience' (*della famiglia*, 19) — a description that could equally well apply to the life and beliefs of Thomas More. Each of these works uses the platitudes surrounding the importance of the old in the shaping and morals of the character of the young ostensibly for a specific purpose; in *della famiglia* to affirm the continuing authority of the father, in the *Dialogue* to bring the young to a deeper understanding of God's purpose. As in *Errors*, each writer is aware of the effect of exile on the old and the need for roots, and each shows painful awareness of the lack of respect in their own times of the young for the old, and the need for the old to guide youth with a restraining hand. At the same time, though they acknowledge the temperance and respect of the young who seek their company, both believe that all old people should father the young, irrespective of direct paternity (*della famiglia*, 39); hence Anthony's paternal care and guidance of his nephew Vincent.

Della famiglia and the *Dialogue* share a looseness of structure, a bagginess due to repetition. The translator of Alberti's work felt the need to punctuate, paragraph, cut the length of the sentences and 'compress' the sometimes 'redundant and embellished phrasing' of the original 'for readability's sake' in the hope that 'an English kind of fluidity replaces the close-knit unity of his constructions' (*della famiglia*, 4). The editors of the Yale edition of More's works in which the *Dialogue* appears experience a similar need to apologise for a comparable long-windedness of expression and structure. They explain the loose and rambling structure of the work as More's dual wish for the verisimilitude of an unscripted exchange taking place over a period of time, but which is also generically distinct as a dialogue between youth and age. Each Book 'has its own decorum, with a lapse in time before each renewal of the conversation' in order precisely to present the universal problem of tribulation from a different perspective. Thus the general application of More's fictionalised setting is conveyed 'by means of deliberate garrulity and conscious digression' (*Dialogue*, lxvii). Much more importantly, garrulity serves as an organising principle for the entire work. I now argue that the seemingly formless ramblings of an old man in the *Dialogue* serve to reinvent the platitudes and paradoxes of old age as a specific principle of organisation.

The circumlocuitous structure of the *Dialogue* proclaims one of the chief characteristics of age — garrulity; that is, what Cicero more circumspectly called love of conversation (Cicero, 1923, 57) but which subsequently hardened into stereotype. In the first stages of the dialogue, Anthony interrupts himself to express the wish that their conversation had been more formally structured, 'in such a maner as lernid men vse betwene the persons whom they devise disputyng in their faynid dialoges' (*Dialogue*, 79). Though esteemed and wise, Anthony possesses the failing that is most closely associated with old age. The structure mimics the rambling conversation of an old man, whose main line of argument becomes submerged in the copious detail of digressionary recollections and stories. In the midst of elaborating upon the nature of penance, Anthony becomes so involved in recounting the strange tale of a tertian fever of his that for a moment he can't remember what he was talking about in the first place, and this he puts down to the talkativeness and abesentmindedness of age: 'I haue bene so long in my tale' anthony tells his nephew 'that I haue almost forgotone for what purpose I told yt' (90). This digression re-appropriates two platitudes of growing old. In the first instance it uses garrulity, the off-side of love of conversation, as a means of widening the perspectives of the topic under discussion and in the second, it serves to blur the boundaries that divide youth from age. The story of the tertian fever spawns the information that a young woman, whom Louis Martz identifies as More's daughter-in-law (lxx), 'more con-nyng' than either of the physicians attending Anthony, correctly diagnosed the fever as a result of having read Galen's *De differentiis febrium* (90). By such means, and as a result of the overarching frame of old age, More is able to bridge the divide between fiction and reality, to challenge stereotyp-ing of the antagonisms between young and old, and to provide a structure that enables the work to thoroughly examine the problem of tribulation not from one, but from many angles, thereby advancing the argument obliquely and playfully, through the negative stereotyping of old men as windbags. Anthony speaks of himself as an old fool who loves to sit 'well & warm with a cupp & a rostid crabb & dryvill & drinke & talke' (78) as he veers off into a story about a man in a cloister who talked too much, vowing all the while not to do the same thing himself. This is the first of a number of Merry Tales which, under the guise of garrulity, exemplify ordeals. More himself faced, and by means of which he is able to untangle true from false comfort.

Garrulity, a topic discussed at some length in the old age literature pub-lished both before and after the *Dialogue* and stereotypically associated with old men, serves also to introduce the question of whether suicide, the temptation most personally threatening to More, is an option.[15] The subject first appears in four separate diversionary tales. The first reference is in the story of a wife who kills herself to spite her husband by goading him into an excess of violence against her, so that he would be hanged for murder (125). In the second an old monk is tempted to martyrdom; he mistakenly believes that God orders him to kill himself (129–30). A rich widow courts martyr-dom in the third by tricking a poor neighbour into cutting off her head and bequeathing a sum of money to the Pope to speed along her canonisation (127). In the fourth, Anthony uses St. Augustine's story of the Roman vir-gins who drowned themselves rather than suffer rape as a caution against suicide, even though in this instance it was inspired by God, who presum-ably had his own reasons for sanctioning their 'temporall deth' rather 'than abide the desoylyng & violacion of their chastite.' In the normal course of things, as Augustine himself points out, 'it is not lawfull for any other maid to follow their sample but rather suffer other to do her any maner violence by force, & commit sinne of his own vppon her agaynst her will

than willingly & thereby sinfully her selfe become an homicide of her selfe'
(141–42). Young girls are thus warned against the Roman model wherein
suicide is honourable, and are persuaded instead to quietly accept the will
of God. In the stories of the wife, the monk and the widow, self-destruction
is made viable by an absurd twist in logic which indicates a shift in perspective from More's youthful classically-inspired radicalism. In *Utopia* suicide
is valued as a way of saving family and friends from the burden of coping
with incurable illness, whereas in the *Dialogue* it becomes a temptation to
be resisted at all costs. Anthony alludes to insomniac terrors of succumbing
to its lure. Whoever is prone to sleeplessness must arm themselves against
this most insidious of enticements to mortal sin, and must

> so compose hym about with a pavice (a shield), that he shall not nede
> to drede this nightes feare of this wikkid temptacion And thus will I
> fynish this piece of the nightes feare And glad am I that we passed it &
> comen ones vnto the day. (157)

More entwines the experience of growing old as a strategic tool in his
main argument with the diversions so tightly that it becomes impossible to
disentangle one from the other without damage to the narrative integrity of
each. This reference to the temptation of suicide enters the main argument
only after it has been diversely illustrated in these stories. It first appears
in an oblique and complex manner. Anthony divides tribulation into three
categories: 'either it is such as hym self willyngly taketh, or secondly such
as hym selfe willyingly suffreth or fynally such as he can not put from hym'
(86). He places the trials to which an aging body is subject in the last category. An old man must resign himself to the trials of a body that is weak
and ailing, and a life that has almost run its course. Old age, bringing with
it the kind of bodily harm 'that a man hath all ready caught & can in no
wise avoyd' prompts Anthony to liken his life to the snuff of a candle 'that
burneth with in the candell styk nose,' at times seemingly extinct, at others suddenly flaring up again 'til at last ere it be lokyd for, out it goeth all
together' (85). His sense of urgency prompts him to resolve to keep to the
point. Each day might be his last, and there is more to discuss than he has
days left to live. But his resolve soon dissipates, and the chapters which
follow deal in a densely allegorical way with the temptation to suicide and
the trial of patience, both of which beset old men most particularly. In
this manner More performs a double task. He reworks garrulity and the
temptation to suicide, impulses to which age is prone, into a complex re-
evaluation of the part played by the frail old body and spirit in dealing with
the trials through which God tests the faithful, and he accomplishes this
by choosing as his foundational structural tool one of the most commonly
assumed failings of old age.

In so doing, the author enables his fictional self to remain in control of
the superabundance of diverse material in the *Dialogue* precisely by means

of circumlocution. He is able to do this because the experiences of constriction coupled with the experience of aging (in the main argument and in the digressions) drive the narrative forward. The causes for tribulation and the need to discern between false and true comfort are topics of surmounting interest to the elderly, while at the same time engaging the sympathy and care of the young. This is evident in the main dialogue and is elaborated, illustrated and developed in the digressionary tales. The argument progresses from point to point as the work visibly takes its shape from the welter of narratives that crowd in on the point being made. More's conveniently multifunctional form of fictionalised biography enables him to deal all at once and in a perfectly coherent manner with old age, ill health, imprisonment, and the religious and political crisis of Henry VIII's divorce from his first wife and, as a consequence, from the Roman Catholic Church. In this work the digressions, specific effects of garrulity, serve an important structural function, and, in their very reliance on the stereotypical features of old age, establish the cornerstones of the main argument.

In later, more straightforwardly didactic accounts of old age the commonplaces and stereotypes, inventively serving More's narrative purposes and signposting the spiritual journey Anthony embarks upon with his nephew, are merely formalised into advice. Old men may attain its idealised status by acquiring wisdom, temperance, spirituality and endurance but they do so by recourse to strategies unproblematically handed down in an unbroken line from the classics through the middle ages and on to the sixteenth and seventeenth centuries.[16] The mutation of commonplace into prescription subsequent to More serves to distinguish his *Dialogue* from normative instructional material at the same time as it exploits the relationship between authors and the condition they all seek to explicate and defend. Simon Goulart's *Wise Vieillard* provides a convenient example of the difference in effect; as a result of divergent aims and methods fiction reinvents the same *aperçus* of age which manifest in the advice manuals as uncomplicated commonplace.

Goulart was a French Protestant divine who wrote his treatise in his own old age as a spiritual consolation for fellow-sufferers. It was translated out of the French by 'an obscure Englishman, a friend and fauourer of all Wise Old-Men'. Dated 1621, and initialled 'T.W,' it bears on its title page a woodcut of Thomas Williamson. On the flyleaf of the British Library copy of this edition is a handwritten note saying that TW is Thomas Williamson. The impulse to personalise the translation, to fashion it to those growing old in England, to instruct English readers on the art of growing old gracefully, how to avoid the pitfalls of age and how to find comfort in the winter of their lives is one that derives from the genre of comfort literatures just as much as it does from antique apologies of age. Goulart dismisses the miseries of senescence and concentrates instead on its felicities. Ripeness of judgement, for example, is found exclusively in old men; honour is 'the Magnificent and Maiesticall reward of their vertue (Goulart,

1621, 87); they are exemplars to the young; they possess true wisdom, and sincere knowledge of God (88); they are in a unique position to dispense magnanimity and true fortitude, which 'are not enclosed in the muscles' or sinews, but 'in the bearing and sustaining of grieuances' (90); the tongues and pens of wise old men (eg Basil, Augustine) never lay still; the 'milde and meeke conuersation' of old men is 'of better esteeme, and more gracious in them'; they are more patient, more temperate and suffer the approach of death more steadfastly (91). There is no infirmity that the old are not prepared to withstand with courage and patience (98–99). He reiterates Cicero's dictum that wise men go willingly to death whereas the wicked depart against their will (103); the Scriptures provide all the comforts that the wise old need (108–17). Above all, Goulart converts More's subtle interrogation of suicide into the stuff of a sermon. However much the wise old might anticipate death as the end of 'some Comedie or Interlude' (162), to kill oneself is to 'make a hazardous proofe of some kind of greatnesse of courage;' but, as Augustine says,[17] it is madness and totally lacking in magnanimity. Old age is a voyage of self-discovery; inability to tolerate adversity lays bare old men's impotence and pusilanimity 'in casting them-seues so into the gulfe and iawes of death' instead of revealing reserves of strength, for 'hee is truely magnanimous, who chooseth rather to beare the burthen of a miserable life, then rashly to rid himselfe, and flye from it, instead of standing and abiding in the place allotted and appointed vnto him' (169). Goulart, in his desire to give old age a good press, enthusiastically embraces the two contradictory positions. On the one hand, 'hee that vfainedly loveth the Lord shall be satisfied with long life'; but on the other, death gives us 'rest and ease' (3).

Even though the *Dialogue* and *The Wise Vieillard* approach age from doctrinally different standpoints, they reach similar conclusions on the matter of how to prepare oneself to die well. As exemplary discourses on age, they each start from the assumption that an old man must battle for control of his spiritual self by reference to St. Anthony in the desert, thereby forging links in a chain of New Testament association. But although each narrative approaches the circumstantial experience of imprisonment as part of a much wider discourse of old age, there the similarity ends. In the *Dialogue*, Anthony and Vincent work together to re-evaluate the commonplaces of the end of life and in so doing to transform the platitudes of old age, which remain platitudes in manual precept, into a wider message for humankind. A major agent in this transformation, literalised in Anthony/More's imprisonment, is the spiritual battle against constriction of the soul. Mankind must forego its addiction to reason in favour of a spiritual source of comfort found only in belief in God's grace. Man must accept the physical constraints of age, and embrace the notion of God as 'the chiefe gaylour (jailer) of this brode prison the world' (*Dialogue*, 4) — an image borrowed from St. Paul's Epistles and later notoriously exploited by Donne in the Holy Sonets. More's deeper consideration that the world, though a prison, is one which the old particularly are loth to give up, 'for as wee well wot that a yong man may dye sone so be we very sure, that an old man cannot lyve long' (4)[18] does not have a counterpart in manual dictum. And though manual givens thrive on paradox, they do not encourage paradoxical observations akin to More's, that though life and the flesh are as a prison, God is 'neyther cruell nor covetouse' since he lets his prisoners 'walk about, [...] & do therein what we will' (272) despite the fact that both More and his fictional self suffer imprisonment, long exile and must face death.

But whereas *The Wise Vieillard* merely lists and copiously examplifies the commonplaces of the end of life, More's comfort in times of tribulation assimilates the trials of old age into the wider experience of pain and violent death, which enables Anthony to inform his nephew that dying from sickness and 'the deth which men call commonly naturall' involves equal amounts of pain, for it is 'a violent deth to euery man whom it fetcheth hens agaynst his will' (301). Anthony says that he himself, locked in a cell in a prison made by men, is no worse off than those who believe themselves to be free in the world. Indeed, he counts himself blessed, because he has far more time than those at liberty to reflect upon the nature of sin, freedom, and the loss of worldly goods: 'Vpon our prison we bild our prison: we garnysh yt with gold & make yt gloriuse' Anthony tells Vincent, and in this 'false perswasion of welth & forgetfulness' we lose track of our own sorry state (273).[19] Anthony's meditation on the effects of imprisonment on the body and soul does, however, find a parallel in the plight of the old who suffer bodily constriction yet convert it into a rich storehouse. By so doing, More and, later, Goulart personalise the commonplace of God the jailer and the prison of the world and the flesh and give it a new, idiosyncratic direction, just as, conversely, in *Errors*, Adriana's experience of confinement and neglect borrow from the experience of the constrictions and disabilities of age.

2 Old and young

The commonplaces and stereotypes of age looked at in the last chapter could not have been formulated without their correlatives in youth. Alberti's *I Libri della famiglia* and More's *Dialogue of Comfort* both seek to instruct the young, and the close relationship between the two resulted in the displacement of the negative effects of age onto the young in *The Comedy of Errors*. Works such as these have as their ground plan the premise that concord between the young and old is a two-way process in which both must play their part. For the young this means obedience, respect and subservience to the authority of their elders. For the old it depends upon good habits learnt when young. For this reason commendations deriving from the classics on an old age well trained up from childhood are widely quoted in the prescriptive literature (see, for example, Goulart, 1621, 100–101; Sheafe, 1639, To the Reader). They share a widespread assumption that the old have a moral responsibility to prepare the young spiritually and temporally. They must also teach them how to behave towards their elders, so that they may themselves reach a discerning old age: 'Hee that will take vpon him the wardship and tuition of some young man, and to haue him well brought vp, doth commit him to a wise old man' (Goulart, 1621, 97; viz. fig. 2.1), and the sooner the educative process begins the better. Henry Peacham expresses this parental duty in the well-worn analogy of sowing seeds in springtime:

> As the spring is the only fitting seedtime for grain, setting and planting in garden and orchard, so youth, the April of man's life, is the most natural and convenient season to scatter the seeds of knowledge upon the ground of the mind. (Peacham, 1622, 32)

In addition to its adumbration of the spiritual lessons teased out by Anthony in More's *Dialogue*, Goulart's *Wise Vieillard* usefully demonstrates the enduring character of ruminations on the commonplaces of youth and age from the ancients onwards at the same time as it hardens into dogma the stereotypes that Alberti, More and Shakespeare variously appropriate and transform. Even though it is not formally structured as a debate between

Figure 2.1 Leonardo da Vinci, Profiles of an Old and a Young Man, drawing. Gabinetto dei Disegni e delle Stampe, Uffizi, Florence. Scala/Art Resource, New York.

youth and age, its generic debt to youth–age dialogues is manifest throughout, as is Thomas Brookes' *Apples of Gold for Young Men and Women and A Crown of Glory for Old Men and Women*.

According to Goulart and Brookes, and most early modern non-fiction writers, the relationship between old and young is one of unproblematic subservience. An old man's experience, wisdom, judgement, knowledge and discretion entitled him to a position of unchallenged authority. Ancient, biblical and proverbial binary formulas of the callowness of youth in contrast to the wisdom and enhanced spirituality of age also find fertile soil in works of fiction. However, the privileging of old men becomes increasingly complex and ambivalent as it migrates from one era to another and from prescriptive to imaginative writing. In the matter of inheritance particularly, the needs of the young become increasingly clamorous, rendering even more precarious the relations between old and young. In this regard, the formal settings for the arguments of age against youth across the genres permit slippage from the security of the idyllic in formal dialogue and pastoral to the uncertainties of a kind of realism that stands against the idealisations of age at the expense of youth. The task of this chapter is look into some of the cultural and generic conditions which promote intergenerational harmony as well as strife in age's spiritual and material legacy to the young.

INHERITANCE

The final section of the *Dialogue* achieves harmony between youth and age only by youth's acceptance of the greater wisdom of age, and age's acceptance of its condition as a return to the innocence of childhood, but not its dependency. The same is true of pastoral. In terms of genre, Stephen Marx places aged authority at the centre of what he calls the pastoral of old age. He examines the role of the dialogue form in its development, finding that the pastoral of old age complements the pastoral of youth in shared assumptions of a world on the edge of 'socially defined reality, remote from center of court and city' (Marx 1985(a), 21–24; 1985(b), 150–187; 239). Here as in the *Dialogue*, the harmony between youth and age depends upon 'exemption from concerns of office;' its goal is to 'maintain the world,' and it explicitly excludes the *vita activa* from its realm (Marx, 1985a, 22). This 'shared exclusion of and by the world' attracts both old and young, who come together in 'a tender relationship of mutual guardianship,' as in Virgil's *Eclogues* (cf. Eclogue I, lines 46–52) which provide an ideal environment for both, in that 'the natural world of poverty, of labor, of winter and rough weather nourishes the simple virtues of hardiness, wisdom, and honesty' (Marx, 1985a, 22). The ideal place for old age to flourish is the countryside or in sequestration.[1] The old may have a (limited) role as wise counsellors to youth at court, but Marx finds that pastoral poetry rejects court city dwelling in favour of the bucolic (25). Any harmony between old and young is fleeting and is a feature exclusively of country living which removes old and young from the ambitious thrust and competition for social advancement characteristic of city and court life (26). The youth–age debates in pastoral evoke a bucolic paradise where, mindful of their classical antecedents, the young hold conversations with the old which take place in an environment ranging through the landscapes of the mind. In Plato's *Phaedrus*, for example, the youthful Phaedrus talks to the aged Socrates on a variety of subjects melding pleasure with wisdom in an idyllic country setting (Phaedrus, 1995, 6; 23–6; 49-53; 83–6). In both pastoral and dialogue harmony between the young and the old is presented as an ideal, for the specific purpose of instructing youth. Similarly, in the Februarie Eclogue of the *Shephearde's Calender*, the mutual antagonism of the young and old shepherds dissolves in story-telling; Thenot's story of the oak and the brier reaffirms the ability of age to withstand the bitter winds of winter (it is destroyed by anger, not cold weather) in contrast to youth's vulnerability to harsh conditions. According to Marx, Spenser adopts Virgil's purpose in the Georgics to codify the practical knowledge of country living and to promote the untutored wisdom found in farmers' almanacs as his structural model for *The Shephearde's Calender* (Marx, 1985a , 33). The country ideal extends beyond the confines of dialogue and pastoral. Taking its model from Cicero, whose Cato recommends agriculture as the ideal pursuit for the elderly, and from Virgil's *Eclogues*, where the old are given as much land as they need (Cicero, 2001, 73; Virgil, 2000, 4), it finds its way into the health regimens of the period and re-emerges in sixteenth- and seventeenth-century drama. Both *As You Like It* and *The Old Law* contain a pastoral motif which idealises the harmony between old and young; in the former, old and young migrate from court to forest, an environment which highlights the contrasting relationships between Adam, the old man accompanying Orlando (the good son) and Oliver (the bad one). A similar pattern and setting in *The Old Law* enable the good son, Cleanthes, to hide his old father in a forest paradise remote from the city world of politics and corruption.[2] Furthermore, the motif of mutual care connects pastoral to tragedy and comedy. Adam, the faithful old servant in *As You Like It*, has his counterpart in tragedy in the figure of the Old Man, Gloucester's 'tenant' who towards the end of *King Lear* delivers the blinded Gloucester safely into the arms of his maligned son Edgar. Lear and Cordelia briefly sing like two birds in a cage, just outside Dover, where they can laugh at gilded butterflies, and Edgar looks out for the blinded Gloucester as he wanders along the cliffs there. In *King Lear*, removal from the factionalist politics of the wicked daughters allows a glimpse of youth and age in mutual care — a motif present also in book six canto nine of *The Faerie Queene* where the 'good old man' Melibae continues to protect his foundling daughter Pastorella (Spenser, 1590, 6: 9, 14–16).

Indeed, considerations of age in dramatic genre in general include city and country-centred environments which originate respectively in Roman new comedy and Roman pastoral. Jacobean city comedy, for example, with its urban setting, draws on traditions giving rise to the stereotypes looked at in the previous chapter, where age is in conflict with youth. The old are 'blocking' characters who put obstacles in the way of young love matches, and who trick the young out of their due inheritance of land and possessions, whereas the young are presented in a sympathetic light and rightly win through in the end. In their championship of the young, these plays affirm life and continuity. The bequest to tragicomedy of pastoral, on the other hand, is to put resolution into the hands of gods and rulers — that is, it belongs to patriarchal authority — hence the classification of *The Old Law* as a tragicomedy where chaos and order are in the control of the ruler Evander, a *deus ex machina* figure[3]. This same pattern is discernible in *King Lear*, where the scenes on the heath in which Lear learns the bitter lessons of care are a sombre version of the idealised bucolic setting in which age instructs youth.

Contrarily, however, there are texts in differing genres which do not only present youth as the bipolar of age. The authors of these texts are also fond of representing relations between youth and age in a series of epigrammatic euphuisms that emphasise the disadvantages each must suffer. This kind of rhetorical equation was practiced by Aristotle, who placed those in the prime of life, as the measure of age, at either end of the central 'perfect age' of man. Thus the young 'take pleasure in living in company and as yet judge nothing by expediency, not even their friends' (Aristotle, 1984, 2: Bk 2, 12, 1389a-b, 2213–14), whereas the old are always suspicious owing to mistrust, and mistrustful owing to experience, and are lukewarm in their affections, neither loving warmly nor hating bitterly (bk 2, 13,1389b–1390a, 2214–15). But the defining characteristic of *akmē*, the perfect age achieved at forty-nine — only one manual refers to this stage in life as middle age (Goulart, 1621, 14) — is the possession of a fully developed mind, bringing with it a rapprochement bearing 'all the advantages that youth and age possess separately' (Dove, 1986, 28–89; Vaugan, 1600, 57). However, the urge to integrate the attributes of each age and a refusal to polarise them is prompted in the didactic literature by the idea that what a person does in youth will have a direct bearing on the kind of old age that person can expect. A parent's most effective bequest to a child is to set them on the road to self-discipline and respect from childhood onwards. Warnings are given to the young to shun 'all shamefull and vnruly passions, to seek 'by the wise gouernment of our selues, to obtaine such an old age, as may bee long, strong, and healthfull' (Goulart, 1621, 35) and to care for the spiritual so that they 'may serue to young and old' (197). Young men are ubiquitously advised to begin laying the foundations to old age in their youth, so that

> men haue occasion to hope well of them, when they see them soberly and constantly frequent the company and are conuersant with wise old men, are advanced to places of charge in the Common-weale or are imployed in the seruice of the Church, or are well seene or experienced in domestiche affairs. Those which see young men thus carefull cannot but greatly reioyce, and assure themselues that after their times humane societie will bee mainetained and kept intire. (198)

An older person will be the slave of pride, intemperance, dissoluteness ava-
rice and vanity if in youth he has not been educated out of treating aged
persons in an ungrateful, sullen, churlish, and insolent manner (198). The
message is conveyed in a wide range of literatures; youth is the incubator
of the ills of old age as surely as 'The Sunne that riseth in the morning
doth set at night.', so 'there is not any thing that doth increase and flourish, but it doth decrease, wither, and waxe old' all the sooner if bad habits
are not scotched in youth (30; Cuffe, 1607, 4, 86; Sheafe, 1639, 198, *passim*). Prescriptive literature exhorts young men to be sober, virtuous, serve
their country commendably and honourably, and never seem reluctant to
do what they are employed to do. Above all youth should

> respect ancient men, bearing with the lumpishnesse and sowernesse of
> those, who haue done them many good turnes and seruices, and who
> are still able to helpe and further them much. (Goulart, 1621, 198;
> Sheafe, 1639, 203)

Rapprochement between old and young with its ancient pedigree and its
voice, transitory but still insistent in dialogue and pastoral, thus results in
a body of generically varied material which attempts to draw together the
divergent experiences of youth and age into an object lesson on what the
old have to offer the young. The importance of the old in shaping future
generations lies at the core of old–young narratives and as such they seek
to account for the whole of a man's life. Edward Calver's verse dialogue,
Passion and Discretion, in Yovth and Age, published in 1641 and centrally
concerned with bequest, illustrates this defining principle. It is a dialogue in
verse and has a narrow didactic aim elaborated around two related biblical
motifs that hinge on inheritance — prodigality and thrift. It is interesting
because of the way Calver codifies commonly held assumptions about the
characteristics and behaviour patterns in each age and their consequences
later on in life into a rigidly balanced set of contrarieties that are formulated along the well-trodden path of youth versus age, but do not involve
youth in conflict with age. Instead, the dialectic of Calver's poem proceeds
from a personification of rash youth in the first instance arguing against
its youthful temperate self — and then, grown old, the foolish 'type' is set
against its opposite, wisdom and discretion in age. Calver's work is relevant
as a distillation of such common binaries in renaissance drama as temperance versus immoderation and prodigality versus thrift. He organises his
oppositions into two sets of dialogue, the one between two younger selves,
temperate and wasteful, the other between these selves grown old. The
implications for what youth is heir to incorporate a view of the vital role
of education in shaping the man, since bad thoughts and habits uncorrected in youth harden and multiply in age. The contest is thus between
contrasting representations of youth paralleled by a continuation of the
same vice–virtue frame into old age.

Calver's dialogue can be fruitfully read alongside fictions of age. For example, he extrapolates two major components of youth-age narratives utilised by Shakespeare in *The Merchant of Venice*,[4] where vexed relations between parents and children arise as a result of the complex issue of inheritance. The play reconstitutes the character types of the penny-pinching old man and prodigal child into typological representations of the good and the bad in youth and old age. Shylock in his old age[5] is a figure of fun to the young Christian traders because he embodies a composite of several stereotypes. As the stock figure of the usurous Jew, who makes a virtue of living by profit and thrift, and as a caricature of the aged miser who hoards his gold and makes his child live in such penny-pinching conditions that she describes her house as hell (*Merchant*, 2.3, 2), Shylock is an old man who, as Christian society would have it, acknowledges the value of human bonds only in so far as he can turn them to profit. His daughter, by contrast, plunges into all of youth's immoderate passions, its voluptuous desires, pursuit of pleasure, and lack of heed to the future. As the stock figure of a father injured, Shylock's double loss of daughter and ducats expresses itself in a comic confusion about values; the loss of his daughter is just as impossible to endure as the loss of the gold and jewels she took away with her. Meanwhile Jessica, representing rash youth, indulges in an orgy of spending without a thought as to where it might lead. In this she contrasts in 'type' to the obedient child Portia, who is level-headed enough to ensure that her desires are obtained within the compass of her father's will. Calver reprises these motifs (along with the land and property motifs in *Lear*, more of which later) by extrapolating and reconfiguring the formulaic patterns of old and young in each of these plays.

Calver's poem singles out the opposed voices of hot-headed, spendthrift, self-centred youth in dispute with its reasonable, thrifty, moderate self and sets them against each other. Similarly, Passion in Age (an object lesson in what happens in age to youth that remains uncorrected) argues with Discretion in Age. These two sets of personified opposites engage in a formally balanced witty exchange in rhyming couplets upon the subject of husbandry. Passionate youth, presenting itself as spirited, cheerful, beautiful, impulsive, and the epitome of nature's perfection, argues that though these attributes are nothing without wealth, it is the task not of their children but of parents, 'now growne staid', to 'care for getting gaine' (Calver, 1641, 1–4). Youth should not need to 'set age before [his] eyes', or 'Be Metamorphis'd thus, in youth turne old, /In heat of Nature, dry, and dull, and cold' (12). Youth should not consume itself in care, but should be prodigal in the pursuit of pleasure while it may. Youth's discrete self, of course, points out that these arguments are based on the illusion that reason can be subjected to will, and that even though youth should rejoice in itself, its natural exuberance needs anchoring in good sense. Youth must therefore practice moderation now as well as in age (6–11, 15–20).

Shakespeare endows Jessica with a number of the more appealing of the commonly held attributes of youth that Calver later codifies, though it is true that her circumstances as Shylock's daughter, which doubly typifies her as the representative of impulsive and prodigal youth and as the victim of the miser, are much more interesting and complicated than Calver's later stylisations for this figure. Jessica is brought up in an overly strict, sober and orthodox household which allows no room for dancing, merrymaking and music. Her father instructs her to lock the doors against the 'shallow fopp'ry' (2. 5, 35) of the revellers and warns her against clambering up to look at them through the casements (2. 3, 31), as though the very sight of them would be corrupting. Launcelot's foolery provides the only relief from the duty and dullness that make her want to repudiate her father (2. 3, 16–17). Jessica, denied any outlet for youthful exuberance, is instructed to 'stop [the] house's ears' (2. 5, 34). Her disguise, elopement and squandering of her father's fortune are a marker of the Passion that leads Calver's intemperate Youth to reject the 'sad employments' and 'fretting cares' of his parents, just as Jessica repudiates her father's 'manners' (2. 3, 19). Now that their 'their youthfull time have spent', it is fitting that the 'care for getting gaine' should be theirs, not his. Their anxiety over money befits their age and position; '[t]he elder for the younger doth provide,/ As by a Law in Nature strictly ty'd' (Calver, 1641, 4). Passionate Youth's failure to curb his riotous living and spending come home to roost in old age; Jessica's come home to roost much sooner. In marrying Lorenzo, she cuts herself from any further direct benefit from her father's estate. In purloining her father's ducats and squandering them in a manner calculated to break his heart, she loses control of the rest and by far the larger part of it; the court awards half Shylock's wealth and goods to Antonio, the other half to the state.[6] Had Jessica remained indoors and bided her time, as Portia does, she would have inherited all of her father's goods and money, instead of none of it.

Portia shows a much cannier appreciation of the laws governing inheritance. Strict observance of her father's wishes, unpleasantly constricting for a short while, give her long-term independent control of a large fortune. Though she pays lip service to handing over her fortune to Bassanio, in practice it is she who determines how the money will be deployed. In her case, initial acceptance of paternal constraint guarantees a future free from domestic and economic dependence on either husband or father. From this point of view, biblical precept in both old and new testaments to honour thy mother and thy father (cf. Deuteronomy 5: 16, Paul's Epistle to the Ephesians 6: 103), temporarily binding on Portia but disregarded by Jessica, ensures that the wayward daughter enslaves herself to the will of a living husband and rewards the obedient child. But Shakespeare's play rewards Portia in less orthodox ways, too; contrary to the pattern of his comedies, she becomes geographically mobile only after marriage which, contrary to patriarchal practices, secures also her financial autonomy.

There is no such sophistication in Calver's two versions of youth though he does permit himself a note of mischief when youthful passion, blithely dismissing Cicero's idealisation of the aged Cato as envy, has the last word, despite Discretion's reasonable and pious ripostes:

> Good and wise counsell, tis, indeed, and fit
> For men of age and gravity [...]
> [...] severest Stoickes, Passion most refraining,
> *Cato* and *Plato*, pleasures most refraining,
> These in their youth were youthfull, though, grown old,
> These, out of envy, must have youth contrould. (20)

Nevertheless the message, based upon precepts governing relations between young and old, parallels in its formulaic patterning the old/young message of *The Merchant*. Drawn from prescription, the message insists that the harmony between youth and age results from good habits learned in the cradle as the only reliable way of securing both worldly and spiritual comfort in preparation for the grave and lays the foundations for domestic and political economies for later life. As we have seen, Goulart's Cicero-driven apology for age, as one example from many, regards the ages of man not in opposition but as a continuum (Goulart, 1621, 30–34; see also Shahar, 2005, 71–75). Each age contains the embryonic ills which mature in the age which follows it: 'It is a wonder, saith Cicero also, if old men bee troubled with infirmities, seeing young men cannot priuilege themselues from them, but are often enough feeble and weake' (Goulart, 1621, 30) and harbour the same vices.

For this reason, Discretion in Youth in Calver's poem subjects will to reason because passion is an illusion, (Calver, 1641, 5) and though it is right that youth should 'rejoice in itself' it should always keep in mind that as youth sows so shall it reap, so it must begin to govern its fortunes and desires early on in order to secure its future self. Fall in love, by all means, Calver seems to be saying (and as both Jessica and Portia do), but make sure there is no danger in it (Portia); youth should not delude itself into thinking it can exercise its power without restraint (Jessica), for 'Excesse in any thing's unfit' (11). Because of this, Calver balances the books in favour of age. The argument, begun by youth's heedless dismissal of care of worldly gain as a vice, comes home to roost in age when, having contemptuously disregarded Discrete Youth's advice to curb unbridled spending, Passion in Age now perceives the wisdom of husbanding one's financial resources:

> I held them much wormes, and in much disdaine,
> That did not value pleasure above gaine [...]
> [...] But were I young againe
> I would, I thinke, not be so mad, or vaine.' (41)

However, corrupting habits of a lifetime are hard to break, so Passion in Age looks around for ways of recouping a squandered fortune. Here Calver realigns the Shylock stereotype of miserly old age operating at the hub of sixteenth-century Venetian trade. Passion in Age runs through the same possibilities of accumulating wealth that motivate Shylock: he could buy land cheaply, secure it by lending money to a 'spendthrift' from whom he bought it in the first place and then 'pawn' it back to him with what remaining money he has left over from the purchase (41). Or he could speculate overseas, or purchase some office or lordship or manor that will command increasing respect and therefore bring in money. In the end he decides to force up the price of corn to sell dearly to the poor, and raise his rents so that his tenants would have to bear the burden of rates and duties that he should rightfully be paying. Built on the same 'type' as Shylock, who is glad to part with the services of Launcelot Gobbo because he is 'Snail-slow in profit', lazy and 'a huge feeder' (2. 5, 44, 45), Passion in Age makes household economies based upon similar views of servants. He can feed servants on cheaper rye or barley, not wheat, cut them down to two meals a day, and not buy any more new clothes for himself. As a result, he reckons to be well on the way to recouping the spending of a lifetime. And he won't spare his body either; like Shylock, he will toil and labour all day for gain, and at night he will exercise his brain awake by thinking up other ways of making money. After all, he has a library full of books on Land Tenure and Usury; and he has his bonds, bills, silver, gold, jewels which are to him more refreshing than meat and drink (42–44). The source of Shylock's 'well-won thrift' (1. 3, 47) resides in the complex stock-exchange world which thrives on bargains and bills and which allows him to build his fortune on a pile of multidimensional bonds, debts and transactions. Calver renders this world of trade in goods, money and people, in which an old man loses everything he has left to bequeath, into a neat formula for keeping want at bay in old age, and at the same time securing a living for his children. The surface moral of the play and the poem is that the value of initiating good habits of thrift in youth is to make provision for the next generation. The play builds this simple postulate into a complex structure in which generic expectations are explored, interrogated and confounded, whereas the poem deals with these expectations according to a balanced formula which by its very nature reduces human actions and motivations to an oversimplified and unified pattern, and characters into stock figures and 'types'. Importantly, though, their common interest in the dynamics of and between youth and age contains, beneath the surface, the fears and anxieties grounded in a particular stage of life about its own future. Each in different ways and for different reasons gives old fathers a heftier punch than the wayward youngsters who oppose them.

INHERITANCE, GENRE AND *THE OLD LAW*

Since balanced judgement belongs to age alone, the pastoral works of Spenser and his predecessors — Alexander Barclay in his 1515 Eclogues,

George Turbervile's translation of the eclogues of the renaissance neo-Latin poet, Baptista Spagnuoli (Mantuan) in 1567 and Barnabe Googe's 1563 *Egloga prima*, a dialogue between youth (Daphnes) and age (Amintas)[7] — all adopt the perspective of age with its practical wisdom and attacks upon the follies, pretensions and vices of youth (Hallett Smith, 1952, 32). From this point of view, according to Marx, pastoral is best understood as a response to society's marginalisation of the old, with the youth–age binary acting as a 'conceptual polarity' like that of body and soul or nature and art, summer and winter, hot and cold, wet and dry, passion and reason (Marx, 1985a, 23–41). However, in the matter of inheritance, these broad perceptions of age and its relationship to youth, present in pastoral and the prime subject matter of Calver's balanced youth–age formula, become more complex and ambivalent in dramatic works such as *Merchant* which probe more deeply into motivation and circumstance and in which the balance of young–old opposites is by no means clear-cut, and even less so, progressively, in tragicomedy and tragedy.

In the May eclogue of the *Shepheardes Calender*, Piers counters Palinode's nostalgia for youth as a time for pleasure and idleness with the pertinent observation that a shepherd's life does not, as with 'men of laye,' depend upon inheritance:

> With them [i.e. laymen] sits to care for their heire,
> Enaunter their heritage doe impaire:
> They must prouide for meanes of maintenaunce,
> And to continue their wont countenaunce'
>   (Spenser, 1985, 76–80),

thereby allowing youth to be spendthrift and carefree. A shepherd, by contrast, must take responsibility for himself and his livelihood early on:

> For if he misliue in leudnes and lust,
> Little bootes all the welth and the trust,
> That his father left by inheritaunce:
> And will be soone wasted with misgouernaunce. (87–90)

Here, the value of what the old have to bequeath to the young is taken for granted and as such is mirrored in prescriptive writers like Thomas Sheafe for whom youth, 'for that it stands most in opposition to the age I treate of' (Sheafe, 1639, 101), looks upon age with a scornful eye. Age, in turn, is scathing towards youth which runs 'the wilde-goose-race without controle, up and downe in the world' (96). *The Old Law* juggles with this truism in a spirit of riotous farce. Like *The Merchant of Venice* and *King Lear,* the play rests upon familiar old/young binaries that turn upon questions of inheritance familiar to early modern society and shares the preoccupations of parents and children in the matter of equitable distribution of property and money among the family surviving a father's death.

These concerns extend considerably beyond the inheritance itself. Sir William Wentworth (1562–1614), writing in 1604, provides a reality check for *The Old Law* and *King Lear*, both of which show the disastrous results of premature transference of inheritance to the young . Wentworth advised his son and heir Thomas Earl of Strafford when he should come to contemplate matrimony to '[t]ake advice of your wise auncyentt frendes befor yow attempt anie thing touching that matter' (*Wentworth Papers*, 20), because his prospective wife's friends and relations will plot and work on him, and corrupt his servants and friends in order to procure as rich a match for her as they can. And while it is a good idea to take a wife younger than himself, he should nevertheless take certain precautions in the matter of her jointure. It would be a mistake to make this too large; upon remarriage, she would be no friend to his house. The way to counteract this is to make his son his executor, show liberality to the wife only through legacy, and above all ensure that her jointure is separate from the heirs' lands. On this point, Sir William informs his son that he speaks from bitter experience; his own mother had her whole inheritance in her possession, and would not assure her land to him after her death. After his father's death his estate was small, and his mother's inheritance of equal value to his. Her jointure out of his father's lands was more than a third and she was her husband's executor. Knowing this, she had before his death removed a lot of money, so her son had only 'the goods and utensells at Wentworth Wodhus' (29). Sir William complains that he had to pay all debts accruing to this property himself, and was obliged to 'defend and kepe my living in such sort as my father left itt' (30). He justifies the sale of his mother's land as

> lawfull very much of the quyett and profit of your house. My mother's perpetuity to me had never fine acknowledged of itt therefore the land being entailed by hir uncle Fr. Gasc[oigne] was by my fines &c lawfully sould and the purchasers haue paid me iustlie. (21–22)

The anxieties over distribution of property caused misery to entire families when sons sacrificed their family's wellbeing to the exigencies of inheritance. Sir John Guise, grandson and heir to Sir Christopher Guise, recounts in his memoirs how his family was forced to move in with an irascible old man in order to safeguard the family interest. In 1642 Sir John's grandfather, 'finding greate disturbance in his wife, greate disorders in his house, age and weaknesse, aproching', and no longer able to fend for himself, summoned John's parents to Elmore, 'never to part agayne.' For John, Elmore was nothing more than 'a spatiouse prison' and his father 'did ill to resume those chaynes.' The old man's 'morosity', his wife's malice, and the 'ill habit' of the servants made his and his parents' life there a misery, but one his father, in order to secure the inheritance, was resolved to endure, 'for which his children may thanke him' (Davies, 1917, 123). The old man himself was a martyr to an unscrupulous woman, and the sequel to this story illustrates another source of anxiety to families — the threat posed by

younger wives. Some years after 1659, Sir Christopher 'fell into a dead pal-
sie on one side, which much impair'd his understanding', and from which
he failed to recover 'to any tolerable degree'. He died in 1671 engaged in a
vexatious law suit against a woman who, living with Sir Christopher in his
latter days, took advantage of his debility to such an extent 'as almost to
cause the ruin of his family' (132). She had been his mistress, had come to
find him, asked for charity, and stayed. Helped by 'treacherous' servants,
she got hold of 'many estates of great value' for herself and her son, and
after his death pretended he had married her — hence the law suit (133).

The Old Law[8] draws upon inheritance quarrels such as these, and
complicates responses to the laws and practices of bequest. Simonides,
impatient to see his father's life ended so he can come into his fortune,
nevertheless dissembles grief in front of his father, claiming that nature
bids him shed tears for him, just as he had shed 'true filial tears' for *his*
father. Entrusted with the care of his mother (though she is only fifty-five,
she wants to accompany her husband to his end) he privately wishes that
they do indeed 'go together' (1.1, 302) so that he can inherit the third of the
property that has been made over to her. A woman could not inherit her
husband's property; landed estates passed over from father to first-born son
but usually with life-long provision for the widow — hence the indignation
of the Guise family at the attempt of a fortune-hunter to lay claim to large
chunks of his grandfather's property.[9] In the play, the contrast between
the two sons is brought out in their reactions to the supposed deaths of
their fathers. Cleanthes, joyful in reality because his father has gone into
hiding, explains that he is so because his father died before the cruel law
could claim him. It is Evander, the maker of the law, who points out that
Cleanthes has now gained '[a] rich and fair revenue' (2.1, 237). By contrast,
his uncle's 'funeral' prompts Simonides to envy his cousin's good fortune:
'what a fine thing' it is to be alive and able to follow 'some seven uncles
thus,/And as many cousin-germans' (2. 1, 245–47) in order to come in to
their legacies.

Simonides, the bad son, jubilantly seizes upon radical changes in the law
which herald a new age 'for those that have old parents and rich inheritance' (1. 1, 34) as an excuse to start spending his father's money. Because
this new law puts to death any man over the age of eighty and woman over
sixty, his father 'cannot live out tomorrow' (1. 1, 26). Every young man
in public office will benefit: 'Are there not fellows that lie bed-rid in their
offices/That younger men would walk lustily in?' (1. 1, 36–37). Churchmen, senators, all who have held office long enough will now be removed to
make way for 'such spirits' as Simonides to 'leap into their dignities' (1. 1,
45–46). In personal terms, the expectant young heir stands to gain doubly;
in addition to his father's estate, he will inherit his mother's jointure.[10] The
playwrights, in satirising the inevitable outcome of social attitudes that
harness the young to the old in positions of private and public dependence,
exploit customary antagonisms between old and young by teaching the old

how to die and the young how to live (1. 1, 345–540). In the play's topsy-turvy world the young envision a new, heady independence, sanctioned by the law and society. In this brave new world 'sons and heirs' can plunge into an orgy of excess, ignoring 'such calves' maws of wit and admonition' (2. 1, 150) from their elders as, for example, to '[t]ake heed of whoring' and 'shun it' (2. 1, 148–51). In confident anticipation of the law's 'firmness', the bad children in the play break away from the elders' restraining influence and immediately begin to enjoy the fruits of their patrimony. Simonides dismisses his father's tailor: 'what son and heir will have his father's tailor unless he have a mind to be well laughed at' (2. 1, 261–62),[11] his butler and his cook. He will have no further need of the services of his father's bailiff, assuring him that he will 'take a course to spend' his father's rents 'faster than thou canst reckon 'em' (2. 1, 282–83). Eugenia, who chose to marry an old man precisely that she 'may soon be rid' of him, has 'waited for the happy hour this two year' (2 . 2, 29), and in order not to lose any more time 'if death be so unkind still to let him live' 2. 2, 30), has anticipated the event by lining up three suitors to supplant him when the law takes its course on his birthday in a few months' time. In her case, 'hot youth' is 'so hast /It will not give an old man leave to die / And leave a widow first, but will make on /The husband looking on' (2. 2, 90–93). Eugenia's advice to her stepdaughter is to 'take age first to make thee rich,' to make full use of her youth while she still has it, and when it vanishes, to manufacture it (2. 2, 139). Yet another example of premature behaviour is the clown Gnotho's trick to falsify his wife's date of birth in the parish registers so he can help an old woman 'out of her pain' (3. 1, 43) and himself into a new wife before the old one's time is up.

All the texts looked at so far use some form of literary dialogue to articulate generational interchanges either by trope or in a topically relevant way as a means of exploring the meaning and experience of old age in matters of spiritual and material inheritance, even though these experiences and relationships to youth may not be part of the grand design of the particular text. With the exception of *The Old Law*, narratives of youth and age, folded inside other, more prominent narratives, need to be extricated. But once exposed, they assume a signal cultural relevance, and nowhere more strikingly so than in the inheritance subtext and its relationship to age in *King Lear* narratives.

INHERITANCE AND *KING LEAR*[12]

Biblical texts from Old and New Testaments exhorting children to honour their parents formed the basis of moral precept and social practice from the Middle Ages onwards (Shahar, 1997, 88), and as such represent a major cultural continuity. Their impact on *King Lear* and *The Old Law* is evident in the first instance in choice of subject matter. Both of these plays embroider plot-lines from Old and New Testament texts that seek to ensure the handing on of land, entitlement and wealth from generation to generation. But whereas *The Old Law* lampoons the general rush to realise parental bequests, *King Lear* is about the ruinous consequences of disregarding the mutual duties of parents and children in the matter of land inheritance.[13] As the Bible says, a child must honour parents 'that thy days may be long upon the land' (Exodus 20: 12) and that 'thou mayest live long on the earth' (Ephesians 6: 2-3). Children had to learn 'first to show piety at home, and to requite their parents: for what is good and acceptable before God' (I Timothy 5: 4) is the surest way to heaven after a prolonged and easeful life on earth.[14] Nowhere is the link between biblical exhortation, generational tensions and social practices stronger than in the inheritance of landed estates. One of the most important areas of conflict between Lear and his daughters is that his gift of land and wealth, along with executive control, clashes with the assumption of a parent's absolute right to lifelong care and respect. In this regard, the story of Ruth in the Old Testament was treated as exemplary. Richard Barnard, for example,dedicating his version to a venerable old lady, Frances, Dowager Countess of Warwick, elevates Ruth into a paragon of obedience to the will of her mother-in-law Naomi, and seizes the occasion to digress upon the absolute need for children to be bound by the wishes of their parents and for their actions to be guided primarily by considerations for their welfare.[15] That Ruth

> would [...] not go abroad without her mother in lawes leaue and good liking: For godly children hold themselues bound to be at the disposing of their parents, yea in all lawful and necessary things

was held up as the yardstick by which parental authority should govern the behaviour of the young in blood and law. Ruth's uncompromising defer-ence to Naomi was quoted as an object lesson precisely because it

> iustly condemneth the sawcinesse of children in law these dayes, who thinke no duety to be due father or mother in law, especially if they be poor as was Naomi here. But what speake I of children in law? I with that a iust complaint might not be taken vp against such as by nature owe themselues vnto parents [...] children will seeke to be nourished of their parents when they are yong, or when they be in need. But if parents haue need of them, Ah how vnnaturall be they! Will they like a Ruth willingly labour for them? Or will they not rather despise them, and get from them, and labour for others? [...] But let children know and remember the Law against a stubborne sonne, [...] and the curse which is threatened against such as despise their parents, that they may feare and tremble, and doe no more so wickedly. (Barnard, 1628, 133–34)

If Ruth's obedience to her mother-in-law and her commitment to labouring on her behalf was absolute and unquestioning, how much more so should be the commitment of a child to its natural parents. Lear's terrible curse that Goneril's 'derogate body' should not bear 'a babe to honour her' (*Lear*, 1. 4, 273) stems from the commonplace that children who dishonour their parents have not earned the right to be blessed as parents in their turn. The force of Goneril's ungrateful behaviour comes in part from the derivation of the word 'pater' from *pascere*, to feed (Trevisa, 1975, 310). According to Trevisa's fifteenth-century translation of *Bartholomaeus Anglicus*, a child's duty to its father arises from the reciprocal needs of old and young; just as a father feeds his children when young, so in his old age, they feed him, in imitation of nature, like the young of the raven and the pelican, who feed off the parent's blood (Trevisa, 1975, 2: 310; Shahar, 1997, 91).

Figure 2.2 Simon Goulart (1621), *The Wise Vieillard*, frontispiece. By permission of the Folger Shakespeare Library.

The changing structure of family life in the fifteenth and sixteenth centuries from extended to nuclear endorsed prescription and biblical strictures to honour parents and support them materially. In northern Europe, the place and role of the elderly in the nuclear household (cf. Laslett and Wall, 1972, 152), indicates that the ideal of reciprocal giving expounded in Alberti's *I Libri della famiglia* (40–41), Calver's verse dialogue, *The Merchant*, *The Old Law* and *King Lear,* that children have a duty to look after parents when they are old and infirm and as a result can expect to be looked after in their turn, was one that no longer reflected the complex nature of reality. Increasingly, arrangements for the care of the elderly had to adapt to the needs of a society in which changing economic conditions and class structures required many different, individually-tailored solutions to the problem. In the fifteenth and sixteenth centuries, the pay-off for honouring and supporting aged parents continued to reside in heaven, but, uniquely, it was now also available on earth, though without basis in law; so fathers had to make their own legally binding arrangements. John Webb the elder, for example, drew up an agreement round about 1600 that his son would manage his affairs and land now that he was too old to labour any more. If John the younger did not prove to be a good manager, the stock and holding would revert back to the father at the end of the year (Houlbrooke, 1984, 90; see Collomp, 1989, 515–18 for corresponding patterns in France and Europe).[16]

Care of the elderly continued to devolve upon the daughters of the house. Girls tended to stay at home or be called back from service in order to look after aged parents. Margaret White lived with her father in Somerset in 1594, 'guiding' him and his household, 'and was continuallye with him in his sicknes vntill his deathe' (Taunton, Somerset Record Office, D/D/Cd 18, f.2, cited in Houlbrooke, 1984, 189) and a century later, in 1695, the Reverend Henry Newcome confidently expected that his daughter Rose would stay with his wife after his death, and provided for this in his will. Rose would inherit sixty per cent of his goods to compensate for her self-denial in the spending of her time and strength 'in painful, tender attendance upon us both in our old age and great infirmities' (Parkinson, 1852, 285; Houlbrooke, 1984, 189). And in 1702 Thomas Greene, grocer and draper of Lancaster aged seventy-four, sent for his two daughters living with relatives in London to help him and their mother 'in his trade and otherways in their old age' (Marshall, 1967, 140–41; Houlbrooke, 1984, 189).[17] Such were the expectations upon which Lear relied when he divided his wealth, and such was the burden of duty, resisted by Goneril and Regan, placed upon the daughters of the house. In what follows, I suggest that *King Lear* contains a response to society's changing family structures and, consequently, copes with a range of anxieties about inheritance not necessarily experienced in medieval times, though still sharing similar directives on conduct.

Given these changes and the ubiquitous advice on the need to provide for old age, it would be clear to an early seventeenth-century audience that

Lear's predicament arose from a refusal on his part to believe that his children would break their filial bonds, coupled with a refusal on the part of his two elder children to acknowledge them. Notably he does not seek advice on retirement options, presumably because he feels this to be beneath the notice of a monarch, who is not only father to his own offspring but also to the entire realm. Thus he forgets in the process another hard-wired social reality admitted even by Plato and Cicero, who idealised old age, that wealth and social position help an old person to bear its the hardships (cf. Plato, *Republic*, old Cephalus, Bk 1, 329–30, 53–54; Cicero, 2001, 16/17). The Knyvett family, for example, flourished in the first half of the sixteenth century as a result of Sir William Knyvett's canny legal arrangements, and there are faint echoes of the Lear story and Middleton and Rowley's play here, too. Like Lear, Sir William lived to the age of eighty at the head of an enormous landed estate. By the terms of his detailed will, his son Edward (like Lear's daughters) had already received 'all the residue of his goods and chattels [...] by a gift [...] heretofore made,' but did not live long enough to enjoy possession of his substantial estates. These devolved upon Sir William's seven year old great-grandson Edmund but without adequate means of upkeep (Virgoe, 1992, 254–55). Just as Edgar cannot not step into his rightful inheritance until the breach with his father heals, so the two parts of Sir William's inheritance, divided by Sir William's will could not be immediately united. As Roger Virgoe points out, 'the prestigious core of the estate was left to his son [Edward] [...], but no attempt was made to consolidate the Wymondham and Buckenham lands [...] in order to reconstitute the original Tateshale holding.' The estate was not brought together until the next generation (Virgoe, 1992, 255).

The Lear story reverberates, too, in other cultural contexts. Jack Goody explicitly relates Lear's situation to prevailing social conditions in pre-industrial society: for the old king, the waning of economic control signifies a loss of resources, diminished bargaining power and as a consequence, neglect by the younger generation. While Lear's transfer of property relieves him from care, it places him entirely at the mercy of his heirs (Goody, 1976, 119). Lear's situation also illustrates Goody's observation that a defining characteristic of gerontocracies is the amount of control the aged exert over women (123), as the circumstances of Margaret White and Rose Newcome, two real life dutiful daughters, illustrate. But the play also challenges Lear's assumption of continuing authority over the lives of his daughters, even though the two elder are married and are thus removed from the domestic orbit of his power. He acts on the supposition that his position as head of family and state is enough of itself to secure him in his old age, and gives away his land unconditionally, evidently not perceiving the need to insert any provisional safety clauses for himself.

The prescriptive literature attempts to mitigate such disastrous consequences as befell Lear by advising the old to safeguard their financial interests against the time when they are no longer able to work. Those who had property were urged not to transfer it to their children in their lifetime in order to avoid dependency upon them and their kindness, since there is nothing as hard and as miserable as poverty in old age. Sermons from the Middle Ages onwards peddled their own versions of the Lear story as a warning not to dispose of inheritance without first making provision for oneself (Shahar, 1997, 95 and 2005, 110) and as censure to ungrateful off-spring who drove the suffering aged out of house and home. For example, Lear stories like the one communicated from a medieval pulpit about a rich man who when he 'vaxed old and feble and unmyghty' gave away all his property to his son-in-law, only to find that his position in the family was completely undermined, found many echoes in the renaissance. Having by degrees skimped on the old man's food and clothing, the story goes, his rel-atives finally banished him to a small house near the outer gate and he had to resort to a trick in order to regain his former position in the household. He made sure he was watched whilst pretending to be counting money in a basket. The spying grandchild reported to his father what he had seen. The son immediately advised his father-in-law to soundly invest it. The old man agreed, saying he would put some by for his son-in-law, and was thereupon reinstated to his former comforts in the main house. When he died no money was found, only a short poem warning men against giving up their possessions (*Middle English Sermons*, ed. Ross, 1940, 89–90).[18] Stories like this are commonplace. Time and again such manuals as Daniel Rogers' *Matrimoniall Honour* warn parents against the folly of attempts 'to make their children great' by 'thrus[ting] themselves out of all, that their children might succeed them in their places, holding the candle to them, while they doe all, and act their parts upon the stage' (Rogers, 1642, 92). Having once lived in comfort, parents find themselves in their old age entirely dependent upon their children's 'curtesie'. Unfortunately, this 'cur-tesie' is so scant that

> the part of their life, which of all others attendance and maintenance, must now become most shiftlesse and desolate. They must come out of the hall into the kitchin, sit at tables end, or in the chimny corner with a poore pittance sent them. (92)[19]

At a time when Lear and Gloucester are no longer in possession of their strength and ability, they are entirely at the mercy of their children, 'cast up for hawkes meat, despised, counted as burdens, wherefore to be eased would be no small joy to their children'. Rogers hammers the message home for parents who are tempted to sign away their property and rights: 'Be wise, you parents, yeeld not your selves captives and prisoners to your children' (93). When it comes to life with his two elder daughters, Lear cer-tainly finds that 'no prison can bee more yrkesome to a parent, then a sonne or daughters house' (93). By contrast, the real prison that he finds himself sharing with his one loving daughter becomes a cage for song-birds; though constricted, a place of harmony and comfort, just as it is for Anthony in More's *Dialogue*, because both receive the care and respect due to elderly relatives. Lear and Gloucester, by the end of the play, can appreciate that it is they themselves who have made the snare in which they are caught. Thus they wrong themselves who and their children by 'putting that into their hands, which God hath denied them'. Like inheritance, 'Love must descend, not ascend', and it is not natural for children to provide for parents. It must be the other way round, so parents must be sure to 'hold stroake sufficient' to secure their children's love and duty (Rogers, 1642, 93). It may well be, as Rogers concedes, that not all children are lacking in a sense of obligation — 'but', as he warns, 'the best will bite' and 'Sure bind, sure find: if you must needs come downe, rather chuse to fall into the hands of God, then your children' (93).

It is clear from the work done by Alan Macfarlane and Cicely Howell that Rogers had good cause for such admonitions; the old and retired who lived under the same roof as the younger generation (Macfarlane, 1978, 136–38, 141–43 and 1986, 321–44; Howell, 1983, 69) did so under varying conditions of autonomy. This was true in Europe as a whole (Collomp, 1989, 510–18; 522–25). William Smith, for example, instructed his executors to sell off all copyhold and divide proceeds equally among his four children (Howell, 1983, 256). Howell's comments are pertinent to *King Lear* in that they identify the point at which inheritance practices broke from their medieval past, and that they mirror the circumstances in which Lear, *pre-mortem* as it were, finds himself:

> In the medieval period fathers seem to have relinquished control of the land before death and therefore the old rule: no land, no marriage, held good; sons were in possession of the land when they married. But by the sixteenth century fathers tended not to retire and sons, when they married, were not yet in possession of the land [...] if one turns to the wills of older men or of widows, one finds that children in their late twenties had still not received their portions and that the heir had inherited the obligation to provide them. (260-61)

The implications of this for the inheriting daughters in *Lear* are evident; it is in their material interests that Cordelia alienates herself from her father and thus her rightful portion of land. In south-east medieval Leicestershire, for example, land remained the sole source of family income and was required to support all adult family members, 'either by supplying each with a share of land where possible, or by supporting one nuclear family and a number of celibate adults' (269), a situation which had changed radically by the sixteenth century, when conditions became less favourable to younger sons' (269). At the time of the writing and performance of *King Lear*, inheritance practice was such that once a father transferred his wealth and property to a son or daughter in a legal document (a will or deed of transfer), he could no longer claim the income from that property. Since there were no legal impositions upon children to support aged parents, parents took care to make provision for themselves by a contract which specified a child's obligations towards their upkeep, itemising exact sums of money, food, clothing, fuel and so on. Without such legal guarantees, fathers could not expect their sons to support them, and Lear's daughters act upon such an expectation. The fact that there were in practice few of these maintenance contracts betokened many different kinds of arrangements, varying in composition according to wealth, status, class and profession. Kirkby Lonsdale records suggest that despite the nuclear structure of families from the peasantry upwards, there might still have been some form of co-operation, with groups composed of several married couples and their closest relatives working a joint holding (Macfarlane, 1978, 74–75; Howell, 1983, 257–69; Collomp, 1989, 517). Goneril sends to her sister for moral support against their father in the expectation that Regan will uphold her decision about the new living arrangements for Lear. Their reluctance to house an aged relative is endorsed by prescriptive literature which counsels young husbands to 'live of thy self with thy wife, in a family of thine own, and not with another', because the 'mixing of governours in a household [...] doth fall out most times, to be a matter of much unquietness to all parties'. Youth and age have different perspectives and objectives, so for the young to 'wholly resign themselves unto the elder, as not to be discontented with their proceedings; or to make the older so much to deny themselves, as to condescend unto the wills of the younger' is a recipe for disaster (Whately, *A Care-Cloth* [...] 1624, sigs. A6-A6v).

Judging by the evidence found in existing wills, Lear's rash and unequal bequest to his two older daughters at the expense of the most-favoured youngest goes against practices which by and large advocate if not equal distribution of fortune within a parent's lifetime, then at least a division, gained by birthright, by which all children get something. Instead, as Laurel Porter points out, Lear stages a competition in which the highest performance earns the biggest portion as a reward (Porter, 1984, 60). Small wonder, then, that the greedy daughters' vocabulary is about money and the law (cf. Regan, 1. 1, 72-76). In the first two scenes of the second act, Lear loses status not so much because of his age, but because of the loss of power resulting from his division of the kingdom, and exposing his vulnerability. Age, for Lear, signifies a 'desire to retire to the comfort of his daughters' care' but for Goneril, Regan and Cornwall 'it represents a pretext for claiming that he is incompetent, an opportunity for seizing power' (Porter, 1984, 65–66).

There is some debate as to whether maintenance contracts were widespread,[20] but whether there were many or few, there was a perceived need for them, and Lear's lack of foresight in not getting anything down on paper with regard to his care once he has given away all reflects this need. The detailed and carefully worded indenture between Sir Robert Plumpton (aged around 60) and his son and heir William is remarkable for the precision of its terms and even more so for its careful and detailed stipulation of precisely the provision that Lear fails to make, to his tragic cost. This maintenance contract (or indenture) was drawn up between father and son 'in the 7 year of King Henry the 8' to determine the balance of ownership and responsibility. William was to be given charge of all household business and goods in order to allow his parents 'to take their ease and reast' (Plumpton, 1839, cxxiv). He was to receive all revenues and profits from the land and its tenants, and upon him devolved the cost of food, drink and wages for the entire household. His was the responsibility of appointing and dismissing all servants, with the important proviso that his father Robert 'shall have thre at his owne pleasure, such as he will appointe' (cxxiv). In addition, William was to pay his father the yearly sum of ten louis, half of which Robert would receive on Whit Sunday, and the other half at Martinmas, or within the next twelve days therefrom. William was also responsible for his father's debts to the tune of £20 yearly, and pledged to give his father a yearly account of all his receipts and expenses 'that the said father may know surely what overplus may be saved towards the contencion of the said debts' (cxxiv–cxxv). He had to consult his father on the letting of vacant farms unless there was 'any break or varience of or in the premises', whereupon the Minister of St. Roberts, Sir John Alan, parson of Burghwalles' must be called in to 'order the cause'. The indenture was signed, witnessed and sealed on 'the day and yeare abovesaid' (cxxv) — that is, 2 May 1516.

Fears for the future continued to prey upon those approaching old age who foresaw a shortfall in financial independence. Foulke Robartes, writing in the early seventeenth century, presents his argument for tithes for the ministry by means of the analogy of the straitened circumstances of the old when they are dependent upon their children's 'curtesie' (Robartes 1623, 114). By contrast, an old man who keeps his estate intact and maintains his independence can afford to be generous. As a result he will be held in esteem: 'his age is honoured, his person is reverenced, his councell is sought, his voice obeyed'(115). Similarly, Sir John Oglander records in 1648 in his commonplace book the fate of Sir William Lisle who, having presumably given all to his son, 'died privately [...] in a nasty chamber (being all his son would allow him for his men, horses, dogs, provisions and for the cooking of them' (Oglander,1936, 124). And, as further indication of how these preconceptions ran and ran, Richard Steele in his *Discourse concerning Old-Age*, points out that old age is attended with contempt, particularly when it is not supported by good estates (Steele, 1688, 171). These writings advise the landowner to keep hold of his property and resist the temptation to hand everything over to children without taking due provision for himself. However, there is a parallel tranche which, like Montaigne, sees it as

> meere injustice [...] [for] an old, crazed, sinnow-shronken, and nigh-dead father sitting alone in a Chimney-corner to enjoy so many goods

as would suffice for the preferment and entertainment of many children, and in the meane while, for want of meanes, to suffer them to lose their best dayes and yeares. (Montaigne, 1894, Bk. 2 chap. 8, 193)

By depriving them of a life in public service, such acts of parental mean-ness plunge children into the 'despaire to seeke' unlawfully the means to 'provide for their necessaries' (193). According to R. N. Foakes, George Petty's translation of Stefano Guazzo's *Civile Conversation* may well be the source for the belief that senile old men should delegate the ordering of their estates to their children, who can cope much better with such weighty matters. Both Guazzo and Montaigne refer approvingly to princes and rul-ers who abdicate and sign over their wealth to their successors (cf. Foakes, 2003, 104–5, 109).

The opening scene in *King Lear* clearly articulates the contrasting implications for inheritance upon retirement. The two elder daughters are already married and living away from the parental home in circumstances which secure their independence, land and wealth. We do not know if they brought pre-mortem dowries to their marriages; the fact that Lear's youngest unmarried daughter is rejected by her suitor Burgundy because she suddenly finds herself dowerless seems to suggest that they did. But in any event, Goneril and Regan are mistresses of the Cornwall and Albany estates and joint owners of sizeable landed property; the addition of one half each of the king's property makes them in effect joint rulers of the kingdom, and, since Lear has made no kind of stipulation about who will look after him in his extreme old age, his gift endows them with a landed power removed entirely from any kind of obligation to their old father. He is king in name only, which means, from the point of view of the accumula-tion of power and prestige through inherited wealth, in effect no king at all, in terms of either power or prestige.

From this point of view, the play provides comment on the need for inheritance contracts as a means of 'placing' the old. Cordelia would 'pre-fer' her father 'to a better place' than in the care of her sisters (*Lear* 1. 1, 276) precisely, it would seem, for the reason that the old who gave away their lands, as Lear has done, were doubly at the mercy of their inheriting children. By giving away his kingdom, Lear has indeed put himself in the way of feeling what wretches feel; he is in the position of the disinherited old with no roof over his head, no way of retaining a following and no means of securing for himself any kind of independent existence. Goneril articu-lates the commonplaces of the age when she points out that in giving away his kingdom, Lear forfeits his claim to respect, and (perhaps unexpectedly) having gained control of one half of her father's lands, feels herself put upon by an old man who 'flashes into one gross crime or other that sets us all at odds'. For this reason she refuses to 'endure it', putting her father in his place by instructing her steward to 'slack of former services' and 'put on what weary negligence you please'. In her household, there is no room for the indulgence of an old man who has shown these unmistakable signs of senility: '[n]ow by my life/ Old fools are babes again and must be used with checks and flatteries when they are seen abused' (1. 3 , 4–21).

In giving away his property and deciding to live out his days in the homes of first one then the other daughter, Lear could be following either one of two practices. His intention might have been to divide land between all heirs, or, if land was scarce, to give it to the eldest and a sum of money for the others.[21] Or it may be that Lear intended to live with his daughters as a lodger, an alternative pattern suggested by the dispute among his children as to who should house him and in what circumstances, for sometimes the terms of a maintenance or retirement agreement specified lodging in the homes of others who contracted to provide food and shelter in exchange for land. The censuses of Ealing, Chivers Coton, Stoke-on-Trent, Corfe Castle and Ardleigh, for example, provide ample evidence of elderly lodgers sharing domestic space (Smith, *Land, Kinship* 1984, 79; Laslett, 1977, 204–05; Houlbrooke, 1984, 191).[22] But it is clear from the outset that Lear has not taken the precaution of stipulating his intentions on the supposition that his authority will continue to be absolute, even though it is unlikely, once he has given everything away, that his wishes will be respected.

Awareness, too, of the role of the church in disposing of family inheritance helps to explain what is going on in the first act of *King Lear*. In *The Development of the Family and Marriage in Europe*, Goody exposes the unintended outcome of church regulation of marriage and its persuasion of unmarried children to abandon family ties in favour of the religious life, thereby diverting family funds into its own coffers. In order to persuade people to exchange the church for their family (and to provide for the church in the same way as members of a family are provided for), it forbade marriage within strictly defined degrees of kinship, encouraged celibacy, promoted the ideal of the conjugal bond, and insisted on the importance of freedom of choice in marriage by the partners concerned. However, this seemingly inadvertently resulted in the enhancement of the position of women as property-holders (Goody, 1983, 103–13; 120–25). Lear's intended bequest of property away from Cordelia, his chosen heir, breaks the main line of inheritance and benefits his two elder daughters as property owners entirely at the expense of the youngest, but at the same time establishes a spiritual rather than financial bond as the basis for harmonious relationship (cf. Goody, 1983, 198–9; 202–04) between his daughter and France, and, later on, between himself and his youngest child. Cordelia, doubly disinherited, nevertheless lands on her feet with France in a godly marriage, and positions herself in twofold capacity as her father's worldly and spiritual heir.

From a third perspective, the play's opening shows that Lear, as paterfamilias and reigning monarch, with full control over the family funds and (though the play substitutes two married daughters for a married son), by advantageous matches for the two older princesses, has augmented the power and riches of his own domain by annexing it through a marriage treaty to the land and fealty of his sons-in-law. From this perspective, the spectacle of Lear giving away all his security and wealth in one breathless moment of vanity and pride is all the more startling, particularly as in so doing he throws away the opportunity of annexing even more lands (Burgundy or, even better, France itself). From the point of view of late sixteenth- and early seventeenth-century politics, failure to secure the friendship by marriage of hostile territory — that is, either Burgundy or France — left English frontiers vulnerable to the threat of Spain. At the end of Elizabeth's reign, Spain was a dangerous enemy to both France and England, yet the Queen's attempts to draw the French back into an alliance met with small success. Though both were hostile to Spain, France's formal peace with the Spanish, and France's need to prevent an agreement for peace between England and Spain, made French diplomatic moves a barrier to either Anglo-French or Anglo-Spanish agreements. With the Queen's death in 1603 animosity with Spain was still alive, but only just. The new King's desire for peace with Spain put a formal end to these expensive and indecisive hostilities, despite national feeling against Spain. Since parliament and the Puritans continued to promote anti-Catholic policies in the early years of James' rule, during which *King Lear* was written and performed, James could no longer afford to sit on the fence with regard to the Catholics. By 1612 he had joined the Protestant Union and married his daughter Elizabeth to Frederick, Elector Palatine. In the first quarto of *King Lear*, the stage directions (Q1, 145) and a passing reference to an invading French army (Q1, 129, 111) indicate that Lear's reinstatement is as a result of the agency of France, a rival foreign power (MacCaffrey, 1992, 243–45; Holderness, 1995, 40; Taunton and Hart, 2003, 696–99, 703–04).

Given these circumstances, It is small wonder that Lear, in the act of giving everything away, has not only relinquished personal authority; he has jeopardised the security of the land, so from the point of view of the ungrateful children in the play, he has abandoned the right to be treated as a rational being who 'by the marks of sovereignty, knowledge and reason' (1. 4, 223–25) can make claims upon his offspring. For his eldest child, he has become an 'Idle old man,/That still would manage those authorities/That he hath given away' and must be reprimanded like a child for irrational behaviour. She has to remind him that 'As you are old and reverend, should be wise' (1. 4, 231). The Fool is quick to point out the folly of 'cutting his crown i' the middle' (1. 4, 153) and the consequences of signing away his property to these two children without making adequate provision for himself. By consigning himself to the 'nursery' of his two elder daughters, Lear renounces his claim to the respect due to a wise elder, since he has put the seal upon his own dependency. In so doing, he at once reverses and accelerates the course of nature; he reverses it, as the Fool points out, by making 'thy daughters thy mother', and he accelerates it by an act which publicly declares that he has entered into that final stage of decrepit old age which brings the very old back full circle to the total dependency of the new-born infant.[23] The Fool hints at this when he compares Lear to the fabled old man who tries to please everybody by carrying his overladen ass to market, and, in anger at the mockery this occasions, he throws the ass into the river.[24] Lear, by analogy, had 'little wit' in his 'bald crown' when he gave his golden one away (1. 4, 154–56), and 'the rent of his land' (1. 4,1 31) leaves him with nothing. The two uncaring daughters believe that they will suffer if they allow their father, in his new state of dependence, to wield an authority he in fact no longer possesses 'with such dispositions as he bears.' Given that he is at the mercy of ungovernable passions, his two elder daughters must take over from him and his followers, and 'i'th' heat' (1. 1, 306–08).

By contrast and contradictorily, both Lear and Gloucester take for granted a child's lifelong obedience to the absolute authority of a parent, thereby linking matters of inheritance to the unassailable authority wielded by the old over the young. Lear experiences Goneril's refusal to house her father's followers as an assault on his reason and sense of self:

> Does any here know me? Why, this is not Lear.
> Does Lear walk thus, speak thus? Where are his eyes?
> Either his notion weakens, or his discernings are
>   lethargied — Ha! sleeping or waking? Sure 'tis not so.
> Who is it that can tell me who I am? (1. 4, 217–21)

Gloucester assumes the right of absolute control over his grown son's business when he snatches the counterfeit letter from Edmund. Both children resist the call on their filial duty. To Goneril, Lear's demands for respect and the retention of his retinue are merely 'new pranks'; his knights and squires are disordered, debauched and bold, and Lear 'as [he] is old and reverend, should be wise' (1. 4, 229–31) enough to keep company with 'such men as besort [his] age' (1. 4, 242). Edmund, for his part, shows his contempt for his father's seemingly weakened grip on the 'real' world and scorns his age, gullibility and superstition. He projects onto Edgar his resentment at having to wait for 'our fortunes [...] till our oldness cannot relish them' (1. 2, 48–49). His elaborate plan to discredit his brother is entirely inheritance-based. Resentful at being 'twelve or fourteen moonshines/Lag of a brother' (1. 2, 5–6) he intends to snatch the inheritance to which, as a younger (and, moreover, illegitimate) son, he has no rightful claim: 'Well, then,/ Legitimate Edgar, I must have your land' (15–16). Edmund, chafing against 'an idle and fond bondage in the oppression of aged tyranny, who sways not as it hath power, but as it is suffered' (1. 2, 49–51), joins Goneril and Regan to form a trio of uncaring offspring who act on the belief that when a father begins to grow old and show signs of that 'unruly waywardness, that infirm and choleric years bring with them' (Goneril, 1. 1, 299–300), he 'should be a ward to the son, and the son manage his revenue' (Edmund, 1. 2, 73–74). By not making legally binding provision for themselves in maintenance contracts or the like, both fathers confirm their dotage and sign their own warrants for harsh treatment.

The dawning of social conscience in Lear, when he confronts his own helplessness and begins to worry about the 'poor, naked wretches, wheresoe'er you are' (3. 4, 28–29) in the hovel during the storm and on the cliffs of Dover, has a specific social context. These central scenes can be understood in relation to the circumstances of the rural poor, who are also likely to be old (Smith, 1984, 75; Wales, 1984, 358) — though the poor are not necessarily old. But whether poor, old, or most likely both, Lear has only now come to perceive their dispossession (Smith, 1984, 73–74; Lesthaeghe, 1980, 531–32). His sympathetic identification with the condition of the disguised Edgar highlights this relationship between poverty (Poor Tom's) and age (his own). Edgar's decision to 'take the basest and poorest shape/That ever penury in contempt of man /Brought near to beast '(2. 2, 178–80) draws attention to the plight of the destitute, and by definition, old, even though Poor Tom is not in this last category. According to Tim Wales, 'the sorts of people on poor relief — the aged, the widowed and the orphaned — predominated [...] in the towns as in the villages' (Wales, 1984, 358). In Cawston, for example, nineteen out of ninety-seven householders considered too poor to pay the poor rates received regular relief. Five of these households were male-headed families overburdened with children. These findings suggest that the most substantial support for the aged came from the community (Wales, 1984, 358). The old, though they 'lived in a structurally dependent relationship to society at large,' were far more likely to have featured among the 'poor' than any other age group of the population, and formed the largest section of those claiming poor relief (Smith, 1984, 77). Lear's descent into extreme poverty and hardship accentuates this relationship between the aged, the poor and society. The Bedlam beggar and the old king together 'outface/The winds and persecutions of the sky' (*Lear*, 2.2, 183). This scene draws together the underprivileged from either end of the social spectrum and accentuates the helplessness of the rural poor at the bottom end and the high-born old at the top. Gloucester, having in the previous scene welcomed Regan and her train into his house, now pledges himself to 'serve' Lear (2. 2, 286) but is ineffectual in dealing with either; his impulse to placate and smooth over the accelerating quarrel between father and daughter comes to nothing. Both he and Lear are powerless to influence the course of events; both humiliatingly have to bow to the dictates of the imperious young. Regan insists that Lear, because he is old, 'should be ruled and led / By some discretion that discerns your state/Better than you yourself' (2. 2, 337–39). Lear is thus put in the position of having to apologise for his age and redundancy on his knees, begging her for 'raiment, bed and food' (2 .2, 343–45). Glossed as sarcasm with an edge of truth in the Arden edition, the spectacle of a king in supplication to his daughter is also a strong visual marker of the dependency of the aged, and entry into the hovel as the only shelter available to him accentuates the penury of those too old and poor to be able to provide for themselves . For the first time in his life, the king is brought face to face simultaneously with what the aged and the poor have to suffer.

Lear is dependent on his daughters' charity just as the aged poor depend upon charitable institutions in the community. The statutory distinctions as embodied in the 1601 Poor Law between the able-bodied poor and 'the lame ympotente olde blynde and such other amonge them beinge poore and not able to worke' mirror Lear's raggle-taggle brigade of down-and-outs to whom he becomes so attached. Lear's impotence comes upon him suddenly, whereas in the sixteenth and seventeenth centuries '[a]geing [...] was a process of gradual withdrawal from economic productivity and self-support.' The urban censuses conducted at the end of the sixteenth century, such as those of Norfolk and Ipswich, provide many examples of people on poor relief having to supplement their income by carding and spinning, as did Mother Ingram in 1597 aged eighty (Webb, 1966, 135; see also Wales, 1984, 367). Regan and Goneril, though unreasonable, reason in the manner of those who refuse their parents shelter in their old age; their house is too small for an old relative 'to be well bestowed' (2. 2, 478), and in any case ''Tis his own blame; hath put himself from rest / And must needs taste his folly' (2. 2, 479 –80). Regan, on the subject of Edgar accompanying Lear's riotous knights, expresses a fear real enough to those facing appropriation of land: 'Tis they have put him on the old mans death, / To have wast and spoyle of his revenues' (2.1, 98–99). Her rapacious harping on property is repellent, but consonant with the drain on income faced by children with dependent parents.

Where extended kinship networks controlled resources, risk of loss or hardship was 'cushioned'. This was replaced by what Lesthaeghe calls 'communal risk devolution' — that is, the burden of relief fell on neighbours, gilds, charitable benefactors, and other organised groups within the community (Lesthaeghe, 1980, 532).[25] Family ties have broken down in Lear's and Gloucester's households, and both old men have to rely on the kindness of those nearby. Kent looks out for Lear, and Edgar, posing as someone near at hand, saves Gloucester from a desperate act, and lack of fellow feeling finally does for the two hard sisters and Edmund. Keith Wrightson finds that the pattern provided by his case study of the Essex parish of Terling in 1671 yielded assumptions that held good for the early modern period as a whole: the 'flexible and permissive system' which held the nuclear family at its centre but did not indicate that kinship 'was in itself an important independent element in the structuring of social relations' (Wrightson, 1984, 332). Lear's wilful (but will-less) disbanding of the separate royal households presumably functioning as nuclear before the play's start is the catalyst for the tragedy that befalls old and young. In reality, neighbours and friends played an even more important role in providing support for the poor, old and needy; Ralph Josselin's main source of support was not the wider kinship group (though uncles played an important part in his early life) but a network of friends and neighbours (Macfarlane, 1970, 82, 149, chapters 7 and 10; Wrightson, 1984, 314). Indeed, neighbours took precedence over relatives as witnesses for wills, for providing financial help (reference to debts in wills was mostly to debts between neighbours) or support as 'compurgators' (swearing to a man's innocence in church courts) and sureties (acting as in a recognizance issued by the Justices of the Peace) simply because they were near at hand, and relatives were not (Wrightson, 1984, 332). But even though 'occupational solidarity' was a key factor in communal assistance, and personal friendship was at the forefront in witnessing wills, those who laboured for their living were nevertheless almost entirely dependent on patronage (331). Neighbourliness was of strong practical importance to Terling villagers, and good fellowship was a critically important social virtue. Good neighbour networks rather than the enduring structures of family and kinship were, as Wrightson demonstrates, the key to social change in the period (332).

Edgar's mad behaviour as Poor Tom 'enforces' (2. 2, 191) the charity of 'pelting villages, sheepcotes and mills' (2. 2, 189); Kent nudges the drenched and deranged king towards the hovel which will 'some friendship .. lend' him against the lack of 'courtesy' from the 'hard house' of his relatives, who deny shelter to everybody (3. 2 60–77). Yet, far from their own home, the Cornwall family claim Gloucester's hospitality and support as an unquestionable right, to which refusal is unthinkable:

> Regan: Our good old friend,
> Lay comforts to your bosom, and bestow
> Your needful counsel to our business,
> Which craves the instant use.
> Gloucester: I serve you, madam.
> Your graces are right welcome. (2.2, 126–131)

Sensing the danger of their arrival to Lear and his entourage, he tells Edmund to distract the Duke 'that my charity be not of him perceived' (3. 3, 15). Indeed, Gloucester's neighbourliness is cruelly misplaced. Cornwall, Regan, Goneril and Edmund deprive him of the use of his own house and perpetrate a ghastly crime upon him that is made even more unspeakable because it is performed against a defenceless old man in his own home.

In sum, the old are warned against the lack of care and responsibility of the young in cautionary tale, prescription, and from pulpit and stage. There should be a mutual moral responsibility which, if neglected, has dire consequences. If education fails, parents can expect harsh treatment from children who have not benefited at a very early stage from parental example and guidance. In pastoral, poem and play, harmony between old and young is a possibility only if the young accept unquestioningly the authority of the old and take on the burden of care when the old are weak and helpless. Mutual responsibility is the keynote of a wide range of literatures which give lessons in behaviour, inheritance practices in family provision and disposition of wealth, land and estates. Calver and the *Merchant* provide object-lessons in loosening the stranglehold of the parsimonious old at the same time as indicating the need to inculcate frugal habits in the young, and tightening controls on their prodigality. Lack of formal and/or legal provision for care in old age in pre-mortem arrangements, along with changing family structures, provide crucial contexts for *Lear* and *The Old Law*. In both, loss of assets and bargaining power results in extreme occurrences and actions, with the old suffering untold hardship in the tragedy, while in the tragicomedy, the prominent narrative of youth versus age exposes, despite the good intentions of the caring son and daughter-in-law, its ineluctable dysfunction.

3 Disgraceful old age (1)
men behaving badly

The contest in *King Lear* between youth and age, then, is both destructive and uplifting. The cruel and insulting behaviour of Goneril, Regan and Edmund, unseemly in any young person but so much more so in a child, is thrown into relief by the caring children, Edgar and Cordelia, who treat their fathers with the respect to which they are entitled simply by virtue of their seniority. But even though Lear's two elder daughters regard their father's old age as a state of physical and mental deterioration and harp on the infirmity of his age (*Lear*, 1. 1, 294), thereby enforcing his dependence on them (*Lear*, 2. 4, 200; cf. Munson-Deats, 1996, 91), and even though Edmund's deception results in painful injury, Lear's and Gloucester's behaviour is also inappropriate and contributes to an overall narrative of decorum and its opposite in which both old and young participate and in which the old behave in a manner becoming to their status and condition only on the point of death. The play's concern with decorum and its major breaches in the lives of its personages is thus the starting point of this chapter, which will show that classical rules of decorum in art and life apply most particularly to writings on old age.

INDECORUM (1) *KING LEAR*

Decorum in the ancient world encompassed principles of appropriateness in art, language and behaviour. From Plato, Aristotle, Cicero, Quintilian and Horace, the renaissance imbibed the refinements of decorum by fusing ritual, art theory and rhetoric with morality, personal integrity and social sense. The desire to mould idealised people into equally idealised roles certainly included old and young, monarchs and their offspring. The rules of decorum, which Cuddon's *Dictionary of Literary Terms* defines as 'consistency with the canons of propriety; a matter of behaviour on the part of the poet *qua* his poem, and therefore what is proper and becoming in the relationship between form and substance', insist that 'action, character, thought and language all need to be appropriate to each other'. Decorum, with its origins in Horace's *Art of Poetry* (1974, line 333) and its association with advanced age and the behaviour appropriate to it and when confronted by it,[1] lies at the heart of the play. Lear dies with dignity but the final stage of his life is not dignified; he does not age gracefully. In a sense he does not need to; he continues in his energetic lifestyle after retirement. He rides, shoots, hunts, and travels long distances. Even after his prolonged exposure to the elements his physical strength is undiminished; he kills Cordelia's hangman with his bare hands. Lear's indecorousness lies not so much in failure to recognise his limitations; he is strong as an ox at the age of eighty and this remarkable physical attribute is reflected in his energetic lifestyle. It lies rather in his desire to be cradled in Cordelia's 'kind nursery' (*Lear*, 1. 1, 124) when his physical condition does not require it. Newton's translation of Levinus Lemnius tells us that there are 'many old me[n], lusty, mery and wel complexioned, strong of limmes, good footme[n], & in their old dayes as fresh & actiue as many young me[n],' (trans. Newton, 1576, 28), and Lear is one of these. As such, he is an exception to the more widespread assumption that at eighty a person is in the advanced stages of bodily decay: 'the older men are, the more weake and feeble they are in every thing they doe and take in hand [...] the synewes, lineaments, and all the members of the body doe shrinke, languish and decay', though it is true that 'some beare their age very well' (Goulart, 1621, 24). These observations render Lear's behaviour problematic from the start. On the one hand he is eighty years old and needs to adopt the life and style befitting a man of his advanced years. On the other, he retains his vigour and has no need as yet of being nursed. Goulart, recycling Cicero, describes Appius as blessed with a pliant spirit, and 'resolued to dare, defye, wrastle with old age.' Like Lear, he displays enough physical strength to retain 'all the sway of Command' in his household, and keep all members of his family in such good 'awe and order, that he was reuerenced of his children, and beloued of his neighbors' (51). Lear evidently aspires to this, yet contravenes the requirements of decorum in his desire to secure two clashing modes of care for his old age — he wants to be coddled even though his physical condition does not require it, and at the same time he wishes to retain the full authority of his position, even though he gives away the means of retaining it.[2]

Lear's autocratic public behaviour exposes faultlines in his actions as a private individual. His intention to keep control of his family after retirement is not (as ideally it should be) arrived at on the basis of the caution, temperance, dignity, patience, wisdom through long experience, authority based on wise judgement, knowledge of the bible and godliness resulting therefrom, that should accompany old age (Goulart, 27, 29, 46, 49, 50, 59, 199; Brookes, 1657, 57; Steele, 1688, 79–129). There are some old men, and it is clear that Lear is one of them, who are 'cumbered and tortured' with passions peculiar to old age, such as covetousness, anger, distrust and impatience. This is because they are weak in spirit (Goulart, 1621, 64, 69). What the old must do, as both early modern manual writers present-day and gerontologists point out (cf. Bevington, 1989, 408; cf. also Holstein,

1994, 822–27; Covey, 1989, 695), and what Lear does not do, is learn to give up the rights they possess over the younger generation with good grace, and make sure that they earn the right to their respect by practising the virtues most seemly to their age. Though in ancient times 'authoritie, honour, respect, or reuerence did appertaine to none but those that were auncient' (Goulart, 1621, 63), the 'wise vieillard' still needs to earn it. In order to be supported in old age, he needs to have lived a blameless life hard to achieve, but still possible (Goulart, 60; Steele, 79). But Lear, used to 'dealing in the currency of wealth and power' (Bevington, 1989, 408), behaves in a manner entirely inappropriate to his age, to his royalty, and to his duties and status as a father. He and Gloucester behave indecorously in these domains and so solicit indecorous behaviour from the ungrateful children.

Lear's physical robustness is at odds with his mental state, and this imbalance contributes to a twofold conflict with all three of his children over duty and with himself over his own desires. This conflict can be expressed both in terms of doctrines of the humours and Freudian psychoanalysis. According to humoural psychology, behaving indecorously is a likely outcome of the predominance of one humour over the others, and can cause obsessional thoughts which sidetrack a man's actions away from what is expected of him. Inconsistent actions and wildly fluctuating speech and behaviour are the psychological effects of this physiological condition. Lear bears the marks of melancholy in his words and actions. The humour that prevails in old age is melancholy, in its dual aspect as one of the four humours and as a disease. It is, of course, possible for a person (young or old) to have a melancholy temperament, like Jaques in *As You Like It*, without it being a distemper of the mind. But excess of one or other of the humours, rendering them unnatural, were deemed to have dire consequences. The worst of these unnatural humours was produced by the burning of choler and yellow bile, profoundly altering the mind and leading inexorably to death. Andreas Laurentius identifies the disease of melancholy as issuing from one of two types of dotage. The one, delirium, is 'a kinde of dotage without any feuer; hauing for his ordinary companions, feare and sadnes, without any apparent occasion'. The other, mania, 'or madnes', is 'accompanied with rage and furie [...] or else with feare and sadnes, and then it is called melancholie [...] We call that dotage, when some one of the principall faculties of the minde, as imagination or reason is corrupted' (Laurentius, 1599, 86–87). Along with the other major writers on melancholy, Timothy Bright, Levinus Lemnius, Thomas Wright and Robert Burton,[3] Laurentius associates the humour and the disease with old age, perceiving a circular relationship between the predominance of melancholy humours in the old and the onset of the disease as a result of diminution of 'spirits and substance' (Burton, 1955, 183; Laurentius, 1599, 86–89). The melancholy humour, like old age, is cold and dry, and causes dotage in old men by the superabundant production of black choler. This is especially true of those who, like Lear, have lived very active lives, full of 'great employment, much business, much command, and many servants to oversee' (Burton, 1955, 183). Burton makes the connection between active kingship and the onset of senile melancholy quite explicit by citing the examples of Charles V and King Philip. Unable to manage their estates, they 'resign up all on a sudden' and are overcome with melancholy 'in an instant' (183). Lear's melancholy is intensified by many of the causes Burton discusses; he exposes himself to rough and foul weather (*Lear* 3, 1–4; Burton, 1955, 209); to unseasonable, violent exercise (*Lear* 1. 3, 8; 5. 3, 7, 1–2; Burton, 1955, 210); and above all to prolonged lack of sleep (*Lear* 3, 1-4; Burton, 1955, 216). This last is both a symptom and a cause, resulting in desiccation of the body, making it 'lean, hard, and ugly to behold [...] the temperature of the brain is corrupted by it, the humours adust [burn up], the eyes made to sink into the head, choler increased, & the whole body inflamed' (Burton, 1955, 217). Lear experiences most of these symptoms (cf. Draper, 1940, 536–38). But the most exacerbating symptom is the 'thunder and lightning of perturbation, which causeth such violence and speedy alterations in this our Microcosm, and many times subverts the good estate and temperature of it' (Burton, 1955, 217). When imagination or reason is corrupted, melancholy results (Burton, 1955, 219; Laurentius, 1599, 87). It is clear from this that Lear suffers the fate of 'All melancholike persons' who 'haue their imagination troubled, for that they deuise with themselues a thousand fantasticall inuentions and obiects, which in deede are not at all' (Laurentius, 1599, 87, see also Burton, 1955, 220–24). Unable to control his concupiscible and irascible passions, Lear's spirits are consumed by ambition manifest in pride, self-love, covetousness (of his daughters' love), immoderate joy, desire (Burton, 1955, 242), hatred (229), sorrow (225), fear (227), anger (233), desire for revenge (231), 'Discontents, Cares, Miseries' (235). The internal disorder of the balance of his humours leads to external disorder; he cannot suppress these rebellious feelings and in the end is destroyed by them, just as the disruption of the balance of his humours and the onset of melancholy adust makes him behave in a way which destroys the balance of his kingdom.

Lear also bears the stigmata of melancholy brought on by twisted or thwarted love. This, the one great cause of melancholy, is the subject of the entire final part of Burton's treatise. In a subsection on love's tyranny (650–59), Burton provides a very long list of those who in ancient legend were unable to confine their love within 'natural boundaries'. Helen of Troy, herself 'not the first petticoat that caused a war', heads an exemplary troup of transgressives, practitioners of bestiality, sodomites, self-abusers, and necrophiliacs. Interestingly, the list contains only one incestuous pair — Cyniras and his daughter Myrrha (650–53). The names on this list all raged with a love that was 'a Disease, Phrensy, Madness, Hell' (651); a love that was a vehement perturbation of the mind, subverting kingdoms and laying its subjects to waste. Though Oedipus is conspicuously absent from Burton's list, it is not difficult to see in Lear the signs of transgressive love, and to attribute therein his unseemly behaviour. Diseased melancholy initially manifests itself as a moment of hubris at the beginning of the play, when Lear solicits unseemly expressions of love from his three daughters. Conceptually, it is not a giant step from this to Freud's notation of inappropriate love-objects and wrong life-choices in 'The Theme of the Three Caskets.' Freud's essay indicates the hopelessness of an old man who craves 'the love of woman as he had it' (Freud, 1990, 247) when all he can expect at his time of life is the embrace of the third of the Fates, the Goddess of Death (241). Lear is in effect making manifest forbidden desires. His desire for love (Eros) is more fitting for a young man, so the unrealisable sexual aspect of his choice must instead be indecorously re-channelled onto his daughters, and sublimated in a love-test, which requires them to compete in expressions of gratitude. According to Freud's account, the conscious choice of love (his youngest daughter) over the unconscious choice of death (Cordelia represents the Death Goddess) is inappropriate to Lear's circumstances, and must be repressed (246–47). Since Lear cannot bring himself to confront the feelings that lie behind his choices,[4] he must endure their consequences without ever coming to understand what lies behind his motives in burdening his favourite child with the impossible demands of an impossible love. What makes this even more striking as an expression of social/cutural indecorum in *King Lear* is the question of what choices are best suited to the particular stage of a man's life, for didactic writers tirelessly promote Ages of Man *topoi* as a lesson in decorum. Each age has its characteristics and appropriate demeanours, to which individuals must conform. The final phase, old age, is further divided into three stages; the green, the old and the decrepit. As a person progressed from the first to the last, their choices, in company with their capacities, became progressively more restricted until, at the decrepit stage, they were in effect limited to two; either to retire from active life and prepare for the soul to meet its maker, or to sink in reputation for the little time remaining here on earth and risk rejection by God when the time comes for the soul to take flight (cf. *Cyuile and uncyuile life*, 1579, 74-76; *Batman vppon Bartholome*, 1582, 70-73; Primaudaye, 1589, 540; Laurentius, 1599, 173; John Bellars, 1935, 46, 50, 81; Sheafe, 1639, Bk. 1, chap. 1; Bk. 2, chaps. 1–5; Brookes, 1659, 61–73, 348–57; Steele,1688, chap. vii; Covey, 1989, 692–8). Lear is caught between a rock and a hard place here, too. His decision to relapse into the nursery of his daughters' care implies that he is ready to accept retirement as a preparation to meet his maker. Yet this choice is not appropriate on any level, since he still retains his physical strength and wishes to retain his retinue, his liberty, and his authority as king. Unable to sink back into the helplessness of childhood, and unable to relinquish the reins of command, he cannot but make wrong choices, and as a consequence offends against every rule of decorum.

Falstaff, ignoring the recommendations of prescription and pulpit, blithely opts for indecorous living. But in *King Lear* the very question of choice is problematic. Freud's discussion of the restrictive nature of the choices can be extended to each of the characters. Lear, significantly, in choosing among his daughters, imagines that he exercises an unrestricted range of options, yet in reality confines his choice to the family circle. The same is true of Gloucester. Reverting to Freudian analysis once more, it would seem that the preference of one child over another implies initially that Lear's and Gloucester's choice is one of youth and love. But each successive scene unravels the comfortable illusions that have allowed these two old men to repress the true nature of their choice, until the final catastrophic shock at the end of the play reveals that both have chosen death. Seemingly both exercise free choice, from which death is excluded; yet, paradoxically, they cannot but choose death, in spite of its absence as a choice. As Asp puts it, 'the latent content (death) of the object they choose is veiled from them at the moment of choice' (Asp, 1986, 193). The message of the play, in Freudian terms, and according to the rules of decorum, is that both Gloucester and Lear must come to terms with death.

King Lear, in its emphasis on age-appropriate behaviour, draws upon contemporary debates on what it meant to be a reigning monarch as well as who should rightfully inherit the realm. Performed at a time when James I, in his speech to Parliament delivered in March 1609, was broadcasting his own inviolability by telling his ministers that kings are like gods, 'for they exercise a manner or resemblance of Divine power upon earth' (Rhodes, 2003, 327; see also Foakes, 1996, 273), the play seems to stage the unimaginable; a king who gives up his crown and along with it his divinely-bestowed omnipotence. However, R.A. Foakes persuasively argues that, despite what some productions and critics might suppose, he does not in fact do so. The coronet that Lear hands to Albany and Cornwall, angrily telling them to 'part this between you' (1. 1, 39), is a third coronet (the other two presumably being worn by Cornwall and Albany on this ceremonial occasion) and one he had intended for Cordelia's consort once she came to her share of the kingdom. The point Foakes makes is that a coronet is an appropriate emblem for a duke or prince, not a king, whose authority is invested in the emblem of the imperial crown (Foakes, 274). There is nothing in the stage directions or dialogue to suggest that the king takes the crown from his own head to hand to the husbands of his two elder daughters. However, even though Lear is God's representative on earth, anointed by holy oil (Gloucester refers to this 3. 7, 58), and remains to his loyal subjects 'Royal Lear', 'Most royal Majesty' and 'every inch a king' (4. 6, 107), he sustains the decorum of his supreme position in show only; his actions soon belie the epithets of majesty. In terms of matching appearance to action and speech on this occasion of state, Kent is also in breach of decorum by his unceremonious outburst 'What wouldst thou do, old man' (1. 1, 146) that ruptures the formality of the opening scene. It is clear from the visual effects that Lear intends to continue as a powerful king, even though he has given away the means of sustaining this role. Lear thus manages to uphold a seemingly decorous position though his actions are indecorous to the point of illegality.[5]

The play initiates its subversive vein by posing the question of the right of kings to choose their own successors and in so doing harks back to Elizabeth's last days. In this respect it intervenes in narratives about the indecorous events surrounding the Queen's deathbed. From this perspective, the play can be read as a thinly veiled criticism of both Elizabeth and James. Was Elizabeth behaving appropriately in withholding her choice of successor till her last moments? Did she in fact do so? And did she make the right choice? The play revisits this sensitive area in the issues it raises regarding inheritance and appropriate behaviour for a monarch. There is no male heir for Lear, just as there was none for Elizabeth. According to the laws of succession Goneril, as his eldest, is first in line. Lear disrupts the direct line of passing on a patrimony; from this angle he has no business wanting to give the largest portion to his youngest. Yet the evidence available from wills suggests that custom permitted parents to distribute wealth as they wanted, and not as the strict laws of primogeniture dictated. The play thus revisits the quandary posed first of all by Elizabeth's refusal to marry and later, much more crucially, her refusal in her old age either to name her successor, or to take the sacraments, or indeed to acknowledge the onset of old age at all, until just a few days before she died — a fiction which involved her entire court (more of this later). Lear's refusal to behave in the manner fitting to old men evokes the profound indecorum of Elizabeth's deathbed comportment.

Lear is guilty of impropriety in feeling as well as in behaviour. He is driven by anger and shame, two emotions associated with aged impotence (cf. Boaistuau, 1574, 213; Barrough, 1601, 22; Coeffeteau, 1621, 620; Goulart, 1621, 76; Bacon, 1638, 174), along with a misguided belief that he continues to wield power over his children and over nature itself (1. 4, 274 and passim). Lear's anger explodes when the reality of his position is brought home to him, that he cannot change the nature of his pelican daughters; nor can he renounce his image of himself as a God-appointed king, with powers more godlike than human. As a consequence, his appropriation of divine wrath is unseemly in the extreme, as is the shame he feels at shedding tears in public. Manifestations of these two extreme emotions of anger and shame, not inappropriate or unbecoming in themselves — Laurentius saw no harm in occasionally 'raising' old men's choler to 'rouse them' and 'warm them up a little' (Laurentius, 1599, 174) — become so in the circumstances in which they arise. They are inappropriate in Lear because he imagines he still possesses a power he no longer has, and unbecoming because, as Bevington notes (1989, 410), when he catches a glimpse of his own impotency, he is overcome by a sense of shame that undermines his estate as a man and as a king (*Lear*, 1. 4, 295–98). Because of this, the play's enquiry into questions of decorum in old age is deepened to include the perception that not only does Lear behave in a manner unsuited to his age and status, but that old age is itself indecorous; it is in condition a second childhood, an inevitable reversion to the dependency of a former state, carrying a raft of unappealing symptoms, and it cannot be avoided.[6] Lear's response to the indecorum of age is itself indecorous; though he pays lip service to his own advanced years he does not regard his retirement as such, because he still intends to hold the reins of power, and he intends his twice-yearly visitations to his daughters to be conducted in the costly and burdensome manner of a reigning monarch, like Elizabeth's near-ruinous visitations upon her courtiers' country estates.

The sense that old age in itself is an indecorous condition is widespread in seventeenth-century writings that feature senescence. The following anecdotes show the continuing resonance and ramifications of the Lear story by continuing to harp on the impropriety of giving away of his property via a route which underscores the unwholesome degeneration of the aged body. The unprepossessing habits of the old from which the young recoil in unfilial disgust notably feature in the ways in which the old are marginalised. So Foulke Robartes compares the lot of clergy entirely dependent upon parishioners' handouts to a father who has given away his estate:

> Hath any man euer seene a poore aged man live at curtesie, in the house of his sonne, with his daughter in law? Doth not the good father in a short time, either by his coughing or spitting or teastinesse or some soon seene vntowardnesse or other, become troublesome, either to his owne sonne, or to his nice daughter in law, with continuing so long chargeable, & so much waited on, or to the children, with taking vp their roome at the fire, or at the table, or to the seruants, while his slow eating doth scant their reversions? But, if the olde man hath estate of his owne, to maintaine himselfe, and to pleasure his children (oh then) hee is had in estimation; his age is honoured, his person is reverenced, his counsell is sought, his voice is obeyed. (Robartes, 1613, 114–15)

The repellent symptoms of a body too full of phlegm and excrement belong to old age which is 'by nature dry but in condition moyste' (Newton, 1576, 88). Old men are full of mucus because 'creatures drain out towards decay', and the dry quality in moist complexions 'maketh colde and dryeth the solide partes of the body: but the Receyuers and conceptacles of the humours it filleth wyth excrements, which thing in Old men is plainly to be discerned & perceyued, who abou[n]de and are ful of Phlegme, spitting & spatteringe al theyr mouth, w[ith] their Noses euer droping and sneuillye' (88). And they are full of shit because 'as lees and dregs doe sinke downe, and lie at the bottome of vessels: so the excrements, noysome humours, and all the miseries of our life, doe settle in old age their last lodging place' (Goulart, 1621, 54).

The relationship between an old man who has given away his fortune and the harsh treatment he receives as a result of his disgusting condition appears in the Commonplace book of Sir John Oglander, written under James I and Charles I, and in the reports of Bulstrode Whitelocke while he was Ambassador to Sweden. In an entry for 1648, while he was Deputy Lieutenant of the Isle of Wight, Oglander compares the deathbed circumstances of two gentlemen, one his brother, Edward Cheke, the other Sir William Lile. Both lay sick for some time. His brother died of consumption becomingly, in a manner fit for a gentleman at the age of eighty, and Oglander provides a verbatim account of his last confession:

> I have been a great sinner. There was no content I denied to myself: I have given loose rein to the flesh. But God out of his abundant goodness, with this long sickness and His grace working upon me, hath called me home and, through faith in Christ, I am become a true penitent and no-wise doubt of his mercy but that, after this life, I shall live with Him eternally. (Oglander, 1936, 123)

This repentance converted him from an indecorous voluptuary to a penitent throwing himself on the mercy of God in his final hour, and earned him a public funeral ceremony attended by a 'great assembly' of the local gentry, with 'gloves and ribbons given to all'. He was gentle and 'so good a fellow that he had 500 gentlemen called him "Father"' (123). Both Cheke and Sir William were 'good drinkers' and 'housekeepers' (home owners) on the Island. But by contrast Sir William, though a 'very good housekeeper' of his estate, was too free and bountiful with the good beer in his cellar, and in his person too slovenly to be thought decorous. He went around dressed more like a farmer than a knight, and was never happier than when 'he dropped at the breeches', that is, when he was at his wettest and dirtiest, presumably as a result of sploshing around in muddy puddles. He ended up giving over his entire estate to his son, who restricted him to £150 and one 'nasty' chamber, allowing him no more for his men, horses, dogs, provisions and 'for the cooking of them' (124).

The third anecdote comes from Bulstrode Whitelocke, nominated by Cromwell to the embassy of Queen Christina of Sweden, who tries to dissuade her from resigning her crown in favour of her son, the Prince Palatine, by telling her the story of 'an old English gentleman, who had an active young man to his son' (Whitlocke, 1855, 352). The son successfully persuaded his father to sign over to him his entire estate, and its management, reserving only a pension to himself. The papers were drawn up, and friends assembled in the parlour to witness the signatures. The father settled down to a pipe of tobacco in the same room, 'where his rheum caused him to spit much.' The son, embarrassed by his father's coughing and spitting in front of so many people, 'desired his father to take the tobacco in the kitchen, and to spit there' (352). The father obeyed, but when the paperwork was ready, refused to sign, saying he had changed his mind, for he 'resolved to spit in the parlour as long as he lived' (352). The Lear story continues thus to resonate through the rest of the century and on into the new, and is used in a variety of ways that show up breaches of decorum in the demeanour of young and old towards each other. According to Edmund Tilney there is nothing more sacred than the 'love towards parentes, which God in the commaundementes, hath rewarded with the longnesse of life' (Tilney, 1568, 105); an enduring sentiment echoed by Richard Steele more than a hundred years later in his observation that for those who have been 'regarded and reverenced,' to be neglected and despised 'grates even the most ingenuuous spirits' (Steele, 1688, 172).

The indecorous (that is, the anti-social, repellent) habits of the old — coughing, spitting, testiness, slovenliness, gluttony — provoked indecorous treatment from the young. They are repelled by the disgusting spectacle of phlegmy old men, who are as a result confined to the kitchen because they deprive children of space, and all because they were over-generous in giving everything away too early, while the young beneficiaries of their parents' estate show no gratitude, and complain instead of the cost of keep. The Lear story continues to occupy front space in the minds of those entering into the vale of years. Handbooks are full of advice to both old and young on how to behave in a seemly fashion on the basis of several commonplaces, running alongside each other. The Ages of Man *topoi* (cf. Hippocrates, Aristotle, Galen), taken up by the Latin poets (cf. Ovid, 1985, 15: 199–216), initiate advice on how to be decorous in old age, and combine with plentiful instruction on how to cope with infirmities by taking appropriate measures such as correct diet and exercise, how to adopt a way of life commesurate with advancing years (cf. Elyot, 1541; Newton, 1576; Cuffe, 1607; Bacon, 1638) and how to suffer aches, pains and loss of vigour with dignity. Above all, the advice on balance of the household and financial independence to the last accompanies copious instruction on preparing for death (cf. Strode, 1618; Goulart, 1621; Steele, 1688).[7]

(IN)DECORUM (2) *THE OLD LAW*

The requirement for literature to rely on graceful self-expression as the surest indication of a life lived with grace features prominently in manuals of style deriving their impetus from antiquity. Vives, writing on rhetoric in 1532, elaborates Cicero's definition of decorum as a match between the language a speaker uses, the conditions giving rise to his utterance, and the relationship between the speaker's subject matter and his character (Vives, 'de decoro' 1532, 2, , 173–96, 174). A speaker's words must always signal his own impeccable sense of what is appropriate to his station in life (Vives 'de decoro', 1532, 2, 176.) Vives stresses the importance of doing things according to the rules of decorum in order to manage one's self-presentation as a man of wisdom, temperance and good character. Rules of decorum thus bear a strong social and cultural weight since they encompass aesthetic and rhetorical measures ensuring fitting expression in speech and behaviour (191). Early modern culture adhered to standards of good taste and correctness that required the organisation of social image and prominent position in social hierarchies (cf. Rebhorn, 2000, 4–5; George, 1992, 163–65), and according to these rules, the disgusting habits and decayed condition of the old are by definition indecorous.

Vives paved the way for sixteenth- and seventeenth-century concern in conduct books with issues of decorum in its social sense. Like their classical models, they define fitting behaviour by its opposites. Both Thomas Wilson and George Puttenham 'stigmatise indecorousness' (Rebhorn, 2000, 2) by insisting that the ideal orator must not employ the kind of language and behaviour that is scurrilous and that descends into rough ale-house jesting (Wilson, 1560, Preface). He should also avoid any of the vices of rhetoric such as barbarism, rusticity and crude innuendo. Above all a writer should eschew language that might identify him with the peasantry. A decorous writer must, by contrast, use the language of the king's court, or at least employ an urban vocabulary in order to avoid the barbarisms of dialect, or the language employed by 'rusticall or vnciuill people' (Puttenham,1589, 120). Wilson and Puttenham both use the figure of the learned clerk or pedant to embody all that they consider indecorous. Both abhor the use of inkhorn terms, believing that true eloquence persuades by use of appropriate language and organisation of material, whereas exhibitions of learning obscure meaning by recourse to jargon, technical terms and foreign words. Abuses of decorum perpetrated by 'English clerkes', those on the fringes of learning who, 'counterfeiting the Kings English [...] wil so Latin their tongues, that the simple can not but wonder at their talke, and think surely they speake by some reuelation' (Wilson, 1560, 162), are class-based; Wilson satirises provincial attempts at erudition by inventing a letter from a man from Lincolnshire peppered with the worst kind of inkhornism that Wilson can dream up (163–34). For Puttenham 'clerkly' means uncouth (Puttenham, 1589, 125) and he adds preachers and schoolmasters to the list of those who defy decency and decorum by committing the cardinal error of using high-flown terms for humble subject matter (115). Obscure language is thus associated with obscure men — that is, men whose origin is base, and who cannot help reveal their obscure origins through the use of 'darke' terms.

Puttenham, however, does not include old men among those committing sins of indecorum. On the contrary, old men

> more then any other sort speake most grauely, wisely, assuredly, and plausibly, which partes are all that can be required in perfite eloquence, and so in all deliberations of importance where counsellours are allowed freely to opyne & shew their co[n]ceits, good persuasion is no lesse requisite then speach it selfe (118)

— an opinion which reveals an interesting anomaly. Puttenham's approval (and Peacham's too)[8] of the gravity of enunciation and subject matter that forms the basis of old men's conversation is an exception to guidelines which exclude the old from the social élite of the decorous. It is based upon the assumption that all old men who express an opinion are grave counsellors of breeding whose origins are neither base nor obscure, and, alone of those Puttenham considers blest with elegant speech, he singles out the old as men whose innate decorousness arises from a combination of age and status. This observation has so far escaped critical notice despite the importance of manners in early modern cultural practice. Perhaps this is because old age itself has so far by and large escaped the notice of literary scholars. Puttenham's association of wisdom and eloquence with age requires closer examination, particularly in view of a reluctance found in the paradigm of manners, *The Courtier*, to consider the aged courtier as a fitting model of either speech, style or gravitas — a reluctance adopted by subsequent treatises on manners and style.

This exemplar of courtly manuals, written by a supreme practitioner of graceful and appropriate behaviour, Baldasare Castiglione, raises important issues on how an aging courtier is to conduct himself in public. He is advised to bow out of all the activities that he has hitherto practiced and perfected; it is now unseemly for him to continue to pay court to ladies, to make music, to compose verses, to take part in games and tournaments, to continue in arms, to take to the dance floor. To persist in these manifestations of courtly style is to make oneself ridiculous, and betrays a gross breech of court etiquette. Displays of indecorum disgrace the aging courtier, and undermine his position as the prince's guide and mentor, a position which of necessity requires him to be more perfect than the prince himself. The aging courtier thus finds himself in an impossible position: behaviour by which courtly grace is defined is no longer available to him, yet not to perform these acts is to forfeit his courtly self and function. A courtier is defined by a set of rules governing his public behaviour and by which his aptitude is judged; take these away, and you take away his identity. Two consequences of this for Castiglione are that by very definition, there is no such thing as an old courtier; and that old age is by its very nature not suited to court politics — an observation whose implications are manifest in a variety of subsequent texts.

The Courtier acted as model for the later, English manuals on court style such as those of Wilson, Puttenham, and Peacham. The author of *Cyvile and Unciuile Life*, even more closely indebted to *Courtier* ideals, explicitly connects aging with the kind of indecorousness Castiglione details. The best age to serve the Prince is twenty-five, and to exercise the body to thirty-five only; thereafter the practice of arms, riding and entertaining ladies are 'seldome seemely' in a man of ripe age, and 'in olde yeares very ridiculous' (*Cyvile*, 1579, 74–75). The old commit the same kind of sins against decorum as do the socially inferior. Decorum is a means of separation from base roots; Wilson and Puttenham sought advancement by means of rhetorical skills, both oral and written. Wilson, himself a Lincolnshire man, managed through the patronage of Sir Edward Dymock and Thomas Cecil, Lord Burghley, to become Secretary of State, and Puttenham married well; his writing was rewarded by Elizabeth I and its compass and definition is used by these and other writers to distance themselves from what they consider to be socially demeaning. Decorum requires also a separation from the condition of life that is most demeaning to a man's perception of his own identity — old age. The contraries of apt speech and behaviour are in many instances the same ones that are used to define the characteristics of senescence. Wilson thinks digression is barbarous; the old are fond of telling long digressionary yarns. The old and the socially inferior are marginalised by unsavoury habits. Phlegmy, spluttering old age is cast upon the very bottom of the social heap, just as are the common sort, whose poor clothing and dirtiness aligns them with the clerks who sully language.

We have already seen how stories and anecdotes clarify this identification. Interpenetration of classical ideals on decorum in rhetoric, poetry and style with codes of behaviour for all the stages of a man's life reinforce their mutual dependency. As Wayne Rebhorn, in a provocative essay upon the anxiety of indecorum in three renaissance writers on style, states, 'the maintenance of decorum is really the maintenance of one's social distinctiveness, a process in which the speaker, presenting himself through language that is erudite, artful, urban and urbane, identifies himself as a member of the social elite' (Rebhorn, 2000, 1). The old are unable to do this. Given that old age alone of all the ages of man was a disease from which one never recovered, how could one carry through into old age the conduct of a life that was, until its onset, graceful and apt? This is the quandary facing writers on old age. Their only option is to deal with it by recommending a retreat into the religious life, passive and contemplative, which seeks to distance itself from the ways of the world. By demystifying the nearness of death, so that it need no longer hold any terrors, the apologists for old age remove the need for direct confrontation with its painful and problematic nature. Like the conduct book writers, whose fear of being thought uncouth themselves leads them to denounce 'vnseemely or misbecomming' language (Puttenham, 1589, 114) as the enemy of decorum and hide behind decorum in order to distance themselves from their own lowly origins, so the writers of old age manuals seek to reinstate the value of this despised yet inevitable condition of life by insisting on its qualities, and denounce those who behave in a way that brings shame upon its venerable estate. And like the authors of manuals of style, they do so in order to avoid having to confront their own decline into the vale of years. Writers on rhetoric find that they are unable to distance themselves from the indecorum of oral and written expression; they have to borrow terms from foreign languages because their own has no equivalent for what they want to express. Similarly, writers trying to rescue the reputation of old age have to deal with the fact that old age is in its very condition unbecoming according to all the ideals of courtly grace, and, like the authors of manuals on style, are faced with the problem of how to invent a fitting and pleasing form of words to rescue from disgrace the condition of which they are writing (Puttenham, 1589, 114). *The Old Law*, because of its dependence on style, manners and cultural imperatives, provides ample illustration of this.

Adapting behaviour to suit individual circumstances and behaving fittingly in old age as regards preparing for death, goes some way towards mitigating the unavoidable disgrace of melancholy and the disease of old age. The two dignified old men in *The Old Law* prepare for death properly. They are exemplars of decorum in their stoicism in the face of state execution. Cleanthes, who honours and respects his father for his resignation, has a fittingly harmonious relationship with him which centrally involves rejection of the unseemly haste (shown by the bad son Simonides) to step into a dead father's shoes. Cleanthes describes his father as

> too old, being now exposed
> Unto the rigour of a cruel edict
> And yet not old enough by many years,
> 'cause I'd not see him go an hour before me. (*Old Law*, 1. 1, 93–96)

However, there are two old men in the play who defy the rules of conduct and (neo) stoic precepts of piety, temperance and patience, through barbarity of language in the one instance, and unseemly behaviour in the other.[9] Gnothos (the low-born clown) and the high-born Lisander (uncle to Cleanthes; more of him later) embark on actions which narrow the rift in the way the high-born are expected to behave and the way in which the low-born, who have not had the advantage of the training of a gentleman, act and speak. The play ends in a display of the kind of indecorum for which the audience has been prepared at the first appearance of Gnothos. The third act opens at the point where the parish clerk has found the entry for Agatha, the wife of Gnothos, who attempts to bribe the clerk to falsify the record by changing Agatha's date of birth from 1540 to 1539, in order to bring her a year sooner to the cut-off age of sixty. Gnothos browbeats the clerk into conceding his superior status as 'the wiser man' and the greater in the parish. The clerk, for his part, exhibits the kind of pedantry that Puttenham abhors in low-grade clerks; he claims expertise in orthography, correct usage of terms, and ability to identify and decipher 'infallible' records (3. 1, 29), and modestly disclaims the 'art to cast a figure' (3. 1, 66). The Clerk's barbarous mixture of inappropriate Latinisms (inappropriate because they are placed in the mouth of a low-born character) is matched by Gnothos in claims to a status he does not possess, and in the ease with which he hoodwinks the clerk into forging the records. In a series of elaborate compliments to each other, in parody of the behaviour of their social betters, Gnothos succeeds in flattering the clerk into falsifying the records, to which the clerk agrees, thinking he is doing a superior a favour. All this is so that Gnothos can behave indecorously in another way; his aim is to get rid of an old wife in order to marry a much younger one. This parodies the rules of decorum as the means by which those of gentle status demonstrate their moral rectitude; he passes himself off as a tender-hearted husband who is 'loath to leave a good old woman' on the grounds that it would be an act of mercy to put her out of her pain, 'for what is a year, alas, but a lingering torment? [...] It must needs be a grief to us both' (3. 1, 39-43). Both manipulate language in a series of manoeuvres that obscure meaning and cloak criminal motives at the same time as they vie with each other to endorse breeding, the prime aim of decorum.

At the end of Middleton and Rowley's play, the draconian ruling to put to death all men of eighty and all women of sixty is revealed as a strategy to test the loyalty and devotion of younger spouses and children. But Gnothos the Clown, unaware of the turn events have taken, enters leading his new young bride at the head of a wedding procession that is tailed by his existing old wife, other old women and a troupe of stragglers who have suffered from the side-effects of the law. Gnothos is confident that the Duke will approve his proactive behaviour. Pointing to Siren the Wench, the new bride he proposes after the law has claimed the life of his old one, Gnothos tells the Duke:

This is my two-for-one that must be *uxor uxoris,*

The remedy *doloris,* and the very *syceum amoris.*
Evander: And hast thou any else?
Gnothos: I have an older, my lord, for other uses. (5. 1, 431–34)

Cleanthes points out the unexpected fittingness of this:

> I do observe a strange decorum here.
> These that do lead this day of jollity,
> Do march with music and most mirthful cheeks;
> Those that do follow, sad and woefully,
> Nearer the 'haviour of a funeral
> Than a wedding. (5. 1, 435–40)

It is entirely appropriate for a wedding procession to be accompanied by music and joyful participants, but it is not at all usual for it to tail off into a funeral cortège. Each part of the procession is decorous in its own way; weddings are fittingly celebrated and funerals are peopled by mourners. In one sense, 'strange decorum', which might ordinarily be considered a contradiction in terms, is, in this instance, an apt description of what unfolds before the spectators' eyes. Furthermore, Cleanthes, the high born young man who makes this observation, describes it in an 'agreeable' and 'becoming' way to celebrate youth and life in the same ceremony that bids farewell to those whose life the law has terminated, thereby showing his breeding and education. Gnothos the (aging) low-life clown, by contrast, butchers decorum in his description of Siren the Wench. He tells the Duke that she is the best of wives (*uxor uxoris*), she will be his cure for sadness (remedy *doloris*) and she will be the provider of love (*syceum amoris*). Apart from being an entirely inaccurate description of the bride (her sobriquet proclaims that she cannot be any of the things Gnothos claims for her), the introduction of Latin terms where English would do just as well is a good example of what Puttenham and Wilson abhor — the infiltration of impure terminology in the mouths of the vulgar and low born in order to apostrophise in an entirely indecorous fashion a woman (a siren, a wench) who is not fit to be a wife in her own person, and who cannot in any case legitimately be espoused. From another point of view, though, the decorum of this procession may be construed as strange in Wilson's use of this word when describing the abominable inkhorn terms so opposed to decent, decorous articulation of thought that the lower classes — his 'Barbarous Clarkes' and scurrilous tavern clowns — are so fond of (Wilson, 1560, 138, 157, 161, 166). Thus the very use of Latin terminology denotes the crude and vulgar (*syceum* signifies pudendum) as well as the inappropriate — a slut cannot fittingly be described as the best of wives. The playwrights use precisely the same frame of reference as the conduct writers to expose indecency, though their aim is to mock it. Gnothos, in his dual function as a low-life clown and as a disreputable old man, expresses himself indecently in various ways.[10] As the stock figure of the clown, he employs the crude vocabulary of his native tongue by investing his Latin phrases with bawdy innuendo, so that his language and gestures are as gross as all low-life clowns on stage. And as a disreputable old man, he expresses sentiments and performs actions that are in stark antithesis to the decorum of old age that requires a dignified retreat from concupiscent desires and an embrace of all things intellectual and spiritual.

The ending of *The Old Law* explicitly identifies decorum in both language and behaviour with the high-born male characters, both old and young. Though some of the young men behave badly, and say shockingly disrespectful things about the uselessness of old age, they do so in comic enactment of the faults traditionally attributed to youth from classical comedy down to our own day — hotheadedness, disrespect for their elders, chafing against their authority, impatience to come into their money and step into their seniors' shoes in the workplace. Yet all three old men — Gnothos and the two old fathers, Leonides and Creon — can be identified with ancient philosophies of Greece: Stoicism and its more radical version, Cynicism. Gnothos' gross behaviour recalls the Cynics' belief that law and custom lacked significance in people's lives. Since they felt bound by no human regulation, they (typically) showed their contempt by behaving outrageously in public. Diogenes the Cynic rationalised masturbating in the market place by annexing this anti-social act to a socially responsible one; he said he wished hunger could be as easily assuaged (Kenny, 1994, 43).

Cynics and Stoics shared moral attitudes, believing in the governance of one's way of life according to the requirements of nature in place of spurious laws devised by stupid and corrupt rulers. Nature's laws were the only true laws, and depended on a kind of double-edged justice that at once respected and denied the individual's rights with regard to public law and order, ownership of land and so forth (39). Leonides and Creon face the end of their life with exemplary Stoicism. Even though Creon adopts a robustly Cynical response to the corruption of Evander's justice in his fulminations against tyranny, he, too, accepts that his life must now end in the manner of the Stoic (*Old Law*, I i, 265–70).[11] The elders' words match their actions in high mindedness. Leonides shows the correct way to face death:

> I have conceived
> Such a new joy within this old bosom
> As I did never think would there have entered. (1. 1, 383–85)

He responds to his son Cleanthes' entirely proper expression of sorrow at the prospect of his father's death as 'the worst of all sorrows' by questioning the power of death over life:

> [...]
> Death? What's that, Cleanthes, I thought not on it [...]
> [...]
> When I die, 'twill be a gentle death. (1. 1, 389–92)

Creon's approach to death is decorous also but represents the Cynics as distinct from the Stoics. He 'understands the worst and hopes no better' from an unjust law, which holds 'white heads [...] cheap' — those who have done service to their country deserve a different kind of recompense. Dark humour, that his wife Antigona calls playing sport with sorrow, emerges not so much at the prospect of losing his life as from the manner in which he chooses to voice his indignation at having to lose it in such a peremptory way:

> Sorrow for what, Antigona? For my life?
> My sorrow's I have kept it so long well
> With bringing it up unto so ill an end. (1. 1, 235–37)

The playwrights make a further philosophical distinction by using the Sceptic's questioning of the law to expose its barbarity and to reveal gross indecorum at the roots of government:

> this day,
> without all help of casual accidents,
> Is only deadly to me 'cause it numbers
> Fourscore years to me. Where's the fault now?
> I cannot blame time, nature, nor my stars,
> Nor aught but tyranny [...]

> And so I must die by a tyrant's sword.
> First Lawyer: Oh, say not so, sir, it is by the law!
> Creon: And what's that, sir, but the sword of tyranny
> When it is brandished against innocent lives? (1. 1, 250–66)

Here Creon raises two points of principle: the loss of perfectly healthy life and the enactment of a law imposed by a tyrannous form of government. His words and actions are fitting for a Cynic and a politician. Like his mythical namesakes the King of Thebes (Sophocles, *Antigone*) and King of Corinth (Euripides, *Medea*),[12] Creon is both victim and antagonist of the law. Like his namesake the King of Corinth who is killed by Medea because he knows she has caused the death of his daughter, Creon is the victim of his own son's plotting. His contempt for a law that intends to rob him of life is also double-edged: it recalls, by contrast, his own impeccable status as domestic lawgiver:

> Antigona: His very household laws prescribed at home by him
> Are able to conform seven Christian kingdoms,
> They are so wise and virtuous. (2. 1, 113–15)

And by substitution, it also recalls Antigone's defiance of King Creon's ruling in Euripides' play, and that king's suffering when he loses his own son and wife.

In *The Old Law* Creon's anger and defiance are given an extra dimension — they take place in the midst of a cultural and political debate on the role and value of the old, a debate which incorporates suitable ways in which the old must accept their debility, and adopt correct ways of outfacing death. According to the literature of the day, the only way in which one can grow old in a seemly fashion is to adopt attitudes embodied in an amalgam of biblical precept and stoicism. An old person's only recourse is to accept old age as a misfortune that cannot be avoided, since it cannot be overcome by human agency. Leonides follows these precepts in an exemplary way, for he accepts death calmly. He refuses to escape abroad, for the simple reason that death is inevitable, and will follow him anywhere (cf. Bromham, 1996, 410). And in any case, he has no fear of death, embracing it despite exhortations from his son Cleanthes to 'fight with death/And yield not to him till you stoop under him' (1. 1, 496–97). Stoic acceptance of death, even though it is by 'the sword of tyranny' (1. 1, 265), is a sermon preached by the manuals to show old men how to prepare for it (cf. Primaudaye, 1589, 540; Strode, 1618, 176–277; Sheafe, 1639, bk. 2 ch.2; Calver, 1641, 49; Brookes, 1657, 72–74; Steele, 1688, ch. 4); both Creon and Leonides face death 'with joy' (1.1). They refuse to travel; it is not wise at their age (cf. Sheafe, 1639, 149), and both meet death without fear.

As a result of the enforcement of the Law, the decorum of the old is measured against a variety of attitudes in the young ranging from the most indecently unfilial to the most spiritually upright. The boys are ranged in a straightforward opposition of bad son/good son, but the patterning is more interestingly complicated for the girls since it functions as the vehicle for still more revelations about how to behave when old . Hippolita, Leonides' daughter-in-law and Cleanthes' wife, is at first presented as a paragon of all the virtues. In a body of literature which imputed evil motives to the wife of the son of an old man (cf. *Dives and Pauper*, 1976, 312; *Mery Tales and quicke answeres*, 1567, 121; Smith, 1984, 46–48), her love for her husband and pity for her father-in-law are notable, and inspire her to labour on his behalf (1. 1, 486–532). Yet, by the gender stereotyping of the age, her love, pity and advice turn out to be flawed in argument and deed. Leonides resists her appeal to him to flee the country by pointing out to her the shame of this in words that strikingly echo Cordelia's reasons for refusing to quantify her love for her father:

> This country hath bred me, brought me up,
> And shall I now refuse a grave in her?
> I'm in my second infancy, and children
> Ne'er sleep so sweetly in their nurse's cradle
> As in their natural mother's. (1.1, 438–43)

It is unseemly for the old to turn their backs on the land that bore them, just as it is inappropriate for old age not to recognise entry into its final stage of helplessness.

Tracing through the patterns of Stoic and Neostoic thought in the play, Bromham shows how these two principled male characters, Cleanthes and Leonides, voice the precepts of a stoicism evolved to harmonise with Christianity, principally through Justus Lipsius' *de Constantia*. By giving the central character in the play, Cleanthes, the name of a philosopher of the Early Stoa, but by setting the action in a country associated with Epictetus, the playwrights may well be signalling, as Bromham believes, that distinctions in philosophical ideas will be examined (Bromham, 1996, 405–06). The result is that different forms of Stoicism, along with different religious denominations, crystallise into cultural forms of decorum, and the debate in *The Old Law* on how to face death, filial loyalty, patriotism, patience and piety participates in all of these aspects of decorum. But what is of equal interest is the setting up of Hippolita as a paragon of familial love and pity at the same time as her weakness as a woman is exposed and chastised. Though she works tirelessly to preserve her father-in-law's life, she cannot prevent an uncontrollable access of joy (at his preservation) and misplaced pity (for Eugenia, who dissimulates sorrow at the approaching end of her old husband's life) from betraying the secret of how his life is preserved. Thus she exhibits the flaws of womanhood; no control over her tongue or her emotions. So while Cleanthes is an example of flawless youth in filial feeling and duty, there is no matching counterpart as an example of flawless young female virtue; by implication there is no such thing. But, interestingly, there is a counterpart for the perfect male elder models.

Antigona, wife to Creon, is a woman of just under sixty — the female equivalent of decrepit old age. According to stereotypes of aging, the onset of old age in women was accelerated; a woman was perceived to age much more quickly than a man; hence gender-differentiated ruling of the law. She perceives herself as old;[13] she has come to the end of her usefulness, and wishes to embrace death in company with her husband. The virtuous, seemly (older) wife is up to the mark, in contrast to the well-meaning but faulty young wife.

INDECORUM (3) MAY-DECEMBER MARRIAGES

According to the exacting standards set forth for the old courtier in *The Courtier*, Lisander's desire to compete with the young blades of Evander's court is unseemly on two counts. In the first place, his age requires a different mode of courtly behaviour; in the second, his marriage to a much younger woman offends against the rules of decorum in society at large. Castiglione sets the standard for seemly conduct at court:

> [A]ge does not prevent [the elderly courtier] having a more perfect judgement, and a more perfect understanding of how to teach them to his prince. So in this way, although the courtier who has grown old does not practise the accomplishments we have ascribed to him, he will still attain his aim of giving good instruction to his prince. (Castiglione, 1976, 320)

The aging courtier's 'final aim is to become his prince's instructor' even though he can no longer take part in 'music, merrymaking, games, arms' and similar recreations (318). Castiglione's point is both parodied and taken to absurd extremes in *The Old Law*, where retirement means retirement from life itself. A well-judged retreat from practice to consultancy for the courtier/artist is just one example of the way notions of decorum affected prescription and practice for the old that was handed down from century to century.

Samuel Bufford continues the game of lampooning old men who think that marriage to a young girl will give them back their lost youth. Writing at the end of the seventeenth century, he discourses colourfully upon the absurdities the old fall into when trying to keep up with the young. The 'Matrimmonial Noose' tying the old and the young together (Bufford, 1696, 19) is unnatural and destructive. The union of brisk and lusty young women to 'an old frigid statue' (20) can only result in the humiliation of the old. When 'a dull Walking Clod of Earth, an Old Doting Fellow of Sixty, [...] fall[s] a Dying, Sighing, and languishing,' he becomes a laughing stock, particularly when he dresses up for a ball in an attempt to appear 'Spruce, Gay and Sparkish [...] with his New Tricks and Fooleries about him' (22). Aping and mimicking the behaviour of the young, he brags about how he can 'Run, leap and Ride', thereby subjecting his young wife to a lot of risible posturing. There can be no comfort or mutual cherishing in such a match. What kindness can she show towards such a 'Boyish piece of Gravity'? What comforts are there in the loathsome society of a 'fond jealous Dotard, who suspects all that either look at or speak to her?' What satisfaction in being kept up all night by 'an unwholsom Neast of Diseases, a Cold lump of Clay, whose utmost Power is only to encrease desires, and set an Edge upon that Appetite, which he can by no means satisfie?' On the other side, what pleasure can he have from a peevish, ill-natured wife who hates him, torments him, cares only for his money, fears his presence? He needs a warm bed and a good cordial to chear up his Old Heart, and his 'Bald Pate [...] gently rub'd By a cleanly young Girl' (28-30);[14] why, there are even some women who give their old husbands a push into the next world. Bufford thus articulates a fear prevalent in writings both earlier and later than his own.

Some eighty years after 1618, the likely date in which *The Old Law* was written, Bufford touches on the enduring problem of a disreputable young wife who goads her old husband into extremes of behaviour which may well push him into the next world. Lisander, maddened by jealousy at Eugenia's encouragement of young suitors who clamour for her hand in anticipation of his demise, hires dancing and riding masters, enrols in a fencing school, and prepares to confound the gallants crowding in on his young wife, ready to claim her the instant the law comes into force against him. Lisander also damages his own reputation by making himself the laughing stock of the callous gallants in his efforts to appear young by dyeing his hair and beard. His attempts at hiding his age, pathetic in themselves, are unilaterally condemned in the manuals,[15] and provide a source of further criticism when contrasted to the quiet dignity which graces the old age of Leonides and Creon. Lisander exposes himself as indecorous in his aspirations, vain, lacking in dignity and full of desperation. Furthermore, 'Dyeing' along with 'painting' relegate him to the contemptible position of women who attempt to disguise the effects of age, and earn him the mockery and contempt of his wife and her suitors. His derisory efforts to tame a 'mangy little tuft' that persists in defying the dyer's art is predictably mocked by his young wife:

Eugenia: I'm sure his head and beard, as he has ordered it,
    Looks not past fifty now. He'll bring it to forty
    Within these four days, for nine times an hour at least
    He takes a black lead comb and kembs it over.
    Three-quarters of his beard is under fifty;
    There's but a little tuft of fourscore left
    All of one side which will be black by Monday. (*Old Law*, 3. 2, 47–53)

The significance of an old man altering his hair colour reaches beyond mere disguise of the effects of age. It is an attempt to counteract the effeminising implications of white hair.[16] He dyes his hair out of vanity and a desire to return to the colours of youth; but also it is to vie with the young blades, to demonstrate that he has lost none of his virility. Eugenia mocks his vanity, and his attempts to assert his manhood.

His quest for 'the secret art to make himself/Youthful again' reaches its climax in his improbable challenge to the 'Gregories':

Lisander: The devil and his grinners! Are you come?
Bring forth the weapons, we shall find you play!
All feats of youth too, Jack-boys, feats of youth,
And these weapons: drinking, fencing, dancing,
Your own road waits you, glisterpipes! I'm old, you say?
Yes, parlous old, kids, and you mark me well;
This beard cannot get children, you lank suck-eggs,
Unless such weasels come from court to help us?
We will get our own brats, you lecherous dog-bolts. (3. 2, 127–35)

His project to out-Gregory the Gregories involves workouts at fencing school till four in the morning (3. 2, 33-34) and concourse with the 'great French rider' and his 'curvetting horse' (3. 2, 43–44). Against all odds, it achieves the intended effect. The stubborn tuft of white hair notwithstanding, he does indeed manage to 'beguile' them all. In a bravura performance, without so much as a pause for breath, he out-dances, out-drinks, out-fences the lot of them, and on their own ground too. The episode ends with a triumphant flourish on the rights of the old to 'love our own wives [...] get our own children,/And live in free peace 'till we be dissolved' (3. 2, 228–29). Farce allows the old to triumph by virtue of the very indecorum frowned upon by society and the conduct and style books, yet it provides an ambiguous response at best to critiques of May–December marriages. Despite his triumph over the Gregories, the matter of Lisander's breach of decorum remains unresolved. The marriage itself is inappropriate, and by its very nature contains the seeds of dissention between husband and wife. As a result, everybody in the fencing, riding and dancing episode is totally beyond the pale of decorum; Eugenia by brazenly parading her suitors in front of her husband, Lisander in his ludicrous attempts to spruce himself up into sparkishness, and the suitors themselves by flaunting their athleticism in mockery and contempt for the old.

The widespread questioning of the decorum of May–December marriages is given tragic as well as comic emphasis on stage and in poetry. While comedy mocks the pretensions of both ages, tragedy explores the uncertainties and pain of being inappropriately coupled. Works as generically diverse as John Ford's tragedy *The Broken Heart* (published in 1633)[17] and six poems entitled 'Elizabeth Fools Warning' take up the theme. The poems, printed in 1659 'for Francis Coles in the Old-Baily,' provide in addition a published testament of lived experience. The matching of the events in the poems with existing records and hence the likely identification of 'Elizabeth of Woodbridge' and her circumstances, together with additional close detective work done by Robert Evans, effectively confirm the events the poems describe (Evans, 2000, 447–515). The real life Elizabeth, tempted into marriage with an old widower in the hope of enhanced wealth and status, found that her expectations of domestic well-being and fine gowns disintegrated all too soon. The widower, influenced by a malevolent sister, stripped his new wife of her finery, gave it instead to a daughter, and thereafter subjected Elizabeth to systematic abuse. The birth of two children, one male the other female, infuriated her husband (who wanted no more heirs) into expelling her from the marital bed; they slept apart until Elizabeth, able to bear no more, ran away. Her husband at first agreed to pay forty shillings for her lodgings, but did not do so for very long. Suffering extreme poverty, she survived only with the help of 'a son' (possibly the son of a first marriage). The poems advertise themselves as 'a true and most perfect relation of all that has happened to her since her marriage' and hence a 'caveat for all young women to marry with old men.' (With, 1659, title page)

Themes in the poems have much in common with those in Ford's play. Both engage with the anxiety and pain resulting from a violent yoking together of a young woman and an old man. The young wife in each is trapped and the old husband's insecurities, far from being eradicated by the possession of a trophy wife, are exacerbated beyond the point of endurance. Like Penthea in Ford's *The Broken Heart*, Elizabeth very soon after her marriage finds herself the victim of suspicion and jealousy and like Bassanes, Elizabeth's husband, Robert With, initially wants to parade her bedecked in lavish gowns and jewels before his admiring circle. Elizabeth is seduced by finery, and is outraged to be stripped of it: 'I loved to go fine I must you tell./Oh! I was fowly cheated by this old slim' (With, 1659, poem 3, line 28). Though the response of the two wives to being a clothes horse dripping with jewels varies, in both texts an old husband ornaments a young wife in order to display her as his possession. Both old men possess the characteristics of 'December' husbands; they are oppressive, jealous, and cruel (deliberately or no). Both are suspicious of their wives, Bassanes to the point of insanity; yet both wish to adorn and parade them as prizes, thereby advancing their own status. In addition, Elizabeth's husband is in full possession of the mercenary and miserly traits associated with old age; he inherits a house from his 'old' wife (poem 1, line 6), and he soon reduces his new young wife to the penurious state in which she first came to him. Both husbands are pathologically afraid of becoming a laughing-stock, and so resort to extreme measures designed to secure their human property, though these measures humiliate and oppress their wives beyond endurance. Both wives are thus punished for the shortcomings (due to the intransigence and irremediable effects of old age) of their husbands.

These two accounts of the woes to which young wives are subject present a tragic counterpart to the comically indecorous antics of the old in *The Old Law* and provide a dire example of the warnings in the manuals of what happens to old men who seek them. Significantly, in the Prologue to *The Broken Heart* Ford distances himself from indecorous, low-life jesting in comedy, declaring his allegiance to the rules of linguistic decorum. The action will unfold according to the conventions of tragedy, and its high-born characters will obey the rules of speech and decorum:

> The title lends no expectation here
> Of apish laughter, or of some lame jeer
> At place or persons; no pretended clause
> Of jests fit for a brothel courts applause
> From vulgar admiration. Such low songs,
> Tuned to unchaste ears, suit not immodest tongues.
> The virgin-sisters then deserved fresh bays
> When innocence and sweetness crowned their lays.
> Then vices gasped for breath, whose whole commerce
> Was whipped to exile by unblushing verse.
> This law we keep in our presentment now,
> Not to take freedom more than we allow.
> What may be here thought Fiction, when time's youth
> Wanted some riper years, was known *A Truth*,
> In which, if words have clothed the subject right,
> You may partake a pity with delight. (Prologue, 3–18)

It also makes explicit (as in the poems) the perception of old age as inde-corous *per se* (cf. With, 1659, esp. poems 1 and 2). The playwright will reinvest tragedy with decorous language which properly belongs to youth. Presented in the form of a fiction, and lacking maturity, youth is neverthe-less capable of a perceived truth which, additionally enhanced by the plea-sure of decorous language, cannot fail to move to pity. The law to which Ford refers is the law of decorum in poetry, which takes his play far from the realm of mockery and the cranky mechanisms of legalism parodied in Middleton and Rowley's play. Taking a stage further Castiglione's view that the life of a courtier belongs to youth, Ford at first sight seems to load the scales in favour of the 'rape done on [the] truth' (*Broken Heart*, 2. 3, 79) of the traduced young bride.

The innate indecorum of old age is set out in the first scene. Orgilus asks permission from his father to travel and so distance himself from the pain of seeing his contracted love married to an old man. Bassanes is from the first mention of his name typecast as an old, jealous husband, like Eliza-beth With's old husband, angry without cause.[18] As a result, the resumé of Orgilus' piteous story snags the audience into sympathetic identification with the plight of a young lover as against the jealous dotage of an old man. Bassanes has 'yoked' his young wife to 'a most barbarous thraldom, misery,/Affliction, that he savours not humanity' (1.1, 53–55). He thinks of her as his possession, which thought

> Begets a kind of monster-love, which love
> Is nurse unto a fear so strong and servile
> As brands all dotage with a jealousy.
> [...]
> So much, out of a self-unworthiness,
> His fears transport him; not that he finds cause
> In her obedience, but his own distrust. (1.1, 60–70)

Orgilus proves to his father that his language is not out of proportion to the feeling it purports to describe by insisting on the twofold cause for the violence of his grief; his continued presence at court intensifies the pain Penthea has to suffer, and augments the 'wild jealousies' of her husband in his fear that her former betrothed 'should steal again into her favours /and undermine her virtues.' By removing himself, he hopes to free her 'from a hell on earth.' (1. 1, 74–75, 80) Here, decorum of sentiment, expression, character, belong entirely to Orgilus, the young lover. By contrast it is clear from Orgilus' description that 'jealous Bassanes' (1. 1, 79) suffers from the dotage linked with melancholy adust, caused by old age.

Bassanes' first appearance does nothing to dispel this negative first impression. Identified as an aging melancholic as a result of union with a young wife, he fits in almost every particular Burton's description in *Anatomy of Melancholy*. Aged male sufferers are 'in an instant' crippled by 'ache, sorrow and grief'. Referring to Cicero and Castiglione, Burton describes how old men regress into childhood, sit around being churlish, and talk to themselves. They are 'angry, waspish, displeased with everything' and become, 'suspicious of all, wayward, covetous, hard.' They are, in addition, 'self-willed, superstitious, self-conceited, braggers, & admirers of themselves' (Burton, 1955, 183). Recalling Shylock's similar fears and strategies to shield his daughter from the lures of the outside world, Act two opens with Bassanes' plan to have a window boarded up because it

> gives too full a prospect to temptation,
> And courts a gazer's glances. There's a lust
> Committed by the eye, that sweats and travails,
> Plots, wakes, contrives, till the deformed bear-whelp,
> Adultery, be licked into the act,
> The very act. That light shall be dammed up.' (2. 1, 2–7)[19]

In terms which fittingly reveal his obsessive fear that his wife will succumb to the blandishments of young court gallants, he threatens to tear out the throat of the very man he employs to carry out the work; he will 'rip-up' the man's 'ulcerous maw' if he gets so much as a whiff of a piece of paper the size of 'a wart upon thy nose, a spot, a pimple' being passed to his wife, and rants against 'city housewives' (2. 1, 16–18, 23) whose services as go-between or, worse, procuress, can so easily be bought. The suspicion occasioned by the distemper of his melancholic old age brands as equally false women at court, who are the means by which social climbers obtain preferment, and women who live in the country, who hide their shame beneath blushes. It also provokes mockery; Phulas invents preposterous court gossip that the king has lost his grey beard (a symbol of wisdom and probity) and grown a pure carnation-coloured one in its place. Phulas thus draws attention to the lack of substance in his master's suspicions, and the lack of decorum in their articulation. This criticism is detailed in his final 'report' from the court:

> Moreover, please your lordship, 'tis reported
> For certain, that whoever is found jealous
> Without apparent proof that's wife is wanton
> Shall be divorced: but this is but she-news;
> I had it from a midwife. (2. 1, 56–60)

Once again, as in *Errors*, the negative stereotyping of old men is projected onto (young) women. In addition, the garrulity which characterises old men is projected onto old women belonging to a category low on the rungs of the social ladder; midwives were known as poor old women who spread gossip from one household to another. Phulas' mockery serves the dual purpose of rebuking Bassanes for his needless jealousy at the same time as it places him among the bad old men whose attitude and conduct the treatises on old age are designed to correct.

Yet Ford does not allow the matter to rest there. Bassanes, like Elizabeth With's husband, typecast as jealous, infirm, angry and old, nevertheless grows in structural and characterological terms in a way that is not permitted to Penthea. This growth starts with his wife's appearance on stage, which has the unintended effect of presenting Bassanes in a more sympathetic light, as one who adores his wife to the point of idolatry. This scene brings into play the complex psychology of human emotions which have their roots in gender stereotypes. These stereotypes are grounded in the nature of each character: relations between young wife and old husband depend just as much on assumptions and ideologies of senescence as on gender stereotypes, but also progress well beyond them. Despite cruel laughter at the expense of old men as angry, doting and jealous, the pervasive tragic irony is more even-handed as a result of its treatment of age and aging than critics acknowledge. The play intends a critique of May–December unions, yet here it shows that husband and wife are well suited in mood and temperament, for Penthea is another melancholic. Furthermore, her foregrounding as suffering subject and object of pity by both playwright and subsequent critics obscures a more subtle message on the relationship of youth to age. In his adoration, Bassanes wants to display her in court as a shining beacon of virtue, and will give her anything, do whatever it takes, to chase the clouds from the 'pure firmament' of her 'fair looks' (2. 1, 88). Having seen him at his worst, the viewer now sees another side of him; his desire to bask in the favour of the beloved marks him out as a worshipper of beauty in the Platonic sense. Yet for all this he cannot bite back a furious aside to her maid. The language of indecorum lies at the heart of this exchange, too; as Penthea points out, the way Bassanes addresses his 'handmaid/Sounds as would music to the deaf' (2. 1, 91–92) and her plea for him to 'change not the livery your words bestow' (2. 1, 101) signifies a desire for words to decorously match her mood and situation. The audience is pre-disposed to hear her only, yet her words, by themselves, are as surly and intractable as her husband's behaviour; the language of both husband and wife is inappropriate to their newly wedded state. She mournfully perceives his wish to adorn her beauty with costly finery as a slur on the purity of her reputation. Rejecting 'gaudy outsides', she proposes a decorum in which sombre dress suits the 'inward fashion' of her mind. Listlessly ill-disposed to engage in a conversation about the marital home with her husband, she cannot budge from her sadness, nor for his sake 'put on a more cheerful mirth,' (2. 1, 117) any more than he can change the causes and outcomes of his indisposition. As a result, neither can avoid indecorous language or behaviour.

Bassanes' unseemly conduct as a result of melancholic jealousy compounded by old age reaches a climax when his suspicions extend to his brother-in-law in an 'unmannerly' accusation of 'bestial incest' (3. 2, 150). Yet this crisis is the turning-point in his fortunes. His wife's perfect humility and submission gradually bring him back to his senses:

> Light of beauty, Deal not ungently with a desperate wound!
> No breach of reason dares make war with her
> Whose looks are sovereignty, whose
>   breath is balm. (3. 2, 162–24)

and the 'sounds celestial' of her voice sooth his torment to the extent that his rage leaves him so that he can embrace the virtue of patience (3. 2, 174). He experiences the cure for love's melancholy (cf. Burton, 1955, esp. 765–70; 777–79). What happens to him is similar to what happens to Lear — sight and sound of the beloved sooth his troubled spirits and his rage leaves him free to exercise his reason and cultivate the virtue of patience and temperance. Form then on Bassanes' behaviour is exemplary and his patience, though tried, is unshakable. The mantle of the 'wise vieillard' restored, he reverts to the responsibilities and authority of an elder. It is he who sends to Athens for medicinal herbs for another ailing old man, the king, administers the last rites and funeral obsequies to Orgilus, and becomes Sparta's marshal. Upon the death of the old king, Bassanes takes on the role of the new queen's adviser. The restoration of order and calm is thus once more entrusted to the old.

The hostile depiction of Bassanes in *The Broken Heart,* and Elizabeth With's old husband in the *Elizabeth Fool's Warning* poems, in contrast to the sympathetic presentation of Penthea and the gearing of Elizabeth's plaint to the young wife's point of view, reinforces the main tenet of this chapter, which is that old age is in itself an innately indecorous condition. Bassanes and Robert With, repositories between them of most if not all of the repellent manifestations of old age, exemplify the concepts of indecorum set out in the conduct books on manners and style. *The Broken Heart* and *King Lear* delve into inner psychological states resulting from humoural imbalances which induce extremes of behaviour resulting from the disease of old age itself. Bassanes' jealousy, Lear's refusal to acknowledge his condition, and the anger fuelling the actions of both old men, stem from melancholy as a pathological condition of their advanced stage in life. Both are enfeebled by age, and the tragic implications of that state, combined with the unseemliness of the behaviour to which it gives rise, may in large part be attributed to another kind of ineffable indecorum — that arising from the tension of enforced marital or familial bonds of obligation between young and old. These same traits of indecorous elderliness, inimical to youth's pursuit of love and beauty, become the butt of satire in *The Old Law* when the old refuse to temper their behaviour and, in order to compete, ape instead the appearance and manners of the young. What is a tragic undermining of male authority in *Lear* and *The Broken Heart* become the means by which the old regain some dignity in *The Old Law,* ironically as a result of Lisander's tricks.Though comically disrespectful of the antics of foolish old men, these tricks are the means by which the old reclaim their position of respect both socially and domestically. However, the message that old men forfeit their authority and claim to respect if they do not conform to the rigid guidelines set down for them in manuals of age and style is itself subverted when it comes to cultural, prescriptive and fictional representations of old women, and to this the next chapter turns.

4 Disgraceful old age (2)
women behaving worse

It is true that even though the prescriptive literature denounces as inde-corous unequal marriages in both sexes, it reserves its worst condemna-tion for old women. It was at a pinch within the bounds of correct social behaviour for an old man to marry a young girl. In olden times, according to Richard Bernard, the author of *Ruths Recompense,* society permitted the coupling of an old man with a young woman, but never the other way round, for in this instance, youth cannot possibly 'affect' age (Bernard, 1628, 290) either in the sense of loving an older woman, or in sympathetic identification.[1] Similarly Samuel Bufford's description of uneven marriages, unsparing in its satire of old men (Bufford, 1696, 30–31), reserves its most stinging ridicule for old women who 'can't forget the pleasures of Youth, but must be sporting and playing still' even though they are at 'Graves Mouth' (32). To see an old, decayed and worn out widow lay aside her veil and set herself up as a beauty when her ugly hag's face with its shrivelled skin looks like so much parchment, a coarse bag containing her crumbling bones, deeply troubles him. To trap a young husband, she must seem 'brisk and Young again' (33); she must affect smiles, simpers, 'antick Tricks, and toyish actions' (34). She has to chatter, giggle and 'chaunt' for 'when the Teeth are fled, the Tongue seldom lie still' (34). She must move her aging body in time to 'every scraping tune she hears' (34), and her discourse must be all about balls, gay gallants, mistresses, meetings, intrigues and wed-dings. 'The defects of her Old Wrinkled Face must be carefully supply'd by *Art,* and *Patch* and *Paint* must be made use of to fill up those Furrows which *Old Time* with his *Iron Teeth* has so well and plentifully bestowed upon her' (34–35). The world will cruelly side with her young husband, mocking her 'for an Old Beast' now 'past Mans use'(39), whilst he will be commended and encouraged to make a fool of her and trick her children and relatives 'out of good Estates' (40–41).

Thomas Hilder's more measured advice, addressing some sixty years earlier those about to get married, is to stick to someone of your own age 'if thou wouldst have a meet helper'; but whereas young girls merely need 'a Dame' to instruct them into being a good wife, an old woman will 'need a Nurse to waite on her in her decrepid Age.' Both 'Divinity and Philosophy'

(Hilder, 1653, 44) find good reasons for an old man to marry a young girl, but condemn a man who marries an old woman. A girl can be trained up into wife and motherhood, but it is 'a sin against God, and Nature too' for a young man to marry a woman past childbearing age. Religion and morality join hands in condemning 'such men as in their youthfull daies' who 'for any sinister end in the world' join with a woman just past fifty, let alone one who is over sixty (45). Hilder cannot quite bring himself to believe in the love of a young man for an old woman. Disagreement in years, he believes, breeds disagreement in life, and a young man who attaches himself to a wife who must needs be 'crazie, unhealthful, unhansome' as a result of old age is 'obnoxious to an inundation of temptations of all kinds from his spirituall enemies (even) to uncleannesse, to unbridled passions, to 'Company-keeping'. A wife's two duties are to breed and to regulate her husband's carnal desires, neither of which marriage to an old woman can achieve; the perverse desires that lead a young man to couple with an old woman are in themselves a gross incontinence that ultimately leads to the company of whores, who are 'deep ditches' (Goulart, 1621, 38),[2] and so 'to the neglect of the duties of his Calling, and of his Family, and so to lavish expence, to the undoing of him and his' (Hilder, 1653, 46).

Burton warns against May–December marriages on the grounds that melancholy old fathers beget sons who are by temperament melancholy. Their sons will be wayward, peevish and 'seldom merry' (Burton, 1955,185–86), but a worse fate awaits old women. The disease of melancholy that is an inevitable by-product of old age may identify them as witches. He explains how, upon the authority of Johnann Weyer,[Gian]Baptista [della] Porta (author of a treatise on natural magic, 1558), Ulricus Molitor (fifteenth century author of one of the earliest and rarest book on withcraft,) and Edwicus (who also wrote on witchcraft), old women who are reputed to be witches are in fact suffering from delusions brought on by melancholy. In this sceptical view of witchcraft, all the activities imputed to them, such as bewitching cattle, riding in the air 'upon a coulstaff out of a chimney-top', turning into animals, magicking themselves into different places, congregating in covens to dance and copulate with the devil, are in fact the illusions induced by this condition. They are not witches at all, but simply crazed into thinking of themselves as supernatural beings who 'can do hurt, but do not' (Burton, 1955, 183). Melancholy in women is a 'natural infirmity most eminent,' particularly among those that 'are poor, solitary, live in most base esteem and beggary', or, contradictorily, 'such as are witches' (183). Burton effectively denies agency to those whose only means of self-assertion resided in witchcraft claims by dismissing their fantasies as the effects of female melancholy, solitude, poverty and the degenerative condition of aging. But this is by no means the end of the story, as Burton himself realised. Received opinion was divided on the matter. Arnaldo Albertini, Jerome Cardin and Friedrich Spee, for instance, attest to the reality of witchcraft, though they doubted whether all who were accused were indeed guilty. Cardin thought that witches were sour old women, suffering from melancholy; emaciated, deformed, pallid, they exhibited the marks of this disease in their fantasies of magical omnipotence (Lea, 1939, 2: 446–47). Though Albertini concedes that witches can, in reality, be transported by day and night by demons and that they enter houses and kill infants, he too notes that for the most part those accused of witchcraft are foolish old women and infirm old men (Lea, 1939, 2: 450). North of the Alps, Johann Weyer placed witchcraft claims squarely in the realms of foolish imagination: old women think they can perform many wicked acts, but delusion and the torture of melancholy makes this a brainsick fancy caused by 'the inconstancy of [their] sex, fickleness, a weak mind, despair, and mental disease' (Weyer, 1563, 41; 1583, 181; Lea, 1939, 2: 502, 491). Reginald Scot blamed the vanity of 'lewd' old women which arose from their lack of education, 'the extremitie of their age' and 'their humor melancholicall', leading to dotage (Scot, 1584, *Epistle to the Reader,* sig. Bivers).

Burton for his part hedges his bets and provides an alternative list of writers (Bodin, Erastus, Danaeus, Scribanius, Sebastian Michaelis, Campanella, & Dandinus the Jesuit) who explode the arguments of the sceptics. 'That Witches are melancholy they deny not, but not out of corrupt phantasy alone, so as to delude themselves and others, or to produce such effects.' What nobody denies is that witches are melancholics. Whether or not there are such things as witches in reality is therefore beside the point; the indubitable evidence is that old women suffer from overactive imaginations brought on by this morbid condition (Burton, 1955, 184). Burton thus provides a psychological rationale for coping with the constricted lives of post-menopausal women whose particular circumstances encourage them to collude in witchcraft accusations, even though their fantasies may well lead to a cruel death (cf. Bever, 1982, 173–77; Normand and Roberts, 2000, 60–62; Roper, 1994, 199–218 and 2004, 57–66; Purkiss, 1996, 145–70).

OLD WITCHES AND HAGS

In generic terms, the unruly hags and witches that flourished on the Elizabethan and Jacobean stage perform diverse structural functions. We have seen how the conventions of tragedy restore equilibrium in *King Lear* and *The Broken Heart* through the cure and reformation of an old man who is the tragedy's chief agent, whereas comedy, as in The *Old Law*, can disregard moral strictures and the codes governing the behaviour of the old. This follow-on chapter continues the 'indecorum of age' argument in three plays which typecast old women as witches or fraudulent hags, but which also invest in them an energetic and articulate response to society's amnesia and persecution. Middleton's *The Witch,*[3] described as 'not on the whole a satisfactory play' but nevertheless one which 'suggest[s] an atmosphere of court corruption, of sexual intrigue and fashionable witchcraft [...] that is both more realistic and more disturbing than has commonly been allowed' (Heinemann, 1980, 111), in effect mocks and subverts the strictures of decorum which measure correct behaviour. By forcing its audience to question the cultural assumptions upon which such rules are made, the play transforms old women's 'phantasies' into a circus of comic grotesquerie, it is true, but it also turns the hags from objects of pity and contempt into agentic beings with the power to transform their own and their clients' lives, moving them into a realm unbounded by social constraint. It is through the actions of the witches that wrongs are punished and wives restored to their rightful spouses. The 'phantasies', seen by Burton as the symptom of diseased melancholia, an unavoidable effect of old age, are here turned upside down and made to work as a vehicle for freedom and empowerment specifically for old women, to whom witchcraft permits control over hostile surroundings and a life-style denied their human counterparts. In this regard, the play compensates to some degree for society's proscription of the old.

It does this in the first instance by exploiting and challenging such attitudes as those of Bufford, Hilder and Burton. The hags are not melancholic, and the fantastical happenings they are involved in are a far cry from the diseased imagination of senile dementia. Their very age (Hecate is a centenarian) releases them from the fetters of decrepitude and transforms them into superhuman beings of extraordinary comic energy in their outrageous pursuit of passion and indulgence of every carnal desire.[4] Thought to have been written at the same time as *Macbeth*, the Hecate scenes echo and complement each other. In Middleton's play, however, they mock not only demonological theories, but also restraining attitudes to old women's sexual longings.[5] Middleton's witches inherit, as Gareth Roberts shows, 'the unsavoury activities of witches in Continental demonologies' (Roberts, 2000, 139), and there are links also with Reginald Scot. The play revisits Scot's stories of witchcraft and shares Scot's scepticism on the validity of popular beliefs. But Middleton collapses Scot's misogyny into grotesquery and farce. Diane Purkiss describes Hecate as comic rather than sinister, with no power in the public sphere. Her power in the private sphere, though real, is, according to Purkiss, devalued as trivial by virtue of the very fact that the play's lengthy displays of witchraft 'lore' are not fully integrated into the main plot' (Purkiss, 1996, 217). There is something in this, but the effects of the witches' interchanges with the characters has consequences for the characters themselves and the final outcome of the play comes about as a result of the witches' (indirect) intervention in human business. Witchy old women, the play seems to say, unlike sad, jealous and phlegmy old men, possess an agency that is denied to their younger selves. They rampage the night skies in a phantasmagoria of omnipotence that soars above the straitened standards of decorum imposed upon old men and young women.

The hags in *The Witch* possess geographical mobility and can regulate male sexual desire; and, like the witches in *Macbeth* they use human body parts to make their flying ointment and to suppress male libido. But their activities extend substantially beyond those of the weird sisters in *Macbeth* to include virtual and real indulgence of sexual appetite. Their lives on the outskirts of Ravenna allow them to sample all the benefits of 'community, agency, freedom and fun' that Ravenna women would not have or, as Roberts notes, at the very least have similar lives on much better terms (Roberts, 2000, 140–44). As a result, Middleton's parody of demonological theory and reversal of the tenets of decorum signifies a liberation in the sexual and social lives of older women. Freed from the treadmill of childbearing, in their post menopausal years they arrive at a place of unrestrained power and self-regulation unavailable to old men (who are enfeebled and constrained by the very rules patriarchy sets in motion) and younger women, who must bear the brunt of male anxiety about heredity and female sexuality. The outrageously bad behaviour of Middleton's witches, all old hags, runs counter to the movement in the fictional and prescriptive literature which brings old men to heel. Old men must regulate their eating, drinking, sex life, daily habits, and their bowel movements (cf. Elyot, 1541, 54, 56–59; Vaughan, 1600, 40; Goulart, 1621, 6; Bacon, 1638, 211–28, 252–55), but old women presumably need not; because they are forgotten,[6] they remain unrestrained. Their lack of presence in the didactic literature is translated as license on stage; they get to inhabit a world which provides Middleton's female audience at any rate with the chance to fantasise about sex and liberty (Roberts, 2000, 141). According to Purkiss, Hecate's 'excessive displays of desire and rage externalise the preoccupations of the main characters, while comically deflating them' (Purkiss, 1996, 219). But in terms of the behaviour checks and health habits of old men, the comedy resides in indulgence and excess rather than deflation. The first time the audience encounters Hecate and her crew, they are 'sweating at the vessel' (1. 2, 9), fanning the flames under the cauldron in preparation for a feast. They are all gathered around it convivially. Each has contributed an ingredient, and each can use the potent brew for her own purpose. The recipe will enable them to fly, and to 'feast and sing' a hundred leagues up in the air, to 'Dance, kiss, and coll, use everything' and have equal share in any young man they lust after 'in incubus' — Firestone can absent himself from the sexual embrace of his mother Hecate so that he can 'overlay a fat parson's daughter' simply by requesting her to accept the substitution of a cat (1. 2, 96, 97) — and they all relive the pleasure in gossiping about it afterwards:

Hecate:　Last night thou gott'st the mayor of Whelplie's son;
　　　　　I knew him by his black cloak lined with yellow;
　　　　　I think thou'st spoiled the youth, he's but seventeen:
　　　　　I'll have him the next mounting (1. 2, 33–36).

In gruesome parody of the culinary preparation of roast suckling pig with herbs and sweetmeats, the dead body of the child thrown into the cauldron is stuffed with magical herbs crammed down its mouth, its ears and nostrils stuffed with various poisons (wolfsbane, deadly nightshade) and soot and bat's blood. (1. 2, 18–19, 37–45). Like the witches in *Macbeth*, they can use this concoction to exact revenge against those who have wronged them. Hecate can punish the farmer and his wife for refusing her flour, 'barm', milk and goose-grease simply by 'roasting' their pictures in the fire (1. 2, 49). The witches in *Macbeth* can punish a sailor by whipping up a storm at sea; these witches can tear up oak trees, hang a man in his own house, destroy cattle, blight land, and 'in one night' transfer property and wealth from one person to another. And they can enact revenge upon persons by causing barrenness (1. 2, 135–49). But what they cannot do is to 'disjoin wedlock;/'Tis of Heaven's fastening' (1. 2, 175–76). When Sebastian enters their precincts, in search of the means to avenge himself of the wrong done him (as in *The Broken Heart*, his pre-contract with Isabella has been violated and he returns from the war to find her married to Antonio), all they can do in that quarter is to 'raise jars,/Jealousies, strifes, and heart-burning disagreements' (1. 2, 176–77). Yet at the end of the play their love charms enable Sebastian to reclaim his pre-contracted bride, the adulterers are punished, and the indirect consequences of the love-charm given to Almachildes to ensnare Amoretta is to advance the harmonious resolution of the Duchess subplot. Demonological theory tells us that these witches have the power to do harm, but as the play shows, they also have the power to regulate the society that condemns them.

In *The Witch* and *The Broken Heart*, resolution comes about through the agency of an old person. In Ford's tragedy, however, indecorum in the behaviour of the old man, Bassanes, is restrictive; to regain society's approval he must transform himself. Inappropriate behaviour thus disempowers old men. By contrast, the omnipotence of the witches in Middleton's comedy is only made possible by bad behaviour, thereby providing another angle on the innate indecorousness of old age; it may be barbarous for men in public office who live by the word, but for women, shut away in their houses, it is liberating and empowering. However, few seventeenth-century playwrights were interested in witchcraft as a crime; rather, they exploited its potential for fantasy. There are no other viable options for old women since as a category they are all but forgotten in the manuals of style, behaviour and health; they feature only in a limited way in narratives specifically restricted to description of unequal marriages. The paradoxical nature of this absence is revealed when we consider that it effectively removes them from society's care at the same time as it liberates them from the constraints of that society, so that they are potentially, and frighteningly, free.

Middleton's witches are carnivalesque agents of licence and misrule, and their ability to affect the lives of the human characters resides precisely in their remoteness from the sufferings of old women accused of witchcraft represented in the 'reality' witch plays (more of this later). Purkiss' take on the attempt to historicise the play by seeing it as a covert representation to the notorious Frances Howard trials is to look at the relationship between Ann Turner, Mary Woods, and Isabel Peel, witches in real life, consulted by Howard for impotence charms. The relationship between a court lady and cunning women form 'discourses of conspiracy' involving women in 'a terrifying network of secret power, power capable of destroying the order of society (Purkiss, 1996, 216–17). Purkiss reads Hecate as a monstrous and inhuman version of Turner; 'she is found *doing* all the things of which Turner [...] was accused' (217). What is hidden in Turner is fully displayed in Hecate. Turner meets her death having repented and thereby securing reintegration into the community. Hecate 'survives the play and undergoes neither retribution nor repentance. Paradoxically, this treatment of the witch-figure eliminates any sign of women's agency and control over their own story' (217). But does it? Here, the question of age as well as class is crucial. The point, surely, is that old women, in reality both isolated in their community whilst totally dependent on it, escape from these bonds in a fantasy which places them on stage as an amalgam of all the most nega-tive stereotypes in which society cast them; they are lustful, incestuous and vengeful as a result of their fellowship with the devil. But all the while, the play invests in them powers denied to the younger characters in the play, and to women in reality. In this way they are able to reclaim the agency and control that society doubly denies them — as old and helpless, and as women. So Hecate is not identified with old women tempted into witch-craft by the devil in order to better their lot. She is named after a classical witch. As a supernatural being beyond the scope of the witchfinder she is at the height of her powers at the age of a hundred and twenty. And as an alternative model for old women, her very apartness suggests the possibility that even though old women may be invisible to society, yet they have the power to affect that society's wellbeing. It is true that Hecate and the hags' actions are malevolent and immoral, and this does indeed suggest that her capability is largely a negative one (218); her energy is mischievous and the power she wields is destructive because it comes from the devil. Yet the outcome of the scenes in which she and her sisters appear is as hospitable and liberating as Roberts suggests (Roberts, 2000, 141), which makes her a figure of interesting ambivalence. In the flying scene, the company of witches communicates the 'dainty pleasure' (3. 3, 67) of riding on a journey of five hundred miles, frolicking high

in the air
When the moon shines fair,
And sing and dance, and toy and kiss
Over woods, high rocks, and mountains,
Over seas, our mistress' fountains,
Over steeples, towers, and turrets (3. 3, 68–73),

leaving the envious Firestone to walk 'like a fool and a mortal' (3 3, 81). In *News from Scotland* 'one aspect of the witches' fearful power is supernatural travel, an intensification of women's usual lack of freedom to travel' (Normand & Roberts, 2000, 61; *News*, ?1591, 310).

The figure of the lecherous crone (represented as *Vice* in fig. 4.1) is not confined to representations of witchcraft on stage; on the contrary, it is ubiquitous in art and literature[7] and derives from theoretical assumptions about the physiology of women and bodily fluids formulated by physiologists from the ancient world — Hippocrates and Aristotle, refined by Galen

Figure 4.1 Virtue Overcoming Vice, photograph of Roman statuette, late sixteenth century. Copyright The Frick Collection, New York.

and Avicenna. According to Hippocrates, human physiology worked on the principle of the four humours (blood, yellow bile, black bile and phlegm) and the four corresponding qualities of heat and cold in combination with either moisture or dryness (Hippocrates, 1923–31, 4: Bk.1, ch. 3–13). Additionally, the humours and their qualities corresponded to the four ages of man, and the four seasons. So childhood (spring) was hot and moist, manly youth (summer) hot and dry, mature manhood (autumn) cold and dry and old age in men (winter) cold and moist; in sum, 'a man is warmest on the first day of his existence and coldest on the last (Hippocrates, 1923–31, 4: Bk. 1, ch. 12, 37). Hippocratic gynaecologists such as Galen worked on the principle that, conversely, old women's bodies grew drier (cf. Galen, 1997, 247; viz. fig. 4.1)[8] presumably, *pace* Dean-Jones, because older women ate less, their stomachs unable to convert nourishment into blood, or because their flesh had ceased to absorb blood from their stomachs (Dean-Jones, 1994, 107). In the Aristotelian schema adopted by Galen and Avicenna, women's bodies shared only the first and last qualities; they were cold and moist after puberty. Though these writers' physiological theories differed only in stating that old age was cold and dry, later medieval writers tended to oscillate between the two. And many sixteenth- and seventeenth-century health manuals explained the characteristics of old age as a mixture; old men's bodies were cold and dry, though lack of control over effluvia rendered them at the same time cold and moist — hence old men's coughing, spitting and runny noses (Galen, 1997, 234). According to Galen, the aging process began at the point of inception, as did women's biological inferiority. In the embryo the semen produced enough heat to give definition to the lack of shape and structure of the female contribution to fertilisation, so that tissues and organs could develop both inside and outside the womb. But at puberty this dehydration becomes damaging to the male body, depriving it of its intrinsic (or 'radical') moisture and causing it to lose heat, thereby accelerating the aging process. For Aristotle and Galen, this implies that in the womb, the male foetus develops faster than the lazy female. Women grow more slowly and die sooner because as an inferior biological species they deteriorate more quickly. Men's greater heat keeps them alive longer, though 'males subject to great toil are short-lived and age more quickly owing to the labor; toil produces dryness and old age is dry' (Aristotle, 1984, 1: 466b 12–16, 741). This inferiority leads Aristotle to estimate that women's decline is accelerated by twenty years (1: 545b 26–31, 861). At the same time, his assertion that the flow of semen and menstrual blood stops concurrently in men and women implies that they begin at the same time too (2: 727a 5–10, 1129; Dean-Jones, 1994, 177), an ambivalence Galen did not attempt to resolve. But his explanation of the role of menstrual blood in conception had enormous implications for succeeding generations. Galen's certainty that humankind's origins in the corrupt matter of semen and particularly menstrual blood, 'a septic and filthy substance' (Galen, 1929, 156), meant that it could not possibly achieve immortality. This particular idea was considerably developed in medieval writings to denote the power of menopausal women to do harm to foetus and child — hence the image of 'Vice' as an old woman (fig. 4.1). According to medieval popular science, menstrual blood, always polluted and destructive, became even more so in childbearing women since it accumulated in the womb. Its lack of flow during pregnancy made it so toxic that mere contact with it made trees, grass and fruit wither and die. The newborn infant was the most helpless of all animals at birth because it was nourished by defiled menstrual blood and once born, it took some time to flush this poison from its system (*Prose Salernitan Questions*, 1979, 155; Shahar, 1997, 44; 1998, 60n10; 2005, 84, citing in each instance Pope Innocent III, *De miseria humanae conditionis*). After the menopause it is even more damaging because, no longer having any means of expulsion, it festers so that women's bodies became defiled in their very composition:

> the retention of menses engenders many evil humours. The women being old have almost no natural heat left to consume and control this matter, especially poor women who live on nothing but coarse meat, which greatly contributes to this phenomenon. These women are more venomous than others. (*de Secretis Mulierum* in Jacquart, 1988, 75).

Retention of menstrual blood also conferred upon old women the power of fascination, enabling them to cause harm by casting the evil eye upon their victims. This natural power to inflict damage on their neighbours and particularly their neighbours' children arose from the toxicity of their bodies and was even more potent if accompanied by malevolent thoughts (Shahar, 1997, 44 and Shahar 2005, 84, citing Diego Alvarez Chanca, *Tractatus de fascinatione*, 1494, Antonio de Cartagena *Libellus de fascinatione*, 1529; cf, also fig. 4.1).

According to Pat Thane, in the ancient world '[t]he ideal of an old age in which the pleasures of the mind, poetry, music, friendship replace those of the body appears to have been widespread among powerful Roman men' but '[p]hilosophers offered no such map of life to women, who are more visible in literature' (Thane, 2000, 42). Georges Minois goes several steps further: '[t]he rage felt by Renaissance man against old age', he claims, 'was given particular vent in paintings of old women, because ageing appears to have an even more devastating effect on women than on men', and 'men of letters threw themselves wholeheartedly into the game' of reviling old women (Minois,1989, 256). It is true that in continental art and literature there is no shortage of negative images of the old. Yet Minois bases his opinion on a few random examples — as, for example, the paintings of Metsys and Manuel which depict the depredations of aged female flesh, and a few poems, such as Du Bellay's *Antierotique*, which express revulsion at the hideousness of old age. On stage, they were sometimes mocked and punished, cast as evil, vain, corrupt — and randy. But he is content to leave the matter there, concluding from a few random samples that aged women were universally condemned. In this blandly unitary view, 'literature was joined by practice in condemning old women; unfavourable prejudice turned them into witches much more frequently than young women' (Minois, 1989, 256).

However, it is possible to gain a much more profound and diverse understanding of the role of old women and their perceptions of their own aging selves in both early modern life and literature. Recent scholarship has identified detailed and varied responses to the processes of aging in both men and women.[9] The two recent compilations of essays by Lynn Botelho and Pat Thane amply demonstrate the premise that growing old in the early modern period was a complicated process, by no means necessarily the onset of dependency and helplessness in its final stage (Botelho and Thane, 2001; Thane 2005), and break new ground in their focus upon the lives of old women. The earlier volume contains a number of essays which show that for old women in particular, the onset of the menopause heralded a stage in life characterised by a freedom and autonomy unavailable to women of childbearing age. Anne Kugler's examination of Lady Sarah Cowper's diary, for example, compellingly demonstrates the strategies this aging noblewoman employs in a self-conscious bid for acquiring and keeping authority. By interweaving literary reflections with accounts of her family, politics and society from the vantage-point provided by her own aging process, 'Lady Sarah used both the literature of the period and her own daily experience as a model on which to pattern her own behaviour as an elderly woman: on the one hand acceding to normative values while on the other manipulating ideology as a device for attaining her personal ends' (Kugler, 2001, 68). Lady Sarah's contempt for women who paint their faces in an effort to appear younger than their years is a case in point. She notes disapprovingly that a female acquaintance of the same age as she 'hath rent her face with painting', and even though she is

> hugely infirm yet affects the follys and aires of youth, displays her breasts and ears adorns both with sparkling gems while her eies look dead, skin rivell'd, cheeks sunk, shaking her head, trembling hands, and all things bid shutt up shop and leave trafficke with such vanities. (72)

Lady Sarah denounces attempts to get noticed by masquerading as young. She prefers to claim respect from wisdom and seniority – in other words, to cultivate the mind in place of youth and beauty now lost (92). Lady Sarah thus adopts classical ideals of male old age, and appropriates the veneration accorded to the elder statesman on precisely the same grounds as respect is earned by sober comportment and avoidance of unseemly interest in continuing sexual activity (72). Lady Sarah had plenty of models of the continuing usefulness of old age in the literatures of ancient Greece and Rome and applied these exclusively masculine models to herself.

It is also clear that the varied and complex images the old had of themselves related to gender. Obviously, art and literature, through stylisation and metaphor, present varied images of a range of subjects, old women included. Old men are objects of reverence in quattrocento painting and subsequent humanist-inspired literatures harking back to Aristotle, Cicero and Plutarch but they, as well as women, are satirised in ancient and early modern drama and poetry, as, indeed, are all other age groups. Thane's study of old age is more far-reaching and she arrives at a more measured conclusion — that 'early modern literature, like that of other periods, presents not a uniform representation of old age as gloomy or otherwise [...] but rather a generally realistic representation of the variety of the experience of old age,' and the complexity and diversity of the experience of old age in both men and women is the starting-point of the only publication to date of cultural representations of age in the early modern period (Thane, 2000, 65; 2005, Introduction; see also Campbell, 2006, Introduction, *et passim*).

Perceptions of old women as lascivious, innately malevolent and harmful to young men, deriving from the physiology of the ancients, find their way into Greek and Shakespearean drama. In *Women in Parliament*, Aristophanes parodies women taking over governmental control and substituting their own brand of communism. One of their new laws, that the least favoured must come first, results in a vulgar and crudely caricatured scene in which three hags, 'painted to look young' and singing lewd songs, accost a young man and attempt to drag him away from his girl, chanting:

> We lady legislators here enact:
> If a boy wishes for a girl's embraces,
> Ere he's permitted to perform the act
> He must exercise himself, rehearse his paces
> In an old woman. (Aristophanes, 1968, 450)

Crooked and disfavoured as they are, Aristophanes' hags gain control of the legislature. They draw up the legal documents, and are entirely successful in acting upon the new law; they drag Epigenes off stage, there to execute their lewd will upon him. This episode, where the will of the old triumphs over the contrary wishes of the young, though presented farcically, has the serious objective of articulating the desire for agency of women over fifty at the same time as it registers disgust at the aged female body.[10] The play's appeal to an audience in antiquity lies in mockery of grotesque and unseemly behaviour in the old, but such spectacles of farce, removed from audience sympathy, were nevertheless staged in their own time before a society which revered as well as reviled the old (cf. Parkin, 1998 and 2005, 31–69). An example of the way in which classical comedy furnished succeeding ages with the hackneyed stereotype of the lecherous old crone, Aristophanes' play relies predominantly on stereotype; neither the hags nor the girl are named whereas their named target, Epigenes, moves a footstep or two away from caricature.[11]

Significantly, the most unsettling images of older women wielding political power that threatens state patriarchy appear upon the Elizabethan stage in Shakespeare's history plays which deal with England's changing constitution and the birth of nationalism. Written and staged in the final years of Elizabeth's reign, they displace onto the figure of the old woman anxieties about succession and disaffection with the self-display and policies of the aging Queen. Eleanor Cobham in *Henry VI, Part 2* and Queen Margaret in *Part 3* are older women whose independent and ambitious actions are represented as dangerously out of control. Eleanor, wife of a devoted husband, Humphrey of Gloucester, who is also Lord Protector of the realm, harbours 'the canker of ambitious thought' (*2HVI*, 1. 2, 18) in her attempt to spread her influence beyond the home and into the arena of state politics. Eleanor's dream of sitting 'in the seat of majesty/In the cathedral church of Westminster' (*2HVI*, 1. 2, 36–40) leads her to exhibit in sumptuous clothing the power she fantasises for herself, so that newcomers to the court mistake her for the queen (*2HVI*, 1. 3, 79; cf. Willis, 1995, 187 and Howard and Rackin 1997: 75). Her challenge to state and domestic authority culminates in attempts to achieve her ambition through witchcraft. She employs the services of a witch, a conjurer and two priests in order to find out what is in store for Henry, the ruling monarch, and his two most powerful nobles, Somerset and Suffolk. Just as the hags in *Women in Parliament* are punished and brought once more under the control of men, so too is Eleanor. She is punished for parading in the finery of a queen by being dragged barefoot in a shift through the streets by male enforcers of the law — Sir John Stanley, the Sheriff and his Officers (*2HVI* 2. 4). Her two transgressions are punished as one because infringement of the sumptuary laws is a visual signifier of her presumption in wishing to play the man's part in the politics of state.

In the *Henry VI* trilogy Margaret of Anjou, unruly, unchaste and self-assertive from the outset, represents even more an unchecked and unseemly domestic authority that becomes a danger to the state. Her punishment, incomplete till the start of *Richard III*, comprises similar rituals of disempowerment. A sexual and military threat in *Henry VI Parts 1, 2 and 3*, her sexuality and ability to wage war collapse in *Richard III* into the mutterings 'of an embittered, desexualized crone' (Howard and Rackin 1997: 98). In this play both the women who strode across the world of politics in the *Henry VI* tetralogy are old, shrunken and confined to the hearth. Retribution for Margaret of Anjou's transgressive acts begins in the final act of *Henry VI Part 3* with the murder of her son before her very eyes. All she can do is grieve and beg for a death which is denied; instead, she is sent back to France. The historical Margaret was imprisoned in the tower for four years and, finally ransomed by Louis XI, died at Saumur in France aged fifty-one, at the mere onset of old age. In *Richard III* her disempowerment is clinched by a brief appearance in Act I in a role reduced to a bitter commentary on the conversation between Richard and Elizabeth, Edward IV's queen. When she steps forward the tigerish queen is toothless; all she can do is curse without effect (*Richard III*, 1. 3, 188–237).

For Margaret and Eleanor the onset of old age means a loss of political agency and sexual power and significantly, Eleanor's humiliation involves also charges of witchcraft. So deeply ingrained was the identification of old women with melancholia and witchcraft that neither Elizabeth's female courtiers nor Elizabeth herself could escape their taint. According to Camden, Margaret Clifford, Countess of Derby, the only daughter of Henry Clifford, Earl of Cumberland (whose wife was niece to Henry VIII and whose name was, evocatively, Eleanor) 'out of her womanish weakenesse and curiosity' resorted to wizards or cunning men in a credulous vanity, and I know not what ambicious hope'. As a result she had 'in a manner' lost the Queen's favour a little before each of them died (Camden, 1630, fol.18). The accounts of Elizabeth's last few days of life, all written some time after her death, vary considerably in the details, yet take for granted that a sixty-year-old woman will be suffering first and foremost from the melancholy of age. John Chamberlain in a letter to Dudley Carleton, on March 3 1603 thought

> her disease to be nothing but a settled and unremoveable melancholie, insomuch that she could not be won or pressed, neither by the council, divines, physicians, nor the women about her, once to sup or touch any physic, though ten or twelve physicians that were continually about her, did assure her with all manner of assurances of perfect and easy recovery, if she would follow their advice; [...] they say she died only for lack of physicke. Here was some whispering that her braine was somewhat distempered, but there was no such matter; only she held an obstinate silence for the most part, and, because she had a persuasion that yf she once lay downe she shold never rise, could not be gotten to bed in a whole weeke, till three dayes before her death. (Chamberlain, 1939, 1,188–89; see also Manningham, 1868, 146)

Sir Robert Carey did his best 'to persuade her from this melancholy humour; but I found by her it was too deep-rooted in her heart, and hardly to be removed.' (Chamberlain, 1939, 1, 188–89, repeated in Nichols, 1823, 3: 604–05 fn3).

Reports from one of her ladies in waiting, Elizabeth Southwell, gives more details of the delusional symptoms of melancholy (Southwell, 1996, line 29). Having fallen 'into extremity', the Queen sat full dressed upon her stool[12] for two days and three nights, and could not be persuaded to eat, drink or go to bed. The only person she would have near her was the Lord Admiral, to whom she reportedly confided that if he had seen what she had seen in her bed, 'he would not persuade her as he did.' She shooed everyone else from the room, and shaking her head, 'with a pitifull voice, said unto him, "My Lord, I am tied with a chaine of iron about my feet;" he alleging her wonted courage, she replied, "I am tied, tied, and the case is altered with me."' Lady Southwell, 'with whom she was very private and confidant,' wrote colourfully that the Queen saw one night in her bed her body 'exceeding leane and fearful, in a light of fire' (Nichols, 1823, 3: 612; Southwell, 1996, lines 20–21). These delusions were, additionally, accompanied by whispers of witchcraft; two of her ladies found at the bottom of her chair the Queen of Hearts with an iron nail knocked through its forehead. They did not dare to pull it out, having identified it as something used in witchcraft (Nichols, 1823, 613; Southwell, 1996, lines 47–50). The whiff of atheism and heresy surrounding the Queen's last days worried Camden enough for him to preface his account by refuting the imputation that 'she dyed without sence or feeling of Gods mercies'. Who could tell, in her profound melancholy, what her thoughts were? But 'it may be iudged' that her 'Meditations were fixed on God, and her thoughts lifted vp to Heauen, the ioyes whereof she was then shortly to possesse.' In response to the Honourable Lady of her Bed-Chamber, Lady Newton, she averred 'I warrant you Madam, I thinke on nothing else' (Camden, 1630, To The Reader, sig.B2).

Traces of witchcraft wafted around the Duchess of Derby and the Queen when they were elderly women. For the demonologists the matter of a witch's age is important. Kramer and Sprenger's *Malleus Maleficarum* stated that the Devil targeted virgins and girls, presumably because older women had more sense (*Malleus*, 1928, 97; Bever, 1982,156).[13] The sceptics, on the other hand, did their best to present witchcraft accusations as a problem of senile pathology, 'the product of dementia rather than diabolism' (Bever, 1982, 155). On the basis of the evidence from records of witch trials, old women were particularly susceptible to the charge of witchraft because 'across cultures and with age they seem to become more domineering, more agentic, and less willing to trade submission for security' (Gutmann, 1977, 309) but this disables their attempts to take on positions of authority in public life, because society regards them as too imperious and domineering. They take to the black arts because they envy young, powerful males: 'the long-closeted anger of old women, generally repressed during their childbearing years, may revive, in others, archaic fears of the "bad mother", as expressed in the persona of the witch' (309, 311–12). Early modern society invested in the witch a terrifying power internalised by those who came up for trial. Since most of the women accused of witchcraft were beyond childbearing age (Roper, 2004, 161), this added agency provided the defining feature of their position in a society which attributed to witches the possession of powers that led to their torture and death. This is strikingly illustrated in the witch trials in England, Scotland and southern Germany throughout the late sixteenth and seventeenth centuries. Lyndal Roper's seminal work on the Augsberg witch trials (1994) and, most recently, those in Nördlingen, Würtzburg and Obermarchtal (2004) takes its thesis from the imagery of nurture interrupted. In the former she uses a psychoanalytic approach to explore the individual experiences of those confessing to witchcraft. These confessions provide in the later work the basis of a historical account of southern German society's fears and persecution of women in the sixteenth and seventeenth centuries which includes a survey of the art and literature featuring a particular stereotype of old women (2004, 162–70). Her account of these trials reveals a profound antipathy between the old women who were accused and their accusers, young mothers (1997, 200–02; 2004, 7–9, 150–52); in the Augsburg trials the older women worked as lying-in maids and their victims were mothers who had just given birth (1994, 199) while in Nördlingen those past their child-bearing years formed by far the largest group of those arrested (2004, 160).

Anger and envy, according to Bacon, are two of the foremost 'passions of the mind' that shorten life. Anger causes spirits to devour the body's moisture, but envy is the worst, for it never rests: 'Envye is sayede to keepe no Holydayes' (Bacon 1638, 171, 173).[14] These two negative emotions were identified as characteristic of all old people but most particularly old women, 'in whom envy causeth them to whet their tongues to kill their neighbours fame with detraction' (Wright, 1601, 74; cf. Steele, 1688, 50–51). The Bavarian witch trials expose anger and envy as the prime motivational forces of both accusers and accused. As Roper puts it, '[i]n the logic of sorcery, where emotions might be externalized on to things outside the person and where feelings had active force, the emotion itself was the wellspring of injury.' In the exemplary case of Anna Ebeler, a lying-in maid in Augsburg accused of witchcraft, the very tasks she was required to perform exposed her to the suspicion of her employers: '[c]ircumstances conspired to make the lying-in-maid appear a likely sufferer from envy and hatred' (Roper, 1994, 214). Moreover, the witch herself explained her behaviour as resulting from envy, and this was 'the breaking point which then catapulted her into a range of other confessions about the Devil' (215). This helps explain why Anna Ebeler declared that she had told the Devil she was too old for sex with him, an unforced detail that derives from related attitudes found in the anti-witchcraft tracts. Elderly women accused of witchcraft were snagged into a vicious circle. Insatiable carnal lust, just as intense in old age as in their youth, made old women particularly prone to the lure of sex with the Devil, since men of all ages were warned against them, and all consorts of the Devil were known to be lustful (Kramer & Sprenger, *Malleus*, 1971, 47). Caught between this and the position adopted by Agrippa, that demonic copulation exists only in the imagination and ravings of old women who are deceived by dreams when asleep and deluded by imaginings of violent lust when awake (Weyer, 1583, 239), Ebeler acknowledges herself a witch yet sets herself apart from her lewd sisterhood. But even though lust was not the motive, Anna Ebeler's testament is imbued with a sense of hatred and alienation which is projected onto the Devil (Roper 1994, 216).

POVERTY: *THE WITCH OF EDMONTON*

Henry Goodcole's account of *The Wonderful Discovery of Elizabeth Sawyer a Witch, late of Edmonton* (1621), the source for *The Witch of Edmonton* by Rowley, Dekker and Ford[15] draws on much the same material, commonplace in misogynist and witchcraft tracts from the late sixteenth century onwards, in its account of an attack on an old, post-menopausal woman. In both play and pamphlet, Elizabeth Sawyer is the object of accusations deriving from a range of witchcraft beliefs which contain the core assumption that old women were most prone to blandishments from the Devil. It proves absurdly easy for Elizabeth Sawyer to gain access to the Devil, even though she is unsure initially of how she should go about it:

> I have heard old beldams
> Talk of familiars in the shape of mice,
> Rats, ferrets, weasels and I wot not what
> [....................]
> Would some power, good or bad,
> Instruct me which way I might be revenged
> Upon this churl. (2. 1, 109–116)

As soon as he hears her blasphemy, he appears in the shape of a dog to claim her as his own (2. 1, 128), and by the fourth act the two have struck up a close bond. Though she sees herself as 'dried up/With cursing and with madness' she evidently does not see herself as too old for sex with the Devil:

> Stand on thy hind-legs up. Kiss me, my Tommy,
> And rub away some wrinkles on my brow
> By making my old ribs to shrug for joy
> Of thy fine tricks. What hast thou done? Let's tickle.
> [*They embrace.*] (4 1, 167–73)

Like Anna Ebeler and the Augsburg witches, the fictionalised and the real Elizabeth Sawyer is motivated by anger and resentment against those who torment her, and espouses the Devil in order to be revenged upon them; anger and envy, which accelerate the aging process, also push her into the Devil's arms. She bewitches cattle, wives, daughters, maidservants (4. 1, 15–17) and 'nurse children.' She congratulates Dog on having stricken a horse lame and 'nipped sucking children' (4. 1, 173–74; cf. Goodcole, 1621, 138). Both Ebeler and Sawyer were in the margins of their community (the one urban, the other rural — a contrast brought out in the play). Both were poor, dependent and angry, and both were objects of suspicion. In Goodcole's pamphlet and the play, Sawyer is accused of everything bad that happens to the other characters:

Old Carter: The witch, that instrument of mischief! Did not she witch the devil into my son-in-law when he killed my poor daughter? [...] He could never have don't without the devil.
Elizabeth Sawyer: Who doubts it?
[......]
Old Carter: Thou didst bewitch Anne Ratcliffe to kill herself.
[......]
First Countryman: I'll be sworn, Master Carter, she bewitched Gammer Washbowl's sow to cast her pigs a day before she would have farrowed, yet they were sent up to London, and sold for as good Westminster dog-pigs at Bartholomew Fair as ever great-bellied ale-wife longed for. (*Witch of Edmonton* 5. 3, 21–40; cf. Goodcole, 1621, 138–39)

Placed centre-stage by their sorcery, Ebeler, the real life and the fictionalised Sawyer all achieve a measure of self-definition that would never have come their way by any other means. In the Augsburg trials the lying-in-maid was suspected of witchcraft as a result of her social and domestic circumstances. She was old and alone, her own family had grown up and moved out of the family home, and one of the few options open to her was to earn a living passing in and out of others' houses, beyond childbearing herself yet still chained to its claims. Elizabeth Sawyer the person and the character are comparably dependent on their community. In one way the unskilled labour that Ebeler, Sawyer and the Sawyer character performed placed them in a position of humiliating dependency; they did not have any status or training, and Ebeler for one was entirely at the mercy of the favourable opinion of the young woman who employed her. But at the same time she was in a very powerful position. She exercised total control over both mother and child, who were entirely dependent upon her, even though this dependency was coupled with the same kind of suspicion Sawyer experiences; in Ebeler's case, since the infant did not prosper, she was the first person to be suspected of harm. Furthermore, these women's age, their widowhood and their solitary state exposed them to the malice and envy of their neighbours. The fact that Ebeler, for example, had given birth to illegitimate children, and her nearness, made her the first person to be suspected if the husband was unfaithful (Roper, 1994, 211–12). In the glare of the publicity of a witch trial, each is under the spotlight and receives the rapt attention of the very people for whom they were up until that moment invisible. Once Sawyer has Dog working for her, she becomes the focal point of the whole community, and seems to glory in the unaccustomed attention; every setback and calamity, from bewitching Sawgut's fiddle to inciting Frank to murder, is laid at her door. Though her final speech is to confess and pray forgiveness, there is a note of triumph in her salvoes against Old Carter, and in her final moments she attains an impressive dignity:

Elizabeth Sawyer: These dogs will mad me. I was well resolved
         To die in my repentance. Though 'tis true
         I would live longer if I might, yet since
         I cannot, pray torment me not; my conscience
         Is settled as it shall be. [...]
Old Carter: Thoud'st best confess all truly.
Elizabeth Sawyer: Yet again?
         Have I scarce breath enough to say my prayers,
         And would you force me to spend that in bawling?
         Bear witness. I repent all former evil;
         There is no damnèd conjuror like the devil. (5 3, 41–45)

But even though she repents, she does so in continuing rage. Her antagonism to Old Carter remains; her last words to him are a sharp rejoinder to his evident wish to press the point of her punishment home by making her repeat her confession.

The proximity of the old to the very young made them more vulnerable than any other member of the community to the charge of malevolence. Ordinarily, the continuing participation of the old in the lives of their children and grandchildren made them respected and recognised, particularly in their continuing role as child-rearers. The Norwich census of 1570 reveals, strikingly, that about a third of households headed by the old also contained children; Thomas Wylson, for example, and his wife Margaret, aged forty-six had five children living with them, the eldest eighteen, the three youngest all under seven (*Norwich Census*, 26; Houlbrook, 1984, 192–201; Pelling, 1991, 77). Widowers sent their children to their grandmothers, and elderly widows, who, unlike their rural counterparts, still rarely (though more often than widowers) lived alone. They either took in lodgers, or lodged in the homes of unrelated people. Children, or younger helpers, seem to have been distributed among those who could not manage on their own but who still retained control of their property (Laslett, 1972, 35, n.50; Pelling, 1991, 85–87). The loss of a husband or wife did not break up the household, nor was it being re-formed around the separate households of married children. If a widow or a widower lived alone, it was through choice; if a sick old person moved in with a married child it was not because the parent necessarily desired or required such a move (Laslett, 1977, 177). According to Laslett, 'the elderly [...] were ordinarily left in charge of the family groups they themselves had brought into being and maintained in their earlier years' (Laslett, 1977, 200). If they wanted or needed extra domestic support, the elderly did not acquire it at the expense of their independence: 'once a man or woman had become a householder, or a householder's wife in England in traditional times, he or she tended to stay at the head of the family' (Laslett, 1977, 199). Instead, they either changed occupation (as a goldsmith and a worsted weaver turned to labouring in 1570s Norwich), or they worked at spinning white warp if they were women, and domestic work like caretaking, sweeping, turning spits or 'keeping' prisoners if they were men (Pelling, 1991, 82–83). Emotional and domestic support from offspring, siblings, more distant relatives or even those outside the family could be attained without loss of independence, the poor often making their own arrangements for support on a basis of exchange (Laslett, 1977, 175; Pelling, 1991, 87). Confirming the findings of Laslett and MacFarlane as regards the small, nuclear structure of a poor family in which close kin were not the main means of support, Pelling's examination of the very detailed Norwich census of 1570 reveals in addition that the old continued working even if they were handicapped and for as long as possible (82) and that there were almost no old women unemployed. For example, Agnes Silie continued to spin and card even though she was disabled in the hand and blind. Weak, lame-handed women were still knitting, carding and spinning into their seventies (81–2, 84).

Yet when things went wrong it was the caring old who bore the brunt of society's censure. Child informers were common at the witch trials (cf. Roper, 1994, 207; 2004, 209; Purkiss,1997, 137, 163–66; in her most recent work, Roper examines in detail the ways in which children were implicated in trials against old women particularly (Roper, 2004, 170–71; 173, 204), and witches infamously targeted children as victims of their malevolence. In Goodcole's account, Sawyer was asked to explain the role and function of two ferrets that she had been feeding with white bread and milk. This was observed by some children 'of a good bigness and reasonable understanding' who then testified against her in court (Goodcole, 1621, 145) — small wonder Sawyer doesn't like children in the play and orders Dog to 'nip' one (4.1, 173–74).

The witch was an old woman whose body had dried and shrivelled; unable to nurture, she either impeded the nourishment of others, or diverted it to herself. Poisonous in herself, her object was to pervert the course of nature by causing babies and cattle to shrivel and die, while she herself flourished. She also destroyed her victims by poisoning them – that is, by interfering with their source of sustenance. From this understanding of the role and function of bodily fluids deriving from ancient literature and science, there arose also the belief that old women had the power to wreck the health of a young man, and, if turned witch, to make women barren. The malevolence of the old thus singled out the young as their victim, and would wreak damage by sucking out the moisture that characterised youth (cf. Kramer & Sprenger, *Malleus*, 1971, 47, 117, 171–72; Bever, 1982, 175; Roper, 2004, 164). The old woman's hunger for semen would suck out a young man's seed,[16] weakening and infecting him with her own impuri-

ties. And no longer able to produce nourishing and youth-enhancing fluids
herself, an old woman's envy (itself a feature of old age) would find its
outlet in acts of malice against the nursing mother (Roper 1994, 208–09).
Post-menopausal women's envy was fuelled by a desire for revenge, as are
witches according to James I (*Demonology,* 2000, 384). The Augsburg
women were accused of turning the mother's milk sour, or of poisoning
the infant — that is, both mother and infant were harmed by the witch's
attacks on the mother's food and for this reason, breast, milk and nourishment were key images at the trials (Roper, 1994, 207–08; 2004, 127, *et
passim.*). In addition to old age, the inability to feel pain removed a witch
even further from the experience of childbirth (Roper 1994, 211; 2004,
173). As a result, she was perceived as cold in body and feeling, incapable
of pity or maternal affection.

APTITUDE AND GAIN: *THE WISE WOMAN OF HOGDSON*

In this as in other ways, *The Witch of Edmonton* bears an interesting structural similarity to *The Wise Woman of Hogsdon.*[17] In both, the witch-
figure appears in the second act, which in each is devoted to unfolding
her circumstances, and each thereafter comes to influence the main action.
Both are voluble old women, both are particularly vulnerable to the taunts
of their neighbours, and both lay claim to a learning they do not possess;
Sawyer, like Wise Woman, dabbles in love charms (2. 1, 245–50) and lays
claim to match-making abilities (2. 2, 272–83), and, like Wise Woman,
appears to have no quarrel with the young people who come within her
orbit; 'witch or no witch', to Young Banks, Sawyer is a 'motherly woman'
(2. 1, 208). On another level, however, *The Wise Woman of Hogsdon* illustrates co-operative arrangements among the real life poor and so reflects a
measure of care and emotional support for the elderly. She has a houseful
of (very) temporary lodgers, and is able to employ a 'lad' to help her run
her various businesses, whereas Elizabeth Sawyer illustrates the estrange-
ment from the rural community of old women living alone. In the context
of witchcraft accusations this very involvement of the old in the lives of the
young contained its dangers; one grandmother, Roper tells us, was accused
by her grandson of poisoning the aniseed water she gave him (1994, 207). In
the *The Wise Woman of Hogston*, however, the young and old are involved
in each other's lives in a way that reflects co-operation and also indicates
wider social issues to do with the ordering of households into economi-
cally viable units of work. Thus while attention to the psychological helps
explain predominant characteristics of the witch narratives in the late sixteenth and seventeenth centuries, and the domestic isolation in which the
female members of the household lived, there are still wider social issues —
highlighted, for example, by the Norwich census of 1570, and the records
of the Royal College of Physicians (both examined by Pelling; respectively,

Figure 4.2 After Jan Steen, A physician writing a prescription for a sick young woman. By permission of the Wellcome Library.

1991, 74–101 and 1997, 67–83) which need to be considered alongside the inner motivations of witch and persecutor.

In early modern society old women were gainfully employed in the town as well as the country. Significantly, the first indications of the Royal College of Physicians' anxiety over the activities of old women came in the plague years of the 1580s. The searchers for bodies were women, employed precisely because they were reliable and mature — though, as Pelling suggests, it might also have been because they were 'poor and expendable' (Pelling, 1997, 70–82; 82). However, once identified and brought in for questioning, they were treated leniently by the College authorities. Though suspected of witchcraft, they did not fit the misogynistic characterisations of the old crone so forcibly represented in the witchcraft texts of the late sixteenth and early seventeenth centuries. In seventeenth-century Dutch painting, the theme of an old woman's industry becomes an offshoot of her piety and quest for knowledge, as paintings by Rembrandt, Lievens and Dou show. These artists represent old women contentedly absorbed in their reading. Rembrandt, using his mother as a model depicts 'An Old Woman Reading' in which the subject familiarly handles the very large book she is poring over (1631, Amsterdam, Rijksmuseum); Jan Lievens, a close friend of Rembrandt, paints his 'Old Woman Reading' as bespectacled and wrapped in an ermine shawl, surrounded by several large tomes, and reading one of them in solitary close-up (Museum of Art, J.G. Johnson Collection, Philadelphia) while Gerrit Dou illustrates the desire to further knowledge in his 'Old Woman reading a Lectionary', c. 1632.

Piety, the acquisition of knowledge and the cultivation of serenity is a feature these paintings share with depictions of old women in specifically medical contexts as wise and informed, a response themed in the Dutch genre paintings as 'the doctor's visit' which records their activities in a quasi-medical context. For instance, Adriaen Brouwer, David Teniers the Younger, Jan Steen (see fig. 4.2), Gabriel Metsu and Quirijn van Brekelenkam considerably complicate the stereotype of old women ignorantly intervening between doctor and patient. In their paintings old women are in command of their domestic workplace, the sick room, as a result of their specialist knowledge and experience (Pelling, 1997, 64–66). Their knowledge of the female body puts them on a par with the doctor (cf. Pelling, 1997, 73, 78).[18] Pelling establishes a connection between these paintings and old women who practiced medicine informally, whose activities the Royal College of Physicians did their best to curtail. The College's prejudice against them was influenced by the stereotype of ignorant old women interfering in medicine, though a much more harmful one was the widespread view that these old women were more experienced and knowledgeable than the academically-biased College physicians, and their cures were a lot less damaging to patients. In all strata of society, from the noblewomen and wives of gentry who kept diaries and recipe books to a wider social range encompassed by the college registers, it was women who were the primary domestic carers in times of ill health. Grace Mildmay, for instance, was one of a number of high-born women who practiced medicine both in and outside the home (Pollock, 1993, 143). In the College registers, women practitioners were classified by what they did rather than to whom they were married, and what their husbands did. As such, they vary considerably from their stock description as wandering lonely old crones ostracised by society and practicing an ad hoc sort of hedgerow medicine. In London at any rate, and in contrast to their domestic sick-room counterparts, these unofficial, specifically female practitioners usually operated from home ground, and bought rather than picked their medicines (Pelling 1997, 74–76).

However, depictions (whether on canvas or in print) of the activities of elderly female practitioners of unofficial medicine, unlike those of old women reading, seem to intimate disreputable activities, in that they combine knowingness with a hint of threat. In the 'the doctor's visit' genre, the pursuit of pious knowledge becomes a question of knowingness. The doctor's helpers, old women shrewd in matters relating to young girls, convey a hint of menace in the underlying motif, and the same is true of the canny old women in comedy. In Thomas Heywood's *The Wise Woman of Hogsdon*, for example, the involvement of a knowing crone (who claims bookish knowledge) in the love complications of the young calls for a rather surprisingly complex response from the audience. Heywood's Wise Woman recalls a variety of genre representations of shady old women, among them Aristophanes' hags, and initially elicits a shiver in her nefarious dealings with the young. Like the hags, she is identified solely according to occupation; she has no other name and is described as 'the witch, the beldam, the hag of Hogsdon', sobriquets which draw attention to her sinister aspect. Yet it is she who stage-manages and finally resolves the love complications to everyone's satisfaction. This ambivalence is deliberate, and owes its being to the particular circumstances of the main plot. Wise Woman's dubious areas of expertise are sought after by a rogue, Young Chartley, to effect a seduction through bogus secret marriage. Like the depictions of old women in attendance on young sick girls in the Dutch genre, the play turns on a youth–age contrast in which the younger woman is helpless, and the older is in demand for an expertise which emanates menace, particularly when allied to the figure of a hag. She first appears carrying a urine sample from a countryman's wife, and singles out the owner of the sample as the first of her clients for that day (2. 1, 20–21, 48). This small episode stages in essence the subject matter of Gabriel Metsu's painting — the doctor's visit, where the old woman carries a chamber pot and a urine basket, confident in her knowledge and experience of medicine of correct diagnosis of a patient's condition from a urine sample. Urine was used in medicine and magic by the wise folk to identify an ailment and cure it. According to received opinion, there was no need for the patient to be there as well, and the scene in which the Wise Woman blithely prognosticates in the absence of the passer of the sample evidently parodies this. As the genre paintings show, doctors also made extensive use of the urinel, a practice endorsed by medical handbooks despite the Royal College of Physicians' disapproval (Thomas 1971, 10, 225), and depicted in the painting (after Jan Steen) in the Wellcome Institute Library, London, very explicitly entitled 'A Medical Practitioner Taking a Girl's Pulse and Examining a Flask of Her Urine.[19] Urine was also used to treat ailments resulting from magical charms. Ann Green of York, for example, claimed in her deposition that she cured her patients' headaches by taking a lock of their hair, boiling it in their urine and throwing it all into the fire (Thomas, 1971, 217). Another would not prescribe any medicine until the patient's urine had been used to bake a wheatmeal cake, together with some swatches of hair and horseshoe stumps, and then put into the fire (Heywood, *Diaries*, 1882, iv, 53–4). Combining the practice of medicine with that of astrology, some cunning persons claimed to be able to name the illness, devise an appropriate treatment, determine precisely the time it would reach crisis, and predict its effects (Thomas, 1971, 339–40). The same recipes for urine were used to confound witches (as a means of detecting witchcraft, not practising it), assuming a sample of the witch's urine could be procured. Once the sample had been boiled, baked or buried, the witch would reveal herself by not being able to pee (Thomas, 1971, 648).

The fact that these old women took a pride in their profession is clear in both paintings and historical accounts, and is endorsed by Heywood's play. The genre paintings depict a reality in which the activities of old women are meant to be taken seriously; the presence of the doctor confirms the legitimacy of the old women in attendance — their assistance is necessary and required. The Wise Woman's first words articulate self-belief and pride in the wisdom and skill she brings to her clients:

> [...] What a toil and a moil it is,
> For a woman to be wiser than all her neighbours —
> I pray, good people, press not too fast upon me. (2. 1, 1–3)

Confidence in her own skills derives from her ability to use urine to diagnose and treat the ailments of those who consult her, and she accounts for her popularity by identifying with other wise women. She gives a roll call of well known London practitioners: Mother Nottingham and Mother Bomby are famous for casting waters; a wizard in Hatfield finds lost goods; another in Coleharbour is good for planetary influences and Mother Sturton in Golden Lane is known for dealing with those bewitched. Mother Phillips and Mistress Mary on Bankside are experts in 'weakness for the back' and astrology, respectively; there is a very reverend matron on Clerkenwell who is an all-rounder, and one in Westminster who detects thieves by use of the book and the key, and the sieve and the shears (2. 1, 20–35). Heywood's Wise Woman has her place among these renowned women, and has her own reputation and following: 'For myself, let the world speak' (2. 1, 37). She is in no doubt that she too is a wise woman:

> Let me see how many trades I have to live by: first, I am a wise-woman, and a fortune-teller, and under that I deal in physic and fore-speaking, in palmistry, and recovering of things lost. Next, I undertake to cure mad folks. Then I keep gentlewomen lodgers, to furnish such chambers as I let out by the night. Then I am provided for bringing young wenches to bed. And, for a need, you see I can play the match-maker.
>
> She that is but one, and professeth so many,
> May well be termed a wise-woman, if
>   there be any. (3. 1, 166–74)

Heywood's Wise Woman says she can tell fortunes, a skill which brings her in line with the practices involving palmistry and forespeaking — that is, bewitching or exorcising the bewitched. This ability brings her closer to activities associated with witchcraft. In the transcripts of the notorius North Berwick witch trials of 1590–91 (Normand and Roberts, 2000,

127–203) it is clear that Agnes Samson, 'the elder witch' in years and repu- tation and one of the chief protagonists in *News From Scotland* (*News,* 2000, 312/3), had a 'long established career' as a wise woman sought out for her skills in healing, divining and midwifery. She cut a dash at her trial; John Spottiswoode describes her as 'most remarkable, a woman not of the base and ignorant sort of Witches, but, Matron-like, grave and setled in her answers, which were all to some purpose' (Spottiswoode, 1668, 383; Nor- mand and Roberts, 2000, 207). The first part of her dittay (trial record) proclaims the diagnostic, healing and foretelling skills which contribute to her reputation as a cunning woman. But her predictions of whether the sick would live or die bring her dangerously near to the brink of legitimate practice. Furthermore, it could well have been her age, conferring senior- ity and authority, that made her the particular target for persecution. In claiming to know James' and Anne's honeymoon secrets she seems to claim agency and occult powers at the cost of her very life. Her precarious posi- tion becomes evident two thirds of the way through her deposition, when she records her first meeting with the devil, after the death of her husband. Until then, though some of her cures involved counter-magic for bewitch- ment, her predictions about health, length of life, storms and damage were performed solely by the power of prayer, and she charmed cattle against sickness by stroking them and saying several 'Ave Marias' (Normand and Roberts, 2000, 208–9).

In addition to her position on the same cusp of witchcraft as the real life Agnes Samson (a model also for Middleton's Hecate), Wise Woman's claim to be able to 'see as far into a mill-stone as another' and to do as well 'according to their talent' as any of those whose names she reels off (2. 1, 21, 36), presupposes a bookish knowledge which she boasts but does not possess. Though fortune-telling could be accomplished by solely natu- ral means,[20] it was more often learned from printed sources (hence Wise Woman's well-stocked bookshelves, and her kinship to the 'old woman reading' paintings), medieval in origin and widely available in Elizabethan times. Debased by village practitioners, divination by various means (read- ing palms, moles on the face, lines on the forehead) was nevertheless a topic for debate among intellectuals (Thomas, 1971, 283). John Falconer ridicules John Trask's claim that it was possible to read a man's fate in his face (Falconer, 1618, 7) a facility elevated into a popular science by such handbooks as Doctor Arcandam's, translated from the French by Wil- liam Warde, who subsequently became Professor of Physic at Cambridge.[21] Heywood's illiterate Wise Woman's fortune telling claims, with their dual origins in nature and books, have a real life precedent in Valentine Staple- hurst, who saw into the pasts and futures of people in Maidstone in 1560 even though he could not read. Neither, it transpired, could John Bewly, 'an olde fellowe' who came to Maidstone in 1662 claiming to be a physician with bookish learning (Halle, 1565, 11–14, 16).[22]

However, Wise Woman's self-belief does not mask from the audience that canny as she might be, she is not necessarily knowledgeable. She owns many books, and flips through them in a pretence at authority designed to dazzle the citizens' wives who consult her. She asks them to wait while she reads 'a little of Ptolemy and *Erra Pater.*' to help her 'cast a figure' (2. 1, 84–85). *The Compost of Ptolomeus* and the *Erra Pater* were both crude works on fortune telling. *The Compost*, published around 1532, containing a pirated version of *The Kalendar of Shepherdes*, translated from the French in 1503 and thereafter reprinted seventeen times, gave information on how to tell fortunes from the stars, and on the influences of the planets on the body. The *Erra Pater*, also published many times between 1536 and 1640, derived from a medieval work on prognostication (Thomas 1971, 350). Both of these popular works are cited by Wise Woman in a bid to ratchet up her status. She evidently considers them influential, though in reality they were being ridiculed by authors as examples of rural credulity; Henry Peacham for example scoffs at the husbandman's use of the 'Erra Pater, and this yeare's almanacke (if he can read)' as being 'the two onely bookes he spends his time in' (Peacham, 1638, 119), while Joseph Hall's superstitious man would never go out without a copy of it in his pocket (Hall, *Works*, vi, 110). The naming of these two rudimentary works exposes the Wise Woman's ignorance in the very act of claiming specialist knowledge and locates her precisely among those early modern village and urban healers whose skills were part of a culture of orally received wisdom; the healer rarely possessed books, relying instead on ritualised forms of behaviour (Thomas, 1971, 272). Wise Woman describes her skills as non-magical, and the 'Ptolemy' she pretends to be able to read contains, in addition to almanacs and prognostications, information about books on magic that were only necessary for the conjuration of spirits, and the Wise Woman knows enough to expressly exclude these from her repertoire (Thomas, 1971, 271–72). However, the boundary between witch and wise woman in such works as Johannes ab Indagine (von Hagen)'s *Brief Introductions* to palmistry, physiognomy and astrology is not well defined, and reflects a cultural blurring of categories (ab Indagine, 1633, sig.E4). The many names for wise persons is in itself an indication of this; there were no distinctions made between the activities of wizards, wise men and women and cunning men, sorcerers, charmers, blessers, conjurers and witches because their healing procedures involved a mixture of handed down skills in midwifery and nursing and the remedial use of plants and minerals with magical charms, spells and incantations (Thomas, 1971, 210). Item 15 in Agnes Samson's dittay informs the court that her father instructed her in the use of prayer in curing the sick: 'if she stopped in her prayer, she would not pass (go) to the sick person, and if she stopped not she would pass and the person diseased would live' (Normand and Roberts, 2000, 233–34). Agnes Samson was convicted of witchcraft for curing and failing to cure the sick because she used devilish means to do both, but Wise Woman is only called a witch, a she-cat, a damned sorceress and so on when things go wrong for those who sought her help in tricking others, such as Boyster (4. 2), when the complications of the fake marriages begin to unravel. She herself only practises non-magical skills.

But even though Wise Woman does not see herself as a witch, her self-proclaimed talents extending merely to the detection of witchcraft but not its practice, she does not entirely dissociate herself from it. Like the wizards of her day who used magic to help their clients recover lost goods, she draws upon a range of strategies to identify thieves and recover stolen goods. She can use polished stones (her boast, as noted, is that she can look deep into a mill-stone) to reveal to her clients an image of the person who stole their possessions, and to manipulate in the manner of an ouija board player a pair of shears stuck in the 'rind' of a sieve, with her own and the victim's forefingers lightly resting on the top part of the sieve, so that they can feel it move when the name of the supposed thief is called out (Scot, 1584, *Discoverie*, Bk. 12 ch. 17; Aubrey, 1686–7, 25; *Wise Woman*, 2. 1, 35).[23] She can also confirm the name of the thief by the key and the book method. Here, the names of the suspects are written on bits of paper and are put inside the ring part of a key inside a book. When the name of the thief was inserted into the key, the book would jump out of the hands of whoever was holding it. These practices involve a white, beneficent kind of magic; the book was usually a psalter or a bible, and there are many examples of its use, since it was a well known medieval method (Thomas, 1971, 254–55). Both methods were accompanied by prayers, or invocations of the saints or the holy trinity. Agnes Samson's dittay transcribes in full the prayer her father taught her (item 32, Normand and Roberts, 2000, 208). The confidence with which Heywood's Wise Woman proclaims her 'trades' and the eager throng who come to consult her thus mirrors reality. According to George Gifford, recourse to wise persons was:

> a commo[n] thing and well tried by experience, that many in great distresse haue been relieued and recouered by sending unto such wise men or wise women, when they could not tell what should els become of them, and of all that they had. (Gifford, 1587, sig. H1verso)

Like Agnes Samson, Margaret Neale cured diseases by prayer in 1597, and therefore 'hath recourse of people to her far and wide', and an old woman in Stowmarket who claimed 'to be able to heal all diseases by "words of conjuration" had people flock to her in great numbers' (Thomas, 1971, 300, citing the account of Bishop Redman's Visitation to the Norwich Diocese in 1597, 133.) In times of trouble, the first thing a man does 'is to bethink himselfe and inquire after some Wise-man or wise-woman, and thither he sends and goes for helpe' (Perkins, 1608, 175), a decision whose wisdom was confirmed when the outcome was good. It follows that Wise Woman, like the real life cunning folk she represents, has plenty of custom-

ers, despite the fact that such evidence as this places her in the category of
the working elderly poor, who had to continue to perform multiple tasks
until they were well into decrepit old age,[24] and she does pretty well out of
it, despite official censure in the statutes of 1542, 1563, 1604 and 1689[25]
concerning the powers of wise folk who claimed to be able to prognosticate
by means palmistry, physiognomy or who:

> tell or declare [...] where Goodes or Thinges lost or stollen should bee
> founde or becume, or shall use or practise anye Sorcery Enchantment
> Charme or Witchecrafte, to thintent to provoke any pson to unlaufull
> love (Statute 33, 1562–3, 4, 447)

or indeed those who 'perform cures of sores' by herbs (Statute 3, 1542,
3, 906).[26]

It is evident that wise women's dabbling in medicine necessarily involved
the deployment of a range of specialist knowledge and skills which ran per-
ilously close to the activities of witches.[27] At the same time as Wise Woman's multitasking establishes her professional credentials, their very nature
expose her as a bogus medical practitioner, and, worse, place her in danger
of bringing down accusations of witchcraft upon herself. That the practice
of these dubious techniques put wise persons at risk of charges of witchcraft
is clear from various contemporary sources. Their expertise, for example,
might include the cure of cattle or a member of the family. John Grave of
Romford, in a court held by the Archdeacon of Essex on 2 May 1592, is
careful to point out that he employed the wizard Father Perfoche to cure
his cattle, and not for the exercise of his reputed magical powers. He was
'solemnly admonished' to keep away from sorcery, and to pay two shillings for court costs. William Moushowe, also of Romford, was cleared of
the same charge and paid the same court costs on the same day (*Lincoln
Diocese Documents*, 1914, 109), and Paul Rigden told the Archdeacon of
Canterbury in 1598 that he went to Mother Chambers when his wife fell
sick, not because she was a sorceress, but because she had a good record of
success (Thomas, 1971, 226, citing A. Hussey, 'Visitations of the Archdeacon of Canterbury', *Archaeologia Cantiana*, xxvi 1904, 21). Wise persons
as well as those who sought their services often specifically denied occult
means of curing. Joan Warden of Stapleford, Cambridgeshire, 1592, denied
witchery on the grounds that her cures administered only ointments and
herbs (Thomas, 1971, 227, citing Ely D.R., B2/12, f.10v; Borthwick, R. VI.
A. 11, f.13), and so did Alice Maton, 1590, who cured cattle by medicine
and drinks, not magic (227). Distinctions based on whether wise persons
used charms or not indicate unclear dividing lines between magical and
non-magical cures. It was not enough to administer natural cures without
invoking God's help, but it was a short step from this to enlisting other,
sometimes undefined, occult powers, including the power of the Devil. The
conviction of Agnes Samson rested upon her own confession of using devil-

ish means to cure bewitched clients; it seems at first glance incongruous, for example, that she was *convicted* of healing John Ker, 'being sick in all men's judgement to the death' by her prayers and incantation (Item 17), but Item 18 clarifies the terminology, for here, as elsewhere, she is convicted of 'healing John Duncan of Musselburgh of his sickness *by her devilish prayers*' (italics mine; Normand and Roberts, 2000, 234). And she is obviously skating on thin ice when she cures the sheriff of Haddington's wife 'who was witched by the witch of Mirrielaws' (Item 23, 234) because the cure involved using the devil's means. Though Wise Woman professes only natural cures, her dabbling in conjuration, 'reading the waters' and forespeaking bring her dangerously close to activities associated with witchcraft; as a witch, Agnes Samson had 'foreknowledge' that William Markeston, Thomas Watson of Inveresk's servant, 'was but a dead man' (Item 1, Normand and Roberts, 2000, 232). Like the white witches of the period (that is, those whose occult powers derived from God, and who therefore did no harm), Wise Woman is consulted by her neighbours from all social classes. But she also conforms to the stereotype of the black witch, like Agnes Samson, in that she is old and, when things go wrong, she is insulted and despised. She is 'beldam', the good wise person, when her work meets with her patrons' approval, but 'witch', 'hag', 'crone' when her intercessions thwart the plans of the rash young men. These epithets evoke a vast body of learned literature on witches.

From this we can conclude that the Wise Woman is one of those purveyors of charms, fortune telling and wizardry condemned from the pulpit (c.1627) by Robert Sanderson, later Bishop of Lincoln, but still slavishly sought by 'our common ignorants' besotted with the opinion of their skill and 'pitifully' gulled by 'their damnable impostures, through their own foolish credulity' (Sanderson, 1854, 3: 117). Every parish had its miracle worker and writers from Reginald Scot onwards confirmed their continuing popularity thirty five years later (Scot, 1584, Bk.1 ch. 2). The countryman, the citizens' wives, Taber and the serving-maid are Heywood's versions of these ignoramuses, stubbornly clinging to their own credulity in the face of all the evidence of Wise Woman's impostures (2. 1, 1–86). But charlatans or no, '[t]he laity went to sorcerers for help and advice, and whether their trouble was physical or psychological they gained comfort and assistance' (Thomas, 1971, 314), and Wise Woman dispenses plenty of both.

Like the cunning-folk on whom she is modelled, Wise Woman's self-delusion is easily fathomed. Second Luce reveals in asides to the audience that the Wise Woman is no real healer or learned practitioner because she merely repeats information she has already been given:

WW: And who distilled this water?
Countryman: My wife's limbeck, if it please you.
WW: And where doth the pain hold her most?
Countryman: Marry, at her heart, forsooth.
WW: Ay, at her heart, she hath a griping at her heart?

Countryman: You have hit it right.
WW: Nay, I can see so much in the urine.
2nd Luce: Just so much as is told her. (2. 1, 6–14)

Wise Woman's trick, despite its obvious transparency, is unfathomable to those who consult her. For the kitchen maid who comes asking if she 'be maid or no' in company with the serving-man who wants to know if he will have her, the matter is resolved by both being ushered into a side-parlour, where he promises to resolve her doubt (2. 1, 46–56). This is not as stupid as it sounds; the maid articulates an area of ignorance common to the poor and uneducated. Resolution of her perplexity is well within Wise Woman's range of competence, as is her claim to have the powers of a witch who can see into people's lives. The citizen's wife who wants to know how many husbands she will have is evidently convinced (2. 1, 80–83) but second Luce's sceptical aside makes it clear that this claim is misconceived: 'If this were a wise-woman, she could tell that without asking' (2. 1, 88–89).

Adopting the attitude of the Royal Physicians in their campaign against unofficial medicine, Second Luce contemptuously dismisses Wise Woman's skills on the grounds that she has no bookish learning:

What can this witch, this wizard, or old trot,
Do by enchantment, or by magic spell?
Such as profess that art should be deep scholars.
What reading can this simple woman have?
'Tis palpable gross foolery. (2 1, 40–44)

Once in her employ, she discovers that Wise Woman supplements her income by delivering illegitimate babies who are baptized by a deacon and delivered to doorsteps — an activity which Second Luce is quick to condemn:

Most strange, that woman's brain should apprehend
Such lawless, indirect and horrid means
For covetous gain! How many unknown trades
Women and men are free of, which they never
Had charter for? — (3. 1, 41–45)

Luce's reasons for entering Wise Woman's employ disguised as a lad, even though she knows her to be a fraud, underlines society's ambivalent response to wise persons. Her plan to '[s]erve her, be't to pry into the mystery of her science' (2.1, 95–56) enables Luce to collude in and exploit the Wise Woman's claim to wisdom and the powers it confers at the same time as exposing them as false to the audience. Even though her fraudulence deceives no-one, she continues to be consulted, and the play gives her considerable scope for influencing its action. Indeed, the play culminates in a masterstroke of stage managing in which Wise Woman synchronises all the complex strands of the plot and brings them single-handedly to romantic resolution. By the end of Act Four when the comic complications are at their most intricate, the Wise Woman magisterially begins to take command of the action.[28] Her flair for the role of *deus ex machina* comes triumphantly to the fore in the final Act, when she superintends the movements and actions of the three sets of couples, ensuring that each is married to the right person in exuberant vindication of her job-description as matchmaker.[29] Heywood's audience had to take Wise Woman's success in physic, fortune-telling, fore-speaking, palmistry and finding lost goods on trust, but had plenty of scope for assessing her ability in matching the right man to the right girl — a virtuoso performance to which the entire last act is devoted. Her inspired choreography presides over the funniest part of the play, as Young Chartley does his best to wriggle out of three successive exposures of his trickery. The young people, having courted the wrong lovers, end up with the right ones as a result of everyone's willing recourse to trades typically performed by elderly women, and Wise Woman's success in remaining in control of the diverse sources of her income enables her to run a sizeable establishment, whose many rooms allow her to diversify even further. It also shows that her supreme confidence in her own talents is not entirely misguided, for it is she alone who sets in motion the happy conclusion in marriage that is the generic requirement of comedy. As Young Chartley, the reformed rake, sums up:

> Nay, mother midnight, there's some love for you.
> Out of thy folly, being reputed wise,
> We, self-conceited, have our follies found.
> Bear thou the name of all these comical acts. (5. 2, 269–72)

Heywood's play thus confirms and enacts patterns of employment for old women in urban England to which his main character refers; Wise Woman self-consciously belongs to a group of professionals consulted for their expertise in dealing with health and relationship problems, and justifies her name and reputation by demonstrably practising the many trades to which she aspires. Furthermore, her circumstances and environment accurately reflect the realities of sixteenth-century town living. The old accounted for a major slice of the late sixteenth-century urban population, though historians face difficulties in accurately assessing their numbers and identifying their occupations.[30] Poor women aged over fifty, at the end of their reproductive life, had still to earn a living and maintain a household. The Norwich census of 1570 shows that the old women listed had stable homes and were still working; seventy-year-old Agnes Brok, for example, married to an out-of-work labourer aged fifty, was the wage-earner of the household; she spun 'smalle stuf & help neighbours at nede' (*Norwich Census*, 30). Heywood's Wise Woman falls squarely into this category of the working old. The Norwich census shows no unemployed women; old women, reacting under the pressure to earn a living, 'seem to have returned [...] to the labour market' once their children had left home, but also because there was social pressure upon them to be employed; the census records censure of a widow of sixty who 'worketh not but go about, & is an unruly woman' (Pelling, 1991, 83). Hence the evident satisfaction with which Wise Woman catalogues her many 'trades.' She is a cut above the elderly poor who had to wash, scour, dress meat and drink and help out neighbours, though she does look after women in childbirth and in other domestic ways, and claims to be able to cure the ailing. She is evidently not incapacitated by advanced age, and therefore does not need to resort to the occupations of the disabled, carding and spinning. Nor does she need to take on a much younger husband as wage-earner. As such, she is in another category of post-menopausal women who 'appear to have been seen as having a positive value in society which men over 50 would have lacked' (Pelling, 1997, 84 and 2001, 34–35), and she is typical of those who could afford to employ a younger person as a live-in help (Pelling, 1997, 87; Smith, 1991, 39–61).

However, there were obvious dangers embedded in the nature of the work performed by old women, and there was widespread condemnation of unlicensed women practitioners of medicine (cf. Cotta, 1612, 24–34; Gale, 1586, sig.D8, D8v) despite a few supporters.[31] John Woodall in his poem in praise of mercury asks of it one 'boone', that 'If th' old wife kill thee with fasting spittle,/suruive to make her patient cripple' (Woodall, 1617, 305–06) and John Halle posed a series of rhetorical questions on the subject:

> what shall we thinke Diogenes would saye,if ye now lived, and sawe so many rusticall craftsmen leave their misteries, and become phisitiens? Or what would Socrates nowe saye, who saide [...] to a paynter that became a phisitien; nowe thou workest subtillye, [...] for wheras before thyne errors were espied, and judged of all men, nowe thou wylt hyde them in the earth, or bury them in the ground. Meanyng [...] that such phisiciens are more like to kil men, than to save or heale them.' (Halle, 1565, 27)

The Norfolk census, contemporary accounts of witchcraft, particularly Goodcole's account of Elizabeth Sawyer, and *The Witch of Edmonton*'s dramatisation of it, measured alongside Pelling's work, Roper's two accounts of the witch craze in southern Germany, and humoral psychopathology, substantially increase our understanding of the role of cunning-folk in early modern rural and urban society. They provide a composite picture of social and cultural circumstances surrounding English and European attitudes towards old women and, it has to be said, persecution of them. This picture is, moreover, satisfyingly rounded out by Normand and Roberts' transcription of and critical commentary upon the dittays of the North Berwick witches, whose circumstances are akin to the real and fictional Elizabeth Sawyer. The real life Elizabeth Sawyer was married, which placed her in dangerous proximity to the young; in the play, she is alone and persecuted for trying to scratch out a living. Here, the relationship of the older characters is one of conflict and malice; it is the aging farmer Old Banks and Old Radcliffe, husband of Anne, who revile Sawyer most consistently. All three of these old people are particularly hard pressed to scratch out a living, yet this does not create a common bond of hardship; Sawyer's attempts to gather sticks are frustrated by Old Banks, who makes her throw them down, and when she refuses, beats her. In his curses he constructs her as a witch long before the devil comes to claim her. She, in turn, is ostracised and angry, and the only way she can get her own back on the old men who beat her down is to claim the identity of a witch.

But even though there are figures of disablement or contempt, the varied stage representations of active old women examined in this chapter do more than raise a shiver or a laugh. *Women in Parliament, The Witch, The Wise Woman of Hogsdon* and even, in part, *The Witch of Edmonton* all articulate a source of cultural anxiety and at the same time provide a potent fantasy of power for old women, the least represented of social groups in their culture. It is moreover an identity squashed under the weight of either physical infirmity or economic hardship or both. Comparably, in the sixteenth and seventeenth centuries, the figure of the comically despicable hag trickled down from the classical ampitheatre into a mainstream theatrical environment whose audience perceived old age both in formulaic terms and as a rich and complex brew of differentiated experiences. However, the comic and grotesque configuration initiated by Aristophanes served in large measure to obscure complex cultural formations in which older women had effective control over their own lives and over the lives of their younger dependents. Old women's lives in different strata of society reveal an agency whose reach was considerably wider than the domestic hearth — and this continuing authority was translated onto the stage intricately and ambivalently.[32]

5   Politics and the workplace

A range of attitudes whose keynote is education inform early modern conceptions of the continuing usefulness in office of the aging and aged. First-wave humanism presents two conflicting images of their role and value as guide and mentor to the young courtier, statesman, churchman, teacher and politician. The one, in which reason and judgment are the baseline for the continuing importance of the old in the training up of the young for public office, filters through from classical prescription, whereas the other pensions them off as no longer useful in public office. In Cicero and Plutarch particularly, the role of the elderly as educators ensures their own active participation in public affairs, and sanctions a politics of age in which, to the frustration of the young, the old hold all the strings.

THE POLITICS OF AGE: IDEALISATION, PRESCRIPTION AND GERONTOCRATIC STRUCTURES

Alberti's *I Libri della famiglia* enshrines humanist values in such classical idealisations as these. The value of a father's role 'is not only to stock the cupboard and the cradle'. His value is much more enduring in that he prepares his son for a life of public service. He must supervise the private and public behaviour of all family members with authority rather than power, with wise counsel in preference to commands, and by using his intelligence and experience as a guide to his family's virtue and honour. An older man knows 'how to steer according to the wind's favour, the waves of popular opinion, and the grace given him by his fellow citizens, toward the harbor of honor, prestige, and authority' (*della famiglia*, 37). If the old want to curb the excesses of the young, and to instil in them due reverence for authority, 'the jewel of old age' (38), they must 'fill them with good counsel and lessons'. They must not follow the example of avaricious old men who, in the name of thrift, make their children unhappy and servile, teaching them 'ugly and low occupations' (38). Memory, example and counsel are virtues with which the old can command the respect, obedience and imitation of the young. To submit to the old, to love and obey them, to respect age and give it all due reverence is the way to achieve public esteem, for 'in the accumulation of years there is long experience of things, and the knowledge of many sorts of conduct, of many ways, and of many human souls'. For all these reasons, the dying Lorenzo expresses regret that he cannot now fully discharge his educative responsibilities (33). The old have seen, heard, and thought through innumerable practical solutions and 'excellent and noble answers to every condition of fortune' (39–40) — an enduring lesson, as Henry Cromwell, major-general of the Irish army at the age of twenty-six and Lord Deputy at twenty-nine, writing in praise of Chancellor William Steele's continuing paternalist instruction some two hundred years later, shows:

> [Steele] read lectures to me of affairs and maxims of state, taught me to carry myself at the Council, gave me rules how things should be managed at the Board [...] and, lest I should forget my lesson, gave men three or four sheets in writing of those rules he thought of most importance [...] I listened to him with a good deal of attention, supposing that, if I got nothing else, I should get his measure. (Thurloe, 1742, vii, 199)

However, in the early sixteenth century neither intellectual nor political strength were so highly valued at court, where the emphasis was much more on performance. The aged artist and courtier, closely connected since both circulated in the same aristocratic milieu, were both threatened by the superior performative skills of younger and more energetic men. According to Castiglione and Vasari the only way aging courtiers and artists can continue in their occupations is by accepting that sentiment, feeling, the senses, are no longer appropriate objects of pursuit; both should abandon the performative in favour of the rational, and rely on their accumulated knowledge for respect and continuing usefulness. They should be content to be revered for superior wisdom and an authority established on the basis of long experience. In practical terms this requires for both to adopt reason and abandon sentiment if they wish to continue to be respected in courtly and artistic circles (Castiglione, 1976, 320; Campbell 2002, 323 34). Erin Campbell argues that aging court artists of the sixteenth century, along with the courtiers, had to surmount the problem of decline of prowess in old age in skills requiring dexterity, strength and nimbleness of foot. Skills demanding a high degree of manual expertise inevitably declined as a man grew older; hence Vasari's criticism of artists such as Titian who continued to work on commission to the detriment of theory in the execution of their works (Vasari, 1987, I: 3, 455), and corresponding praise of artists who retired before the onset of physical deterioration and who, like Michaelangelo, painted and sculpted purely for pleasure in old age; (Vasari,, 1987, I: 3, 384, 385).[1] Hence, too, Castiglione's similar recommendation to aged courtiers to move from performance to consultation and example (Castiglione, 1976, 107–11). Both Vasari and Castiglione perceive old age as a time of stylistic deterioration. For the artist

> the public display of physical decline drew attention to the manual basis for art, which in turn put pressure on the learned image of the artist, producing what could be called a crisis of identity [...] Hence, there is a corresponding sentiment that the principles of art, expressed both as theoretical study or *disegno*, are the means to ensure the transcendence of old age. (Campbell, 2002, 324)

The courtier, too, needed an intellectual basis for the practice of his art, since dancing, practice of arms, painting, drawing, composing sonnets to a mistress, were felt to be exclusively the preserve of the young. Old courtiers who lose the capacity for execution, and old artists who no longer have an 'eye' or a 'hand' for painting, are nevertheless still able to form abstract judgements. Thus Tommaso Laureti, Michaelangelo and Vincenzo Danti in their old age devoted themselves to architecture (Mancini, 1956–57, 233; Danti, 1960, 1: 238–39; Campbell 2002, 236–37) and so indicate an alternative route for the aging artist away from painting and sculpture, which require keen eyesight in assessing proportion and manual dexterity in the depiction of forms and shapes, towards architecture, whose principles of mathematical abstraction require powers of reasoning and judgement that are undimmed by age. Similarly, Castiglione's advice to the aged courtier is to make himself useful to the prince as guide, tutor and role-model (Castiglione, 1976, 319–20; Campbell 2002, 326–27).

But the argument in *The Courtier* for continued usefulness at court is fiercely contested, and much of Castiglione's discourse on the characteristics and effects of advancing years reverses Alberti's adulation of masculine old age. Castiglione rationalises his hostility to aged counsellors by enumerating the ways in which they fall short of the ideal of the youthful courtier and therefore the aging must be removed from the orbit of the prince. They inhabit a bygone world which in their minds can never be surpassed by any present reality. This is a fault 'committed by all the old without exception', and constitutes one of the chief objections to their continuing in public office; since their powers of recall colour their present perceptions, their counsel to the prince is unreliable. The blinkered vision of seeing nothing praiseworthy in the present and nothing blameworthy in the past, the preference of past values over present ones, the belief that they did things better in their day and that everything has been deteriorating since, makes them unsuitable counsellors. Maturity of age, with its long experience which 'in all other respects usually perfects a man's judgement', in this matter distorts it to the extent that it blinds him to the truth that if the world were always growing worse and if fathers were generally better than their sons, society would long ago have become unalterably corrupted. Then as now, they are charged with radically misunderstanding the quality of the youth of their day (Castiglione, 1976, 107).

Castiglione has the physiology of Aristotle and Galen ready to hand for this particular fault in old age. Deterioration of the organs and senses cause loss of memory and poor judgement. The 'bright, clear thoughts' of youth give way to only a faint memory of past pleasures, 'those precious hours [...] when, so long as they last, heaven and earth and the whole of creation seem to be rejoicing and smiling as we look, and a gay springtime of happiness seems to flower in our thoughts as in a delightful and lovely garden' (107). The old, in the winter of their lives, have lost the capacity (if not the desire) to enjoy life, a constraint which affects an old person's ability to recall pleasures accurately. Castiglione uses the trope of the ship of mortality to illustrate the supposed untrustworthiness of judgements made by those whose senses are blunted by old age: they are like those sailing out of harbour who seem to experience themselves and their ship as standing still while the people on land move farther away. The illusion of past pleasures is like this; they recede while 'we, sailing away in the ship of mortality, cross the stormy sea which engulfs and swallows us up one by one; nor are we ever permitted to regain the land but, constantly assailed by hostile winds, eventually we come to grief upon a rock.' Old age, 'the senile spirit,' is an unsuitable vessel for the pleasures of life. It is pointless to seek them, and to maintain one's position at court (108), given the crucial role the courtier plays in shaping the prince's thoughts, actions and accomplishments (317–319). Since the courtier needs to be more skilled and more perfect in virtue than the prince in order to instruct him, an older man would be useless because his courtly accomplishments and attitudes, formed in a bygone era, will be out of date (317). The prime virtues to be fostered in a young prince — justice, generosity, magnanimity — cannot by definition be entrusted to courtiers advanced in years, since they are the very opposite of the character of old age, which is faulty in judgement, penny-pinching and mean of spirit (319).

Yet even though the old view court life in former times, along with past pleasures, through rose-tinted spectacles,[2] there still remains a limited role for the aged courtier, despite his lack of relevance in a milieu composed of aspiring and accomplished youth. The courtier, in similar vein to the doctor whose objective is to make men healthy, aspires to make his prince more virtuous. Unbecoming as it is for an elderly courtier to be a frontline practitioner in music, merrymaking, games, arms, and the art of love, he can still instruct the prince. For even if he is too old to participate, his years of practice and experience have brought more knowledge, finer judgement and a more perfect understanding of how to instruct his prince in these accomplishments. The old become exemplars in virtue through merit and authority, and as such make the best advisers and tutors to the prince after all, since 'only rarely does wisdom not wait upon age, and especially as regards what we learn from experience' (320). His continuing usefulness in the politics of court life depends upon retirement from the competitive arena of love. If he showed the feelings and aped the actions of a young man in love, he could not instruct his prince. Love intrigues would make him negligent in his duties[3] and besides, he would expose himself to contempt and derision. Deprivation in the happiness of love thus becomes a virtue indispensable to the education of the prince; sacrifice of love augments the old courtier's perfection in freedom from its snares, and ensures his continuing fitness for court politics (323–28).

In the real world of Tudor, Stuart and Carolingian public affairs, however, age held on to the reins of power in prescription and practice. The authority of the old, promoted in tracts, sermons, and dialogues between old and young, resided in their value as educators and had its source in the credo that the young had no investment in knowledge, which belonged exclusively to age and should therefore be passed down to receptively passive youth (Thomas 1976, 207–10). The church, the universities, government, Inns of Court, civil authorities in towns and local communities — all operated in hierarchies underwritten by the seniority of age. Public institutions were gerontocratic; young men had to go through the ranks in the teaching profession (Thomas, 1976, 208; *Wentworth Papers*, 21),[4] the law, (Thomas, 1976, 211), and the governing body of schools (208–09). Apprenticeships took a long time to complete; the statute of artificers was drawn up to safeguard the interests of 'ancient householders' and 'aged artificers' from young upstarts in the trade (Thomas, 1976, 214). In church, the front benches were reserved for the elders in the community while the young sat at the back. Richard Carew, writing in the first few years of the seventeenth century, records that games and feast-day celebrations depended upon age differentials, where age, not wealth held precedence (Carew,1953, 144), while the most senior positions in urban government were ranked according to seniority in age (Thomas, 1976, 209).

The belief that the young were not ready for politics had its sources in ancient formulations for government. Plato's *Republic* , his *Laws*, Cicero's belief, echoed by Plutarch, that the wisest politicians could only be found among the old, provide just a few instances of this truism, and led Gerrard Winstanley[5] to want to keep anyone under forty away from public office (Winstanley, 1941, 543). He prescribed in favour of the creation of a new category of general Overseers aged sixty plus (551), who 'shall be freed from all labor and work, unless they will themselves,' so they can devote themselves entirely to law enforcement (577).[6] Arise Evans for his part, wanting to show his readers 'a form of Government that hath not been yet made known to the world' but prefigured in Christ's Gospel (Evans, 1659, 28), did not want to see 'the chief of Great Britain and Ireland enter into his Power and Government until he be above fifty years of age' (29), nor anyone below fifty elected to Parliament (30).

Pro-age political ideologies from Plato's *Republic* through to More's *Utopia* and Bacon's *New Atlantis*, writings which place the aged at the centre of the state's educative projects and organise their ideal societies around the bedrock of aged authority, experience and wisdom, informed Elizabethan understanding of comic action as one in which old men should instruct and young men should be full of the imperfections of youth (Whetstone, 1578, 1, 59–60). And they led Gerard Winstanley, writing in the interregnum, to organise his ideal Commonwealth in *The Law of Freedom*, 1652, around the premise that 'all children shall be educated and trained up in subjection to parents and elder people more than they now are' (*Works*, 1941, 515). The education of the young, like all apprenticeships, was to be a long drawn-out affair, and was institutionalised in Tudor, Stuart and Carolingian governments. According to Thomas, between the years 1542–1642, the average age for Privy Councillors, Tudor and Stuart Treasurers, Lord Chancellors and Lord Keepers, Speakers of the House of Commons and most judges was 'never less than fifty-one' (Thomas, 1976, 211). In the sixteenth and seventeenth centuries particularly, Thomas finds a 'sustained drive to subordinate persons in their teens and early twenties and to delay their equal participation in the adult world' (214). It is certainly true that in 1620, James I proclaimed that knights and burgesses should be experienced men of integrity elected to Parliament for their gravity, ability and high intellectual quality. Thus by definition 'young and unexperienced men that are not ripe and mature for so grave a Councell' were excluded (Larkin & Hughes, eds., *Royal Proclamations*, vol. 1, 494). The resulting debate in the Commons on this matter was on whether to exclude anyone under the age of 21 from election as Knight or Burgess to Parliament, 'he beinge unfitt to dispose of other mens estates who cannot dispose of his owne' (*Commons Debates*, 1621, 2: 460; 4: 446; 5: 221; 6: 205). These directives were issued at a time when power was very much in the hands of James' younger favourites — Robert Carr, Viscount Rochester, later Earl of Somerset and then George Villiers, Marquis, later Duke, of Buckingham, so the insistence on the need for age and experience in office could well be interpreted as defensive.

So for an early modern audience the youthful takeover of positions of high authority in *King Lear* and *The Old Law* is shocking and execrable from the point of view of institutionalised codes of practice, interesting and exciting from the point of view of repressed youth. But a glance at the ages of the holders of these important offices shows that the matter was not quite so clear-cut. Were these offices earmarked for those in real old age, or for those who had reached the perfect age of man (cf. Primaudaye, 1589, 537; Dove, 1986, 14) — that is, the middle years? Fifty, according to early modern typologies, was the onset of old age for women only; for men, it was the perfect age (Dove, 1986, 28, 34, 36). Shakespeare's history plays are ambivalent on the effects of young men at the helm of army and state. The clashes between young men in high office and older more sedate statesmen reflect youth's challenge to the gerontocratic cast of Elizabethan politics rather than a plea for the young to take over the running of the nation; at the same time, the plays do not gloss over the shortfall in political acumen of the older generation. In *Henry V*, for example, it is possible to account for the young king's actions as issuing from the corrupt and self-interested counsel of older men — churchmen, at that, and Henry's rationalisation for war, delivered to soldiers as thoughtful and more experienced than himself, as the outcome of youthful naïveté and political, if not military, inexperience. As they embrace Aristotle's neat division of rule between young men in charge of armies while elder statesmen supervise the safety of the realm (Aristotle, 1981, 417), so the plays simultaneously show the terrible results of young and inexperienced men heading army and state and the bad faith of greedy over-politicised churchmen as well as the uneasy consciences of those who usurp the king. Above all Shakespeare's history plays depend upon the analogy of the state to the family, and assume the right of the most senior member of each to govern. Thus, King Henry in *Henry IV* parts 1 and 2 who continues to regulate domestic and public affairs from his deathbed, and the figure of John of Gaunt in *Richard II*, whose wisdom continues to exert an influence beyond the grave, are good examples of old age's continuing engagement in public affairs. Yet destabilised readings are possible on this score, too; elders are liable to censure and loss of office if they should 'vent their passion' in the manner of Richard II, or become envious (like the Bishops in *Henry V*), or wilfully set themselves up against the Law, as does Henry IV (cf. Winstanley, 1941, 552).

King Lear emerged in an environment in which old men unambiguously held the reins of power, and it challenges this throttling of scope for the younger generation. Particularly in the 1590s, the counsellors to the aging Queen who enforced rigid adherence to order and degree were all in their sixties and were reluctant to step down from their privileged position as mentors and controllers of the excesses of the younger members of the court. This was mirrored in the wider social scene, where preachers and poets played their part in maintaining the status quo by appealing to Christian humility, through promotion of the myth of the wheel of fortune and by constant reference to classical ideals of old age (Marx, 1985a, 213). Then as now, political leaders were active long after the usual retirement age. In industrial and pre-industrial societies old age does not hinder continuation in office; even senility does not necessarily lead to a changeover in leadership or council. The investment of royal authority by Divine Right could not easily be overthrown,[7] and it is more difficult to 'strip the aged of the insignia of office', though real power may lie elsewhere.[8] Jack Goody provides good reasons for this; the continuation of the old in political office delays the problem of succession, and guarantees some sort of order in difficult times of transition: 'an interest in peace postpones the transfer of title' (Goody, 1976, 127). The principle of changeover at death only was certainly in place during Elizabeth's final years, which witnessed the deaths of most of the councillors appointed in her early years on the throne. Camden notes each of these deaths as they occur in each year of her reign. They come thick and fast from 1596 onwards.[9] 1598 saw the deaths of Philip of Spain, aged about 70 and Thomas Stapleton, Richard Cosins and Edmund Spenser, 'three more 'worthy countrymen' (Camden, 1630, 131, 134). In that year, too, William Cecil, 'being spent with continuall discontentment of mine, the gowt, and old age' wrote to the Queen in 'sorrow and anguish of heart' to beseech her to let him give up 'his Offices of Magistracy'. Despite the Queen's comfort visits he died an enviably quiet death a few days later, 'when hee had liued long enough to nature, long enough to his glory, but not long enough to his country' (Camden, 1630, 127). By 1602, Richard Hooker, Lord North, treasurer of the Queen's household, Henry Herbert, Earle of Pembroke, Henry, Lord Norris, Peregrine Berty, Lord Willoughby of Eresby, and Alexander Nowell, dean of St. Pauls, had all met their ends (Camden, 1630, 134).

The circumstances surrounding Elizabeth's death provide a telling illustration of actual rather than ritual strength up to the moment itself of changeover. The many varying and often contradictory eye-witness accounts leave readers with the distinct impression that the transition of England's body politic from one monarch to another was far from unproblematic.[10] Uniting in one person the power of church and state, Elizabeth held on to the reins of power to the very moment of her death. The French ambassador's report had the Queen robbed of speech from 18 March, six days before she died (Birch, 1754, 2, 507) whereas Chamberlain regarded it as 'obstinate silence' (Chamberlain, 1939, 1, 188–89).[11] Clapham, meanwhile, explained it as an affliction of the mind, but which did not betoken loss of understanding (Clapham, 1951, 98). But what is clear is that Elizabeth contrived, whether by speech or gesture, to issue last-minute directives to her bishops and councillors.[12] Robert Carey and John Clapham's version of the moment in which the Queen named her successor is that she assented to James by placing her hand to her head and drawing around it the shape of a circle, 'discovering thereby as it was said, what she had long before concealed' (Clapham, 1951, 99; Carey, 1972, 59). Alternatively, a manuscript attributed to Robert Cecil's secretary reports her as perfectly able to speak on March 23, the day before she died, whereon she told Nottingham, Cecil and a third unnamed privy councillor that her seat was the seat of kings, and she 'would have no Rascall succeed' her but a king (Nichols, 1823, 3, 607). A third account, that of her seventeen-year-old Catholic lady-in-waiting, Elizabeth Southwell, attributes her silence to a sore throat (Southwell, 1996, line 69) and has her die 'ynstantlie' after her meeting with her Council (line 77) to whom she obstinately refused to name her successor. It was only after she breathed her last that 'the Councell went forth and reported she meant "the K of Scots"' (lines 77–78).

Coinciding with the deaths of those whose tenure of office spanned her entire reign, the death of the Queen marked the transition from Tudor to

Stuart rule by a changeover from elderly female to young male; it did not betoken a change in either gerontocratic policies or practice. It is true that on occasion gerontocracy was not accepted so meekly (on the surface, at any rate) by aspiring younger statesmen and courtiers, who found their ambition thwarted and their creativity blocked. During the interregnum, much younger men were appointed to positions of heightened responsibility; Fairfax was commander of the New Model army at thirty-three, Ludlow became military ruler of Ireland at the same age, and younger judges and mayors began to be appointed. However, the Restoration brought things back onto the ageist track with the appointment of a Lord Chief Justice and two new archbishops in their seventies (Thomas, 1976, 212–13). According to Thomas' calculations for the hundred years between 1542 and 1642, the Privy Council was composed of members aged between 51 and 61, and Lord Chancellors, Treasurers, Speakers of the House of Commons, Lord Keepers and Judges were appointed in their fifties. Secretaries of state were usually in their late forties, Bishops and lawyers in their forties, and Chief Justices of King's Bench in their early sixties. (Thomas, 1976, 211). In 1597, the aging Elizabeth told the thirty-four-year-old Robert Sidney that she thought him 'too young for any place about her' (Collins, 1746, 2: 31).[13] Officers of state had all to be 'grave and sad men who are above the levities of youth, and beneath the dotages of old age' (Waterhous, 1663, 361).

POLITICS, TRADITION AND JUSTICE IN *THE OLD LAW*

The Old Law enacts these reservations about the value of the old in office at the same time as it gives currency to the gerontocratic ideals of Cicero and Plutarch which confirm their enduring usefulness to the state. Tony Bromham has shown how this play would have been understood to audiences of its own day as 'having extensive reference to a current legal controversy and also to a particular moment in factional court politics' (Bromham, 2001, 118). In addition, the play makes a connection between the scandalous courtship of Frances Howard by Robert Carr before she sued her husband, the Earl of Essex, for divorce on the grounds of impotence and the influx of suitors to Eugenia, headed by Simonides, before her old husband is dispatched by the law. Eugenia describes her husband as one 'whose strength lies in his breath,/Weakness in all parts else' and this is by no means the only hint at his impotence (*Old Law*, 2. 2, 144–45; 176–77, 180–81). Once married, Howard and Carr were condemned for the murder of Sir Thomas Overbury. Howard was pregnant, but the rumour was that she was feigning pregnancy in order to stay execution. In the play, appearing only seven years after the trial, Eugenia's avowal that 'next to procreation fitting' she would 'either be destroying men or getting' (4.2, 295–96), in its 'chilling' image of murder and conception, strikingly communicates a specific reference to the Howard case (Bromham, 2001, 118). This topical connection, with its attendant relationship to age matters, is further emphasised by the reversed pairing of the Eugenia/Lisander strand in the main plot (to do with a young wife's desire to dispose of an old husband) with the Gnotho and Agatha sub plot wherein a husband schemes to dispatch his old wife (Bromham 2001, 122–23). However, the play's foundational concern with age has no referent in the topical relationships. Eugenia and Gnotho are each legally tied to an aging spouse that they are reluctant to include in their plans for the future, and with some reason, since Lisander may be impotent and Agatha is no longer of child-bearing age. The play thus maintains two contradictory positions harnessed to a third; derision of old age, exposure of the heartlessness of the contemptuous young, and the role of the law in paradoxically creating, encouraging, regulating and finally punishing generational strife.

The 'current legal controversy' to which the play alludes concerns the conflict between Sir Edward Coke, the Lord Chief Justice, and King James I (Bromham, 1984, 327–39) and may serve as an introduction to the means the play employs in dealing with its central concern of challenges to and negotiations of the primary role of youthful obedience to the wisdom and experience of the old in politics. James I's absolutism in the years following the Oath of Allegiance in 1606 (which insisted that Catholics deny the power of the Pope to excommunicate or depose him as the lawful king) placed in conflict the authority of the state with the right to uphold religious belief and conscience and led to challenges of the royal prerogative by defenders of the Common Law. Edward Coke, the Lord Chief Justice, was required to stand down from the King's Bench in 1616 because he challenged the King's 'learned counsaile' (Chamberlain, 1939, 2: 36) in the Chancery courts and his right to 'review and call in question what judgements soever passe at the common law' (36). This order by the King, issued on 26 July 1616, upheld the Court of Chancery's right to imprison those who did not obey their injunctions over and against Coke's popular championship of the principles of common law (cf. Holdsworth, 1903, 1: 461),[14] ultimately deriving from God himself, and therefore beyond the scope of man to challenge or alter however convoluted it might be (Prest, 1972, 143; Bromham, 1984, 336–37). For example, going against Francis Bacon's advice, Coke insisted that the King should not interfere in legal matters, and refused to sound out judges' opinions before a trial (Bromham, 1984, 336–37). Middleton and Rowley's play pits the 'old law' of God and nature against the 'new' law which placed the king above the workings of the law, gave him the right to preside in the Star Chamber, and to interfere in trials. It places advocacy of each of these positions into the mouths of the two youthful male leads. Simonides, one of the most ambivalent and flawed characters in the play, upholds at its beginning the 'new' law that enables a ruler to override the law by stating that whoever is 'above the law may mitigate/The rigour of the law' (*Old Law*, 1.1, 310–11). Cleanthes on the other hand, as the youthful upholder of God's law (as opposed to those made by man), is subjected to the judgement and sentence of the newly appointed youthful judges. Cleanthes protests lengthily, and his view is upheld by Duke Evander, a *deus ex machina* figure who directs the action and reinstates the authority of the old (5.1, 270–405).

Cleanthes' evocation of the Last Judgement when all will be required to account for themselves before God goes against the argument of the treatise *God and the King*, anonymously printed but attributed to the King, which states that the 'higher bond of duetie' to a sovereign is part of but higher than the law of nature which requires children to obey parents, for it places a subject's obedience to his monarch over and above 'priuate families' (*God and the King*, 1616, 3). In other words, duty to political regimes is above both family and law, but as Bromham convincingly argues, this imperative is reversed in *The Old Law*, where a son's (and daughter's) duty to a father is shown to be paramount (Bromham, 1984, 334). Thus the arguments for political obedience are put into question because they issue from the mouth of Simonides, the bad son (*Old Law*, 5.1, 236–43). In the final resolution, the 'old' law is both upheld and denied in favour of the elderly. In its sense of the law of God, laid down in the Old Testament and decreeing that old men should be honoured above all others, it is upheld; but it is denied in its sense of a law dealing summarily with the old.

More broadly, the play's social/cultural significance appears in its decision to confront the question of what the state should do with the 'useless' elderly in a manner both akin and opposed to the tragic intricacies of *King Lear*. Simon Goulart, in his encomiastic study on old age, writes disparagingly of a 'very rude' ancient Roman proverb in which men of threescore were to be

> cast downe headlong, from the top of a bridge to the bottome, because they were dotardes, and men past labour and vse, and fit for nothing; or because in times past, the young men of Rome (as Ouid thinketh, in scorne) would iustle old men as they mett them vpon narrow bridges, that so by drowning them, they might not stand n their way, to crosse and oppose them, or giue their aduice in their doings and counsells' (Goulart, 1621, 45–46)

This 'Roman' custom has a long pedigree. The tradition of putting the old to death is mentioned in diverse classical, medieval and early modern texts. Pomponius Mela, a Latin geographer writing in AD 43 described how some societies

> slay their own parents and near relations before they reach the time of decline and old age [...] But when old age does appear, those so afflicted depart from society , they wait for death. The philosophers among them, however, through their study of wisdom, do not wait for death to

arrive, but, instead, often cast themselves onto the bonfire — his they consider to be some glorious ending. (Mela, 1997, 129)[15]

Pliny the Elder records in AD77 that when old people among the Hyperboreans (thought to live beyond the North Pole) were tired of living they flung themselves off a high rock into the sea (Westwood, 1985, 240).[16] The story to which Goulart refers appears in Ovid's *Fasti* (a verse treatise on the Roman calendar) and describes a custom of the Vestal Virgins to throw thirty plaited rush figures of old men from the bridge at Sublici into the Tiber (Ovid, 1931, 621). Ovid's explains its origins in the former practice of young men hurling feeble old men from the bridges, 'in order that they themselves alone should have the vote', but censures those who subscribe to this story: 'he who believes that after sixty years men were put to death, accuses our forefathers of a wicked crime'. In answer to the invocation to Tiber to inform the poet of the truth and origin of this rite, Tiber replies obliquely, telling story of 'the Arcadian Evander' who came from far (Ovid, 1931, 623–34; Bett, 1952, 97). The naming of the lawgiver in *The Old Law* as Evander thus has multiple intertextual resonances which suggest the wide classical lexicon of its authors and their attention to stories of the old in public contest with the young.

The myth continues to live in medieval and early modern literature, with strong evocations of the old age theme in both *Lear* and *The Old Law*. In a twelfth-century Latin story an old man surrendered his property to his daughter's husband, and like Lear, was treated increasingly badly until he was driven out of the house. He pretended he had a chest of money. When the family opened it, however, all they found was a mallet, with the following inscription: 'With such a betel (club) may he be smitten, so that all the world know it, that gives his son all his goods and himself goes a-begging'. The story was evidently in circulation. A Herefordshire almshouse in Bargates, Leominster is fronted by a figure carrying a hatchet and inscribed underneath by this verse: 'He that gives away all/Before hi is Dead,/Let em take this Hatchet/And knock him onye head' (Westwood, 1985, 240). This rhyme and the tradition behind it are of course much older than the 1737 almshouse over whose portals it appears (Westwood, 1985, 240–42). The English version of the rhyme is retold (without rhyme or mallet) by Abraham de la Pryme about a man in Winterton, and the Prussian version tells of a Count Schulenberg who saved the life of an old man being clubbed to death by his sons at a place called Jammerholz or 'Woeful Wood'. The old man lived another twenty years as his hall-porter — so much for being 'of no more use'. Similarly, a Countess of Mansfeld in the fourteenth century rescue the life of an old man on Luneberg Heath, while George II saved a peasant in the Göhrde Walde from being beaten to death by a grandson who had already dug the old man's grave (243).

Aubrey conveys the early modern version of the myth (Aubrey, 1686–87, 19) as a country story of a club called 'the Holy-mawle' which, according to popular tradition, used to hang behind the church door for a son to 'fetch' when his father was seventy, 'effoete, & of no more use' to knock him on the head with (19). Mallets associated with hitting old people on the head survive in the accounts of German scholars of the nineteenth century concerning the front of a house at Osnabrück and on the city gates of several towns in Silesia and Saxony where they used to hang, accompanied by verses almost identical with the Bargates rhyme. Grimm, for example, identifies these mallets as the hammer-symbol of the German thunder god, once suspended outside heathen temples, which 'with the coming of Christianity found place on churches and gates to cities as symbols of good luck' (Grimm, 1888, V. 4, 542; Westwood, 242).

Present-day mythographers record the survival of a memorial version of the Holy Maul in Shropshire and Staffordshire, along with the tradition of 'Valhalla cliffs' in Sweden (Bett, 1952, 97), as recounted in the Saga of Göttrek and Rolf (Elton, 1882, 91).[17] It was the custom for the aged who had grown tired of life though still in good health to travel there and to be pushed over into the lakes below by their children. If they were too weak to travel under their own steam, tradition has it that a son (or any male kinsman) could save them the ignominy of dying in bed by beating them to death with a 'family club' (Bett, 1952, 97; Elton, 1882, 90–93). This custom of putting the aged to death was practiced among the Wends, the Slavs, the Prussians, the Westphalians, the natives of Iceland (Bett, 1952, 98), the Hyperboreans who lived behind the Rhipoean hills beyond the North Pole, the Swedes, the Pommeranians, the Poles and the Prussians, who, in addition to the old and infirm, 'unhesitatingly' put to death in infancy 'all the daughters except one [...], the sick and the deformed' (Elton, 1882, 92; see also Westwood, 1985, 240).

King Lear and *The Old Law* powerfully evoke these tales. Gloucester travels all the way to Dover, to put an end to his life by asking a stranger (who, significantly, turns out to be his reviled son Edgar) to lead him to the edge of the cliff, and in *The Old Law* the old must be pushed over a high promontory into the sea. It seems that the playwrights were responding to complex and ambivalent attitudes on the matter of age by recourse to the myths of Valhalla and the family cliffs.[18] England at the end of the sixteenth century saw the death not only of the most powerful and long-serving monarch, but also of the deaths of the most powerful and influential men who had served her. As noted earlier, the years 1598–1617 record the ends of significant figures in the reigns of Elizabeth and James respectively. These deaths perhaps more than any others heralded the end of an era which began in religious uncertainty and ended with the triumph of Protestantism and therefore the routing of Catholic hopes. Furthermore, the deaths occurred in the years immediately preceding the staging of *The Old Law* of the last of the councillors that James inherited from Elizabeth. Robert Cecil, Earl of Salisbury died in 1612, and Thomas Egerton, the Lord Chancellor died aged seventy-seven in 1617. Both were succeeded by younger men. These events form the background to tensions between the generations in public life and push the conflict between youth and age in *The Old Law* into another area of topical significance.[19]

In addition to its topicality and its treatment of specific political issues, the play reappraises ancient doctrines on the value of old age in politics. This is suggested in the first instance by the use of well-chosen Greek names for the characters (cf. Bromham, 1994, 510–11). Deriving, like the subject matter of *Coriolanus*, from North's translation of Plutarch's *Lives*, the names in *The Old Law* evoke the political stances and public personalities of ancient Greece. The good son, Cleanthes, is aptly named after the stoic philosopher whose only surviving work, *Hymn to Zeus*, provided renaissance writers with the means of combining pagan stoicism with christianity. Simonides the bad son is named after the rapacious and opportunistic Greek poet Simonides of Amorgos and Ceos, who used the iambus 'for satire and controversy' (Hammond 1967, 172). He was invited by the tyrant sons of Peisistratus to their court (183), and praised the tyrants Felon, Hieron and Theron as founders of Western Hellenism (271), thereby confirming an association with tyrannous rule. This, coupled with his belief that fast-changing circumstances made men evil (274), aligns him with Simonides in the play, whose opportunism propels him into endorsing the end of his parents' lives. Even more to the point, the naming of the older characters associates them with just laws. Creon and his wife Antigona, whose names evoke the Sophoclean tragedy in which a child sacrifices its life to save the reputation of a father by upholding divine over human law, create a link with Cleanthes' attempts to save his father from a cruel man-made law. Creon also recalls the Greek poet Anacreon who 'laughed at life and death with [...] courage' (275) and praised patriotic self-sacrifice. The Spartan King Leonidas who led the forces against Xerxes at Thermopylae and died there in defence of his country (231, 236) is the namesake of Cleanthes' father Leonides. The naming of Eugenia's reluctantly aging husband, Lisander, suggests this character's ambivalence — he gains the sympathy of the audience but also their contempt (Bromham, 1994, 511). The Spartan commander and statesman after whom he is named, the historic Lysander, had a healthy contempt for the power of gold. Unlike his fellow countrymen, whose cupidity earned them the warning from the oracle at Delphi that 'love of money and nothing else will destroy Sparta' (Hammond, 1967, 441), he 'endured poverty very well' and was not at all enslaved or corrupted by wealth, keeping 'not one drachma' of the riches he imported after the war with Athens — an ambivalence reinforced by the fact that 'he filled his country with riches and the love of them, and took away from them the glory of not admiring money' (Plutarch, *Lives*, web page). Yet 'to those who loved honest and noble behaviour in their commanders', Lysander was duplicitous and self-interested, managing most things in the war by deceit, extolling what was just when it was profitable, and when it was not, using that which was convenient, instead of that which, was good; and not judging truth to be in nature better than falsehood, but setting a value upon both according to interest. (Plutarch, *Lives*, web page)

He tried to alter the Spartan constitution by stealth (Hammond, 441;) and dealt cruelly with his enemies (Hammond, 417; Plutarch, web page).

The naming of Evander, instigator of the law against the old, rounds off a chain of associations in its double evocation of the Evander in Strabo's *Geography* who 'planted' a colony from Arcadia to Italy (Strabo, 1854, 1: 343; Bromham, 1994, 511) and the Evander in Virgil's *Aeneid* who was the pious builder of the first citadel of Rome. The choice of Evander for the lawgiver in the play is not accidental. It reassures the classically educated among its audience that resolution in *The Old Law* will not disadvantage the old; Aeneas encounters the aged but impoverished King Evander[20] whose generosity and help is tendered in recognition of the resemblance between Aeneas and his father Anchises, and Evander regrets that

> [...] the chill blood that creeps within my veins,
> And age, and listless limbs unfit for pains,
> And a soul conscious of its own decay,
> Have forc'd me to refuse imperial sway.
>   (Virgil, *Aenid*, bk. 8, web page)

Apt naming of the *dramatis personae* thus provides an economical point of entry into the play's exploration of the politics of age, and of establishing conceptual links with the ancient world in which the role of elder statesmen was prevalent — and contested.

The play opens with a discussion of Evander's recently inaugurated law condemning to death all men over eighty and women over sixty because they are deemed to be no longer useful to the state. The characters range themselves on the side either of those who condemn the law, or those who welcome it. The latter are jubilant because it allows them to inherit their parents' wealth immediately, with no constraints placed by terms of wills and conditions of inheritance, whereas the former must resort to illegal means to safeguard the lives of their parents. The play thus stages a reversal of order in which the law-abiding but morally corrupt range themselves against the morality and humanity of the lawbreakers.[21] Critical of youth in positions of power, the playwrights use the immediate scandal of the fall of the king's favourite Robert Carr and his replacement by Villiers, Marquis of Buckingham in the King's private affections and public promotion to comment upon familiar ground covered by the prescriptive literature of bipolar attitudes; suspicion of the young in positions of authority, restiveness and anxiety about monopoly of key positions of power by the old.

It is for this reason that Simonides places all his hopes in the strength, permanency and forcefulness of the new law. The opening scenes present hope for the young: 'Here's a good age now/For those that have old parents and rich inheritance!' (*Old Law*, 1.1, 34) and a forceful critique of gerontocratic political structures. The law will clear the way for 'younger men to walk lustily in' to positions encumbered by 'fellows that lie bedrid in their offices;' churchmen, lawyers and senators past 'even the second infancy' will be removed from office at last, making way for young men 'to leap into their dignities' (1.1, 38–45).

The lawyers extol the virtues of the new edict, declaring that never, in the living memory of the lawgivers of Greece, has there been the passing of a law 'more grave and necessary' (1.1, 55). The First Lawyer explains the shortcomings of what has gone before:

> Draco's oligarchy, that the government
> Of community reduced into few,
> Framed a fair state; Solon's *chreokopia*,
> That cut off poor men's debts to their rich creditors,
> Was good and charitable, but not full allowed;
> His *seisactheia* did reform that error,
> His honourable senate of Areopagitae.
> Lycurgus was more loose and gave too free
> And licentious reins unto his discipline —
> As that a young woman, in her husband's weakness,
> Might choose her able friend to propagate,
> That so the commonwealth might be supplied
> With hope of lusty spirits. Plato did err,
> And so did Aristotle, allowing
> Lewd and luxurious limits to their laws. (1.1, 59–73)

In terms of inaugurating just and good laws, its promoters claim, the new legislation expands the statutory changes made by Draco and Solon designed to promote political well-being in the state, and corrects errors in policy made by Plato in *The Republic* and *The Laws*, both models for genrontocracies in More's *Utopia* and Bacon's *New Atlantis*. These writers put their faith in improving mankind by controlling conditions of birth and public service and by championing age in office. In so far as it interrogates formulations of constitutional law as distinct from the laws of nature, Aristotle's critique of the Spartan constitution (Aristotle, 1981, 139–47) provides an important point of critical reference for the play, and in so doing indicates its affiliation to the education theme. The 'lawgiver' Lycurgus who was its founder framed the constitution largely around the existence and function of the board of Elders, twenty-eight individuals over the age of sixty elected from the aristocracy. Their extensive sway in politics was grounded in absolute and enduring supremacy over the judiciary and administration. Aristotle points out the drawbacks to their authority. Though these men may well have come from a respectable background and were trained to a degree of excellence, they were old, with decaying mental powers which rendered them unfit to have 'lifelong supreme power to decide important cases' (146). If the education they received in their youth should fall short of the standards of excellence required of such an office, then even Lycurgus himself would doubt their credentials as 'good men'. In practice, the Elders were corrupt, maintaining their positions by bribery and favouritism. They too therefore should be subject to the kind of scrutiny they provided of all other offices, but from which they were themselves exempt. Furthermore, the manner of their election for appointment to the highest position in the political hierarchy was 'childish' and 'all wrong', for a man deemed worthy of the office should not 'himself solicit it' (147). The best kind of holder of high office is the man who is best fit for it, yet Lycurgus 'begins by making the citizens ambitious and then uses their ambition as a means of getting the Elder elected,' even though misplaced ambition and cupidity are at the root of most acts of injustice (147).

Initially the play renders problematic Aristotle's dictum that the system of selecting Elders from the aristocracy has shortcomings in that those in power may not necessarily be the best educated or the most fit to rule, though ultimately it questions his assumption that the old are unfit for office by virtue of their age. By placing the explication and enforcement of the law in the hands of rapacious young lawyers, the play's action reverses Plato's requirement in *The Laws* that judges should be fair-minded, well educated enough to train up the young, and above the age of fifty on appointment (Plato, *The Laws*, webpage, book 7, 147–82). The relevance of Evander's new edict, which guarantees improvements to the physical well-being of the state by putting a limit on life, to the question of whether society should abide by the laws of nature or man, is manifest in the first scene when the young enthusiastically welcome the edict as an improvement upon nature.[22] By culling those who are no longer useful to the state, the law concerning the old perfects nature by doing nature's work in a speedier and more systematic way; it 'shall finish what nature lingered at' (*Old Law*, 1.1, 123). The law is predicated upon a narrowly functional view of the nature of humankind described by Aristotle in which old age is seen as a condition of unstoppable decay. Nature in old people is corrupt (Aristotle, 1984, 1, 760–61); his critique in *Politics* of the Spartan law issues from this understanding of nature, and the play indulges the viewpoint that old men, corrupted by nature, are no longer of use to society. In a later section, however, Aristotle meets with a contradiction when he concedes the value of the old and the inadequacies of the young in certain spheres of government. If in the ideal constitution all citizens participate equally in its running, then old men will have to be soldiers even though they no longer have the constitution for it, and young men will function as judges and 'statesmen' despite youth's lack of balanced judgement. Yet if these age-groups do not perform these functions they will not be doing what it behoves citizens to do. Aristotle resolves this by proposing a succession of age-related activities; citizens will be first soldiers, then judges and statesmen, then be finally pensioned off into the priesthood (Aristotle, 1981, 414–17). *The Old Law* shows what happens when this principle of succession is bypassed and young men supplant the old as judges. The Duke has had to promote the youthful courtiers into chief ministers of justice since all the old ones 'he hath sent a-fishing' (*Old Law*, 5.1, 23). They must pronounce judgement upon Cleanthes for the crime of concealing his old father, a perversion of both nature and the law: 'Never by a prince were such young judges made/But now the cause requires it, if you mark it' (5.1, 20). Hippolita and he have to plead their case before judges whose lack of years do not suit their calling and who 'sway' themselves with equity and truth they have not been in the calling long enough to have earned, so it is unlikely that the young couple will witness 'Once in [a] lifetime [...] grave heads/Placed upon young men's shoulders' (5.1, 60–64). Cleanthes confirms that old men make the best judges, and that Heaven has no deputy in this upside down world where young men sit upon the bench formerly occupied by their fathers (5.1, 208–28).

Plato, Cicero and Plutarch carve out a prominent niche for the old in state affairs, but Aristotle advocates a more even-handed distribution of authority. He concedes that the old are past use on the battlefield and so cannot defend their country (that is the role nature assigns to the young (Aristotle, 1981, 416; cf. *The Old Law*, 1.1, 150–77); they are past the age of procreation, so can no longer provide 'further issue to their posterity' (1.1, 156); but the play denies the old their right in sharing political responsibility on the assumption that they are all in their dotage, so can no longer hold authority or expect to be consulted in matters of state; their lives are grown burdensome to themselves and their heirs. So they must give up their prominent positions to the young, who claim to work for the good of their country yet 'wanting the means to maintain it, are like to grow old' (1.1, 162–3) before they can come into their inheritance. As for women, they have never performed public service for their country; they are never called upon to defend it, or to advise the government. Their only social use is to provide for posterity by giving birth, which they cannot do at the age of threescore.

The play thus parodies the notion that man-made law puts right the shortcomings of a society which, in the Platonic scheme of things, overvalues age, and disregards its limitations (1.1, 116–75). But as in *King Lear* there runs alongside another view of nature; Leonides extols the virtues of his daughter-in-law in terms that presuppose the benevolence of the law of procreation that passes on good qualities from parent to child. The wonder of Hippolita is

> That the strong tie of wedlock should do more
> That nature in her nearest ligaments
> Of blood and popagation! I should ne'er

Have begot such a daughter of my own.
A daughter-in-law? Law were above nature
Were there more such children. (1.1, 401–06)

The play promotes familial duties by suggesting that qualities of compassion and care may be inheritable, but the laws of society, especially with regard to marriage, may perfect nature in creating an environment combining what is most beneficent in nature with what is most valued in society so that a woman who is not a blood relative can possess more qualities and perform more good actions than a child. This is the proper way in which society perfects nature, as opposed to believing that nature can be altered by man-made but inhumane laws.

The nature versus law argument is further expounded in the discussion on whether Leonides should flee the country in order to escape the harsh strictures of the law. His son and daughter-in-law think he should 'build up' his 'decaying fortunes in safer soil' (1.1, 423), for any country which allows its senior citizens to breathe would provide 'better soil'. But the argument is given another turn. The old man refuses to evade the law and exile himself from his own country, which has nurtured him like a mother; the land that gave him birth must also be his grave. Old age, a second childhood, needs a mother's care, for 'children/Ne'er sleep so sweetly in their nurse's cradle/As in their natural mother's' (1.1, 442–43). However hospitable a foreign country might be, it can never provide the care of a mother. Even though Epire is proving to be an unnatural mother, she is still better than a stepmother. While the divine institution of marriage can improve upon the offices of nature in providing a man and his father with a wife and daughter-in-law of perfect virtue, it is not, by analogy, possible for the old to prefer a stepmother over and above a mother. The old are not able to find solace in an adopted country because their motherland, the soil on which they were born, bred and brought up, however imperfect, must also be the soil in which they are buried.[23] Cleanthes finally prevails upon his father to counterfeit his own funeral and take refuge in a nature retreat. Leonides is thus persuaded to make preparations for a natural death by cozening the death that will be legally imposed on him (1.1, 529).

In pre-industrial societies politics and religion coincide in one aged person, who in a sense is the keeper of language and culture for the ensuing generation. Since the power of the old resides neither in war nor reproduction but in custom (Goody 1976, 3, 127–28), they continue to hold on to power solely by means of 'ritual strength' — that is, by exclusive ownership of accumulated knowledge and the fact that they are on the threshold of everlasting life — which gives them a unique spiritual cachet and makes them 'givers' but also receivers, in that they will get their reward in heaven. The old change the world by words because they are unable to change it by any other means; their lack of physical strength make their blessings and curses all the more potent (128). The play recognises the shortcomings of society's investment of religion and politics in one person, then parodies, and finally affirms it. In the opening scene the claims of religion in formulating laws governing society are resolutely absent. The irreligious young joyfully proclaim that there can be no reason for deferring reinforcement of the law; '[w]hy now', Evander enthuses, 'methinks our court looks like a spring /Sweet, fresh, and fashionable, now the old weeds are gone' 2.1, 38–39) and the First Courtier sychophantically agrees: ''Tis as a court should b / [...] When men pass not the palsy of their tongues /Nor colour in their cheeks' (2.1, 40–44), while the Second Courtier ecstatically expresses the wish that Evander may never grow old, he 'stand[s] so well for youth' (2.1, 37). Furthermore, the law can be enforced even before the shut-off age of fourscore; if a father exhibits signs of dotage and a son can

> [...] bring good solid proofs
> Of his own father's weakness and unfitness
> To live or sway the living, though he want five
> Or ten years of his number [...]
> His defect makes him fourscore and 'tis fit
> He dies when he deserves. (2.1, 21–26)

The impulse to eliminate the old from politics is ratified by the record of births in the 'church-book', the parish register — yet the Bible, the other meaning of church-book, 'overthrows it' (1.1, 136). The lawyers' belief in the clarity and perfection of the law over biblical exhortation to care for the lives of innocents is thus based upon the (spurious) assumption that experience kills innocence, a virtue to which a person of fourscore cannot aspire, by virtue of the many years s/he has clocked up (1.1, 129– 38). In the early scenes, Cleanthes' hope that there may be some loophole in the phrasing of the law — ''Mongst many words may be found contradictions' (1.1,139) — suggests a means of evading its strictures, yet therein lies a double paradox; in the same moment as the new law relating to the old exposes the corruptibility of those who practice the law, one of the lawyers accepts a bribe to provide a means of evading the law. He builds in a quibble based on the different stages of a man's life; a man comes of age at twenty-one, which can be taken to mean that the counting starts not at birth but at a man's coming of age: 'by that addition,/Fourscore he cannot be till a hundred and one' (1.1, 207–08). And at the same time as the lawyer and courtiers (for whatever reasons) attempt to put a wedge between the law and religion, Antigona, Creon's wife, insists that her husband's judicious and devout running of his household as a Christian one is proof enough of his sound judgement at the age of eighty and thus should ensure his continuing value to the state. But while rulers embody both religion and politics, when statesmen grow older they experience a separation of the two, as William Cecil did, desiring to retire from the active world of policy making and retreat with his thoughts into a contemplation of how he can serve his maker (see above). Creon makes this movement explicit:

[...] I confess
I'm troublesome to life now, and the state
Can hope for nothing worthy from me now,
Either in force or counsel. I've of late
Employed myself quite from the world, and he
That once begins to serve his Maker faithfully
Can never serve a worldly prince well after. (2.1, 97–103)

CORIOLANUS

The virtuous old men in *The Old Law* have a limited part in the various comic actions of the play; deprived of 'ritual strength', they subside into resignation and submission to the will of the young, and their old wives are little more than ciphers of virtue and endurance. Yet, as already noted in the preceding chapter, recent scholarship unveils a very different and complicated picture of the realities of old people's lives in the early modern period. In fiction, too, old women are included in considerations of the question of the ideal age of the politician, and whether there is such a thing as being too old for politics. This takes place in Shakespeare's reworking of the antique theme in *Coriolanus*. In this play, ancient ideologies of old age have a central role in the formulation of a politics of state which positions an older woman at the centre of both public and domestic politics. In a manoeuvre by now familiar, Shakespeare reworks his sources in *Coriolanus* by transferring onto a woman past the menopause the attributes so greatly prized by the ancients in old men.

In Cicero's universe, the pinnacle of old age is reached when the libidinous clamour of the body is stilled, and the maturity of years confers the highest powers of authority (Cicero, 2001, 72). Plutarch's treatise, entitled *Whether an old man should engage in public affairs* and written in his own old age, also argues for the continuing need for old men to remain active in politics (Plutarch, repr.1998, 10: 75–153). The hallmarks of age — mature experience, wisdom, judgement and preference for moderation — are indispensable to the individual and to the state. The mental powers of the old are sustained by a life of quiet reflective domesticity, and while still in office are maintained by constant practice, with the young in subsidiary roles until they too attain wisdom through maturity.

In an awesomely lengthy sentence, Plutarch begins his 'address' to Euphanes on old age thus:

But inasmuch as our shrinking from the contests of political life and our various infirmities furnish innumerable excuses and offer us finally [...] old age; and since it is more especially because of this last that these excuses seem to blunt and affle our ambition and begin to convince us that there is a fitting limit of age, not only to the athlete's career, but to the statesman's as well, I therefore think it my duty to discuss with you the thoughts which I am continually going over in my own mind concerning the activity of old men in public affairs, that neither of us shall desert the long companionship in the journey which we have thus far made together, and neither shall renounce public life, which is, as it were, a familiar friend of our own years, only to change and adopt another which is unfamiliar and for becoming familiar with which and making it our own time does not suffice, but that we shall abide by the choice which we made in the beginning when we fixed the same end and aim for life as for honourable life — unless indeed we were in the short time remaining to us to prove that the long time we have lived was spent in vain and for no honourable purpose. (77, 79)

Here Plutarch insists that age, though an infirmity, is not a barrier to continuing public service, and that old statesmen should not be put out to pasture. On the contrary, they should not renounce the public life to which they are accustomed in favour of retirement, an unfamiliar condition far removed from the choice of a career of honourable service to the state since youth, and one which would deny the value of their long years in office.

This treatise is not the direct source for *Coriolanus*; as we all know, that is North's translation of Amyot's French rendition of Plutarch's *Lives of the Noble Grecians and Romanes*, 1595 edition. Nevertheless, his treatise on old age informs alignments and attitudes in both the public and the private realms of Shakespeare's play. At the centre of its political crisis are five old people, one of them a woman. The two tribunes of the people (Sicinius Volutus and Junius Brutus), Cominius and Menenius, are all in continuing positions of authority, thereby endorsing Cicero's and Plutarch's belief in working to one's last breath. These older figures stand apart both from the people they represent and seek to pacify, and also from the central figure of Coriolanus, the youthful warrior who rejects traditional communal responsibilities.

The two tribunes of the people, Cominius (consul and, despite his advancing years, commander of the army) and Menenius, senator and fatherly protector of Coriolanus, valorise Cicero's and Plutarch's advice by continuing in positions of authority. However, Shakespeare presents them ambivalently, suggesting on the one hand that they are respectable figures of state, yet on the other, questioning their assumed right to be obeyed on the grounds of patriarchal seniority — and questioning also their right to be regarded as wise old men. Menenius, an old patrician and a traditionalist, accustomed to taking responsibility for the state and its citizens, embraces the plebs in his fatherly concern; he tells them that 'most charitable care/Have the patricians of you [...]/The helms o'th'state [...] care for you like fathers' (*Coriolanus*, 1. 1, 51–52; 63);[24] and for their part, the citizens deem him 'worthy,' 'honest enough' and one who 'hath always loved the people' (1. 1, 39–41). Yet Menenius' gesture is hollow, for it is the plebs alone who are undergoing a grain shortage. The fact that this claim to caring is made by an elder, upon whose wisdom and experience the state depends, cynically undermines classical prescriptive literature on old age. Cicero confers upon the old the role of pilot of the ship of state, for 'while others are climbing the masts, or running about the gangways, or working at the pumps, he sits quietly in the stern and simply holds the tiller. He may not be doing what younger members of the crew are doing, but what he does is better and much more important' (Cicero, 2001, 27). His Cato has 'never refused an audience to anyone who wished to consult' him (41). Guidance and council are the prerogatives of age in Plutarch, too, where it is always the old and wise who are called upon to proclaim assembly law and are sought out for advice. To endorse this, Plutarch cites Augustus Caesar's response to the clamour of youth: 'Listen, young men, to an old man to whom old men listened when he was young' (Plutarch, 1998, 85). Menenius' compromised position as a wise old statesman is accentuated by the fact that he withholds corn, the source of provender, from the starving citizens at the same time as evincing a concern for the comfort of his own stomach; he is 'well understood to be a perfecter giber for the table than a necessary bencher in the Capitol' (*Coriolanus*, 2. 1, 66–67) and himself admits to loving 'a cup of hot wine with not a drop of allaying Tiber in't' (2. 1, 38–39).

Cicero's Cato believes in lifelong adherence to and practice of virtues which confer dignity and courtesy at the end of a long career (Cicero, 2001, 17, 19). The wisdom and influence of the old, he says, should preserve the state (32, 35). It is only fools who ascribe their own vices and follies to old age and it is the duty of the young to acquire virtue through the precepts of their elders and to begin doing this while still young enough to get into habits of healthy living and moderation in diet.[25] These good habits, learnt early on in life, will help them later to combat the debilitating effects of age. Because Cato has done this, he is profoundly grateful to old age, which has increased his appetite for conversation, not food and drink (57). Senile debility, moroseness, a troubled spirit, fretfulness and being hard to please (25) result not from the condition of age itself, but from character weaknesses in intellect and resolve uncorrected early on in life. A drowsy, slothful, inert old age is the harbinger of forgetfulness, credulity and carelessness only to those who have allowed their mental faculties to fall into torpor (25).

The fact that Menenius and the two tribunes fail to match up to these ideals of the wise *senex* highlights the implausibility of a politics whose representatives are unreliable on the one hand and self-indulgent on the other. In the gossipy lead-up to Coriolanus' triumphal return to Rome, when Menenius and the tribunes discuss Coriolanus' faults and virtues, Menenius *faux-naif* opening gambit to the two tribunes, 'you two are old men: tell me one thing that I shall ask,' makes it appear that he wishes to draw upon the tribunes' wisdom and experience as old men, but is in fact the prelude to listing their vices: 'In what enormity is Martius poor in that you two have not in abundance?' (*Coriolanus*, 2.1, 14–15). These vices, stereotypically attributed to old men, deny them the public honours which according to Cicero's Cato are indispensable to elders who had power 'not only in their speech, but in their very nod' (*Cicero*, 2001, 75). Menenius' accusation that the tribunes are 'censured here in the city' for being irascible echoes 'Cato's' list of character faults. If they had any self-awareness at all, says Menenius, they would recognise themselves as fools, whose abilities are 'too infant-like for doing much alone' (*Coriolanus*, 2.1, 20–36). But in his harangue to the tribunes, Menenius exposes his own shortcomings as a wise old counsellor of youth. His self-image as a bluff and honest statesman ('what I think, I utter, and spend my malice in my breath' 2 1, 43) who likes his wine undiluted, takes sides with the plaintiff ('something imperfect in favouring the first complaint' 2.1,40) before hearing all sides of the case ('hasty and tinder-like upon too trivial motion' 2. 1, 40–41) and a bon viveur (one that 'converses more with the buttock of the night than with the forehead of the morning' 2. l. 41–42) define him negatively against the Cato ideal, that old men should be temperate in their speech and habits and moderate in their drinking, and should cultivate reason and good judgement (Cicero, 2001, 89). Menenius and the tribunes are all three imperfect politicians, none of whom are 'Lycurguses' (*Coriolanus*, 2. 1, 44), for though the two tribunes try to promote new policies in the manner of Lycurgus, they do not succeed, and can hardly be called wise lawmakers. But Menenius is no Lycurgus either, for his desire is merely to maintain the status quo. The pronouncements of all three are self-deluding and disingenuous, and sometimes stupid. The message is that they should know better, having the advantage that age confers on wise judgement. In the very act of rounding on the tribunes as 'a brace of unmeriting, proud, violent, testy magistrates, alias fools, as any in Rome' (2.1, 35–36) Menenius compromises his own position as a wise counsellor.

An additional context for the dominance of age appears in the election scenes (2. 2; 2. 3). Predicated upon contemporary parliamentary practice, they show that the constitution of political power on the basis of seniority was in the process of evolution. Here too considerations of age, though not made explicit, underwrote the selection of representatives to an office still committed to maintaining the status quo. In James' first parliament, only one member of the Privy Council was under forty; the majority were over fifty, one third were sixty or over, and two were over seventy (DNB).[26] In the matter of age as an adjunct to constitutional matters, Shakespeare 'nudges' Roman politics in a contemporary direction (*Coriolanus*, 2000, 28). In Plutarch's society, highly status-conscious and politically quiescent, the election of consuls to the senate was based not on what the candidates stood for or promised to do, but on their personal honour and seniority. But Plutarch's rendition of the clash between senators and citizens is made to signify even more importantly, in that the confrontation is also one between youth and age, and the matter is considerably complicated by the fact that the tribunes are invested not only with the confidence of the people but are given additional weight by their seniority in years — a weight denied the patrician candidate. His election, usually explained by critics in terms of ideological, personal and social matters, is also based upon considerations of age. The continuing importance of classical precedent in debating parliamentary procedures indicates that matters of age underpin the events of ancient history, which Shakespeare draws upon (*Coriolanus*, 2000, 31). To highlight the contemporary relevance of the election process and its radical nature in *Coriolanus*, and to accentuate the continuing use and importance of classical models for English parliamentary procedures, Lee Bliss compares an anecdote from Elizabeth's last parliament, where it was argued that the Speaker of the House was analogous to that of the Roman consul in senate, with a similar anecdote from James' first parliament, where the king showed his hostility to oppositional voices by referring to them as 'Tribunes of the people' (Cobbett, 1806–12, 1: 1071–72; *Coriolanus*, 2000, 31). It is interesting (though Bliss does not notice this) that the analogy hinges on age. Elizabeth, an aging queen at the end of her reign, had accumulated enough political astuteness to allow her spokesman to claim the same privileges as a Roman consul in senate. James, new to the throne of England at the age of thirty-seven, had not the poise to hide his unease when speakers in the House voiced independent viewpoints. Significantly, Henry Yelverton was castigated as 'the *old* Tribune of the house' 'for arguing against purveyance' — that is, the crown's right to purchase carts and goods at below market prices — and, of course, for indirectly criticising the royal prerogative (Bowyer, 1931, 123nl; *Coriolanus*, 2000, 31).[27] In *Coriolanus*, the task of warning the citizens of their impending loss of 'liberties' and 'prerogative' falls to the two old tribunes in a way which accentuates the relevance of age to contemporaneous events, recalling specific procedures in early seventeenth century parliamentary debates, all of which the play takes up and re-examines. In this instance, the relevance of age may be added to an already complex and ambivalent situation.

* * *

> [Just] as teachers of letters or of music themselves first play the notes or read to their pupils and thus show them the way, so the statesman, not only by speech or by making suggestions from outside, but by action in administering the affairs of the community, directs the young man, whose character is moulded and formed by the old man's actions and words alike. (Plutarch, 1998, 117)

Plutarch (and ancient precept in general) strongly emphasised the exemplary educative role of the old in shaping correct public behaviour in the fledgling politician, whose character is moulded by the actions and words of the experienced older man. How else could a young man

manage a State rightly and persuade an assembly or a senate after reading a book or writing in the Lyceum a school exercise about political
science, if he has not stood many a time by the driver's rein or the
pilot's steering-oar, leaning this way and that with the politicians and
generals as they contend with the aid of their experiences and their
fortunes, thus amid dangers and trouble acquiring the knowledge they
need? (117)

Menenius presents himself to Coriolanus as just such an educative guide,
yet his instruction is ineffectual in the matter of Coriolanus' election as consul. The crucial events in Acts two and three, where the trial precipitates an
insurrection, depend upon political dominance based on seniority. Coriolanus' attempt to suppress the will of the people ends in his own dismissal.
The young candidate is routed, and it is left to the elders to negotiate a deal
that will satisfy both patricians and citizens. However, Menenius is in a
doubtful position as instructor in crowd-management. Acting as mentor
to a young man 'ill-schooled /In bolted language' (*Coriolanus*, 3. 1, 326),
his advice is to dissemble his revulsion against the populace at least until
he has secured their support. Ultimately he fails to give Coriolanus the
mature counsel that will help him retain the citizens' vote. The matter of
the grain returns to haunt him, and he is neither able to prevent Coriolanus
from expressing his contempt for the citizens, nor to persuade the tribunes
to 'temperately proceed to what you would /Thus violently redress' (3. 1,
221–22). His attempt to 'try whether my old wit' can patch things up 'with
cloth of any colour' cannot match up to either Cicero's or Plutarch's idealisations of the role of the old in continuing to shape policy by wise guidance
to the young. As we have seen, the tribunes are exposed as manipulative,
and Menenius, mired in outworn tradition, is besides too tarnished by his
duplicity to succeed as a figure of *gravitas* in the Cato mould.

However, the play does contain an image of wise old age and, unexpectedly, it is enshrined in a woman. Representations of old women as crones
and malevolent destroyers in the drama and poetry of the late sixteenth
century,[28] drawn from classical stereotypes of old women as sad, bad or
invisible,[29] have led critics to unexamined and undifferentiated block typecasting of old and young women as nature's incorrigible degenerates. However, configurations of female old age with wisdom, based simultaneously
upon classical mentoring prescriptions for older states*men* and fundamen-
tal though hidden biological distinctions between young women and old,
encourage a reappraisal of the role of Shakespeare's Volumnia.[30]

Ancient society sometimes widened the scope of influence for the older
woman, occasionally conferring, in Thane's words, 'certain honorific
roles' upon her (Thane, 2000, 42). Tim Parkin in 'Aging in Antiquity' (Parkin, 1998, 19–42) finds that while in classical literature old women were
depicted in an 'almost monotonously negative' fashion, in reality a post-
menopausal woman benefited, for the first time in her life, from a freedom

to move beyond the family circle denied to the child-bearing upper class woman:

> As widows in particular, in both Greek and Roman society, women in old age might in fact enjoy considerable authority, in practice if not also in legal theory, because they controlled the family wealth to some limited extent. (37)

However, Parkin goes on to point out that this was not due to an enhanced status, but rather because a woman beyond her child-bearing years became invisible to the male rule-givers; it was simply a matter of indifference as to whether or not she now complied with the social strictures that were imposed upon her during her years as a child-bearer and object of male desire. The older woman in Greek and Roman society could do more or less as she pleased because nobody cared; thus she was doubly marginalised (37–38). But according to Galenic physiology, women became more like men (and therefore less threatening to them) after the menopause; as they aged, the balance of the humours shifted so that their bodies took on the characteristics of the male. They lost their youthful plumpness, they dried out, and they acquired more heat. As a result, they became physically stronger and healthier, and likely to live longer than men, which, in theory, gave them added agency (Pelling, 1997, 63–88; Thane, 2000, 22, 54; Dean-Jones, 1994, 107, 246–47). This feature of the aging woman in antiquity is paralleled in the sixteenth and seventeenth centuries by Margaret Pelling's findings with regard to the Royal College of Physicians' efforts to curb the activities of older women as medical practitioners. As noted in the preceding chapter, Pelling shows that the college's desire to control their activities, assumed to be equivalent in stringency to the witchcraft prosecutions of the period, in fact showed 'little of the witch-hunting fervour that one might expect, even in England.'[31] Rather, the role of the older woman in society was much more complex, reflecting a range of attitudes. Post-menopausal women were not, either in antiquity or in the early modern period, uniformly perceived as physiologically-impaired burdens, and the Galen-inspired physicians of the Royal College were increasingly forced to acknowledge the advantages of post-menopausal women; they lived longer than men and, like men, they were both experienced and wise (Pelling, 1997, 84).[32] Volumnia fits into a comparable cultural framework.

As we have seen, discourses derived from classical literatures complicate assumptions about the nobility (or debility) of a masculine old age. But what of cultural assumptions which give older women scope not available to younger women in shaping the future, whilst in the very act of typecasting them as the hags of literature? Though Volumnia has (with some reason) been depicted as a suffocating mother and the mother-in-law from hell, from the point of view of discourses on age, she furnishes one of the few examples in the drama of the period of a woman elder shaping policy and influencing public events. There is no precedent for this either in Cicero (he does not mention women at all) or Plutarch, who contemptuously relegates women to the domestic sphere.[33] But Shakespeare, perhaps with Elizabeth I in mind, and by accepting Livy's description of the mother of Coriolanus as an 'aged woman' (Livy, 1919, 1: 347), collapses representations of motherhood into the aged female figure, thereby significantly altering his classical sources. This enables him to examine the possibilities for post-menopausal women as educative agents in politics.

The position of old women in medicine and in the structure of late sixteenth-century households provides a useful analogue in trying to understand the range of roles Volumnia performs. These social and cultural realities enable a review of her dominance in both private and public. In this regard, her role as head of household and educator in a single parent family is important, though neglected. Indeed, a mother's continuing education of her son beyond his coming-of-age was not unknown. Theophilus, Seventh Earl of Huntingdon, records that he was educated 'according to the direction of his mother, being wholly domestic' until he reached the age of twenty-one (HMC Hastings Mss;, IV, 1947, 353, cited in Charlton, 1994, 131).

There is considerable evidence to show that the composition of households from the late sixteenth century was nuclear rather than extended (Laslett & Wall, 1972, 152) and as such performed 'social, economic, even educational and political' functions (156). If adult children and their parents lived in the same household, it was because the children remained with the parents, rather than supporting them (Pelling, 1991, 74–101); this held true for all levels of society. 'Our ancestors,' in Peter Laslett's words, 'do not seem to have had much truck with resident mothers-in-law' (Laslett & Wall, 1972, 152). Property ownership gave them bargaining power and continuing independence and control of the way they lived (Pelling and Smith, 1991, 12; Laslett and Wall, 1972, esp. 123–58; Laslett, 1977, 175–79 ; Thane, 2000, 120). The census of Ealing in 1599 shows that of the eighty-six households listed, there were only three where old parents lived with their children (Thane, 2000, 124–45). The old continued as head of household, with the well-to-do 'even less likely to be living with their children' Laslett (1977), 200–212). And women over fifty did not necessarily experience loss of status accompanying the end of their reproductive years; on the contrary, there were positive gains for the individual and for society (Thane, 2000, 26). Furthermore, Volumnia belongs to a category whose independence was strengthened by a classical Roman law still in force in the early modern period whereby a child's property merged with that of a parent. Use of this law guaranteed the power of the head of family (Macfarlane 1986, 80).[34] From the point of view of ancient and contemporary family practice, the older woman was able to sustain a powerful and independent position.

Feminist critics, taking their cue from the ground-breaking work of Coppèlia Kahn and Janet Adelman, have rendered the effects of Volumnia's relationship with her son as disabling and monstrous, and her impact on the state disastrous, precisely because she cannot exercise power in her own right but must live out her ambitions through her son (Adelman, 1998, 23–45; Kahn, 1981, 151–72; Wheeler, 1981, 211–13; Wheeler and Barber, 1986, 303–05. Sprengnether, 1986, 89–111). In concentrating solely on her overbearing motherhood, however, these critics have ignored her equally important position as independent head of household. They have also bypassed her role as her son's sole educator. As a single mother, the responsibility for her son's education has devolved entirely upon her. This education has shaped Coriolanus in the mould of the Roman patrician who wins honour on the battlefield. The importance of this kind of responsibility is revealed by the findings of Kenneth Charlton on mothers as educators (Charlton, 1988, 1–20; Charlton, 1994, 129–56; Chartlon, 1999). As nourisher of her husband's seed, a mother's responsibility to her child began at conception. During pregnancy, she should never 'give herself to anger' and should 'avoid any intemperance in eating or drinking' — an injunction which, incidentally, provides an interesting gloss on Adelman's insights into the shaping of the text by images of deprivation and oral neediness (Adelman, 1998, 24–26). Contrary to the Aries and Stone theses that upper-class mothers wet-nursed their offspring, there was a fairly widespread practice of mothers breast-feeding their children in the belief that the education begun in the womb continued at the breast (Charlton, 1988, 14).

Coriolanus imbibed the warrior ethic at his mother's breast, for Volumnia has assumed the early modern mother's responsibility, sanctioned by all the literature on the Godly Household, to train her young child (and her servants) 'in the way wherein he should walk and he will not depart from it when he is old.' (Proverbs, 22. 6; Charlton, 1988, 3). Despite St. Paul's injunction against women educators: 'I suffer not a woman to teach, nor to usurp the authority over man' (Timothy 2: 12; I Corinthians 14:34; Charlton, 1988, 3), in the sixteenth century it was rather Aquinas' exhortation to women to carry out their teaching duties in the privacy of the household that was widely recalled (cf. Erasmus, 1529, passim; Whitforde, 1537, sig. B i; Bullinger, 1541, chapter xxi; Kempe, 1588, sig.E iv; Greenham, 1599, 160; Perkins, 1600, 72; Charlton,1988, 3). Volumnia's instruction on heroic masculinity in the schoolroom seemlessly elides into instruction into affairs of state. In private conversation with her daughter-in-law, she reveals that her ambitions encompass both the private and the public sphere. She has pushed Coriolanus into danger in order to win the end goal of her particular kind of patrician education, the amassing of honour and fame:

> When yet he was but tender-bodied and the only son of my womb, when youth and comeliness plucked all gaze his way, when for a day of kings' entreaties a mother should not sell him an hour from her beholding, I [...] was pleased to let him seek danger where he was like to find fame (1. 3, 4–11)

and 'to a cruel war [...] sent him' at an age when most children were still at their mothers' knees (1. 3, 7–8). She glories in the fact that the effects of her teaching have born such fruit on the battlefield of Corioles (*Coriolanus*, 2000, 48),[35] a success that has been passed on down to her grandson who 'had rather see swords and hear a drum than look upon his schoolmaster' (1. 3, 50–51). She made Coriolanus a soldier (3. 2, 109) and her continuing educative role is now extended to include lessons in political expediency. Having taught him at the breast to value honour and violence, she now teaches him how to win votes by affecting humility:

> [...] say to them
> Thou art their soldier and, being bred in broils,
> Hast not the soft way which, thou dost confess,
> Were fit for thee to use as they to claim,
> In asking their good loves; but thou wilt frame
> Thyself, forsooth, hereafter theirs so far
> As thou has power and person. (3. 2, 81–87)

Thus Volumnia extends her role as educator into her son's maturity, pro-longing her son's dependency. In so doing, she is able to influence policy. Perceived ancient norms gave due weight to the mother's part in instilling custom-enshrined notions of honour. As Sir William Cornwallis notes

> You shall hardly finde a father now a daies, that will care rather how his sonne is dead, the[n] dead, that prizeth his valour dearer than his life, yet in times past, mothers had that hardines that they hated more that he should be wounded in the backe then dead. (Cornwallis, 1601, Ll 3r-v)

Volumnia's unfeminine aspirations and her continuing ability to form and enact sophisticated political judgements in the public sphere derive from her post-menopausal status, and also from the fact that she car-ries on as head of household in the private, domestic sphere, still actively engaged in the education of her son beyond adulthood. These continuing functions include Virgilia, and with the same expected outcome (obedience and dependency). The first words Volumnia utters to her daughter-in-law are instructions: 'I pray you, daughter, sing, or express yourself in a more comfortable sort.' Virgilia should be rejoicing in her husband's absence, since it is spent in winning honour. She cannot be permitted to retire upon Valeria's arrival, but must stay like an obedient child until she is dismissed. When Virgilia tells the women that she 'will not out of doors,' Volumnia treats her like a petulant schoolgirl, telling Valeria to 'let her alone [...] as she is now, she will but disease our better mirth' (1. 3, 1–2, 64, 94–95).

Volumnia's activities as a post-menopausal woman publicly represent-ing patrician values and as continuing instructor to her son and his family unfortunately align her with the consuls, who see no future in a more con-stitutional basis to the republic (4.6) and reject the prospect of working with the tribunes and people. But Volumnia's appropriation of both public and domestic leadership counterbalances what Bliss sees as the suppression of the private in favour of the 'public world of valour and fame' (*Coriolanus*, 2000, 52). In contrast to Virgilia's silent domesticity, Volumnia continues until the last to manage her son's feelings and decisions through instruction and example, and exerts influence through command of forensic rhetoric (52). Just as the astute old politician Ulysses instructs Achilles on the difference between innate honour and the honour that can be given or won, so Volumnia (another astute old politician) continues to use her position as a single educating mother to initiate her grown-up son into the pragmatics of the concept, reminding him that 'Honour and policy, like unsevered friends,/ I'th'war do grow together' (3. 2, 42–43). In investing Volumnia with this magisterial role, Shakespeare extends her 'private and domesticall'[36] instruction into the public realm, thereby making *Coriolanus* in more senses than one a reflection on early Jacobean educational practices as well as representing political conventions common to the age.[37]

Early modern people believed in preparing for a peaceful and comfortable end to one's life in the bosom of one's family and community.[38] Once this was no longer possible, the individual could only look forward to a lonely death. In this regard also, Volumnia persists in her active role as educator and female elder to the very last. Her ultimate act as exemplar is to bring home to her son the impossibility of a peaceful old age if he continues to align himself with the Volsces. Crucially, she intervenes in Coriolanus' abandonment of his public identity; that is, she intervenes at the moment when he finds his self-construction as Rome's defendant has no meaning or continuity in his alliance with the Volsces (in their midst, he is without name or title 5.1,13). He has forfeited the value conferred upon him by the Roman patricians. From the point of view of the play's subtext on senescence, it is no surprise that Coriolanus chooses not to prolong his life into an alienated old age whilst his mother continues to shape events and furnish counsel. In her public role as Rome's ambassador and in the most dramatically powerful scene in the play, she persuades her son to 'frame convenient peace' (5. 3, 191) and upon her return is acclaimed as 'the life of Rome' (5. 5, 1). But wearing the public mantle of the classical model of *masculine* old age, and in the name of private maternal bonds and educational responsibilities, she has one final lesson to teach her son; the impossibility of an honourable old age for someone in his position. So Coriolanus' death, though dreadful, is, according to the precepts of the ancients, inevitable.

Summarily put, while all the texts examined in this chapter exhibit complications in the role of the old in politics and the workplace, in *Coriolanus* they emerge as unresolvable ambivalences that not only hover around age but also around gender. By installing an older woman at the centre of both public and domestic politics in his play, Shakespeare reworks his sources by projecting onto a woman past the menopause, the attributes so greatly prized in old men by the ancients.

Epilogue
The Triumph of Age:
All's Well that Ends Well

My aim in this book has been to show how works of fiction intervene in and complicate discourses of old age. By way of epilogue to this argument, I want to present Helena and the King of France in Shakespeare's *All's Well that Ends Well*[1] as occupants of two contradictory but cross-fertilising positions which thrive simultaneously in manuals whose rhetorical structure reinforces the opposition between youth (vigorous but heedless) and age (feeble but wise). So far I have argued that while other plays of the period rely on antagonisms between the generations (Shakespeare's *King Lear* and *The Merchant of Venice*, Middleton and Rowley's *The Old Law*, and John Ford's *The Broken Heart* are just a few), there are others (for instance, Shakespeare's *Comedy of Errors* and *Coriolanus* and Thomas Heywood's *The Wise Woman of Hogsdon*) which expose the gap between youth and age as artificial. In pushing the relationship of old to young away from the normative youth—age binaries into more inclusive and complementary areas, *All's Well* in particular enacts a process that was perfectly acceptable to early modern writers on age, who perceived that the moral, intellectual and spiritual strengths of the old could occasionally be present in the young, just as they believed that it was possible for the old to retain their physical vigour. Thus it was said of Hermogenes that he 'in his childhood was an old man' (Carpenter, 1597, 230; cf. also Goulart, 1621, 197; Sheafe, 1639, 'To the Reader'; *Resolved Gentleman*, 1594, 13–25), and Bacon begins his essay on old age with essentially the same observation: 'A Man that is *Young in yeares*, may be Old in Houres, if he have lost no Time' (Bacon, 1638, 130). In other words, if old age is not dependent on years so much as upon knowledge, attainment, religious devotion and control of appetite, it is possible to combine youth with wisdom, and to be physically energetic in age (cf. fig. 2.1).

As a case in point of complex structures of identity formation that go beyond the mere registering of ambiguity, the manner in which the King's recovery in *All's Well* is brought about illustrates the co-existence of intergenerational strife and tolerance, and its outcomes enforce mutual recognition and respect at the same time as they describe tension and antagonisms. Furthermore, the King's recovery restores to him the blessing of youthful vigour, prized above all by the old, through the agency of a young woman, so that he is able once more to exercise in matters of state the wisdom of long years of experience.[2] The old in this play do not abdicate responsibility as they do in *King Lear*, nor are they put out to graze in a geriatric Garden of Eden, as in the ending of Middleton and Rowley's *The Old Law*. They retain their benevolent power to shape the destinies of the young to the very last, bringing the callow Bertram more into line with noble ideals, and shield and support Helena at every turn of the plot. The King's cure thus represents a cross-over from more than one category into another.

The more normative impulse to regard old age as a disease and an unnatural condition (in contrast to youth, whose disorders are corrigible) is expressed by Montaigne:

> What fondnesse is it for a man to thinke he shall die, for and through a failing and defect of strength, which extreme age draweth with it, and to propose that terme unto our life, seeing it is the rarest kind of all deaths and least in use? We only call it naturall, as if it were against nature to see a man breake his necke with a fall [...] a man may peradventure rather call that naturall which is generall, common, and universall. To die of age is a rare, singular, and extraordinarie death, and so much lesse naturall than others: It is the last and extremest kind of dying: The further it is from us, so much the lesse is it to be hoped for: Indeed it is the limit beyond which we shal not passe, and which the law of nature hath prescribed unto us as that which should not be outgone by any: but it is a rare privilege peculiar unto her selfe, to make us continue unto it. (Montaigne, 1603, 162–63)

Old age is an unnatural condition, since nature's laws decree that people die before their allotted span in war, or from famine and disease, which constitute normative patterns of mortality. This being the case, to reach old age is a 'rare privilege', and, Montaigne goes on to argue, it makes sense for a man to be given responsibility and permitted to 'manage and dispose of his owne goods' (163) at a much earlier age than twenty-five; people should begin to take control of their own lives much sooner, given that it is customary to send men out to pasture at the age of fifty-five. *All's Well* intervenes in this debate by enabling the interaction of youth and age on multiple levels; the medical, the physiological, the spiritual and the social.

The play begins in melancholy reflections upon mortality, and nostalgia for lost youth; it includes a young man who is not yet ready to take responsibility for himself, or his goods, and a young woman who manifestly is. The King's life, about to end in disease, as a result of the 'honorable and glorious' (Montaigne, 1894, 163) action of a young person who exhibits the kind of mind that is 'full growne and perfectly joynted at twentie yeares' (163), is brought back into full vigour. Despite its muted beginning and whispers of the Countess's imminent death towards its end, the play turns

Montaigne's ideas around in other ways, too, showing an alternative to the inevitability of shrinkage in mind and body (163). The frailty of age is not permitted to mire the judgement of the older characters, or to prevent them from helping construct a better social reality for the young in their charge; they continue to the play's end to exercise political authority. In this, the play seems to extend to women also Goulart's observation that 'the counsell and sawe of old men hath in it somewhat, I know not what, that is pleasing to heare, gracefull, and of venerable regard and well liking' (Goulart, 1621, 100; cf. also fig. 22).

A further dissolution of the binaries of youth and age occurs in the mutual recognition and respect of the older characters for the younger. The impulse to iron out the antagonisms between young and old is a persistent feature of the prescriptive literature. Ideally, during their lives in office old men accumulate piety, knowledge and experience which they need to pass on as cultivated wisdom to future generations of rulers and public servants. For this reason, youth should not scorn old age but must be conversant with old men and seek their company for instruction and guidance (cf. Guazzo, 1581, 2, 32v–33; Goulart, 1621, 50, 97; Sheafe, 1639, 203–04; Steele, 1688, 267). Sheafe explains this process in an elaborate correspondence trope. As winter is the season when all the profits arising from the husbandman's duties and labours accumulate — when his barns are full with corn, his hives of honey and wax, and his storehouses with fleece ready for warm winter clothing, so the thriving paterfamilias stores up everything necessary for the provision, comfort and smooth running of the household, 'as then the Ants heape is growne great for succour and food'. By the time a man reaches the winter of his life, his store of wisdom, experience and spiritual wealth is replete, ready to 'crowne this age with all manner of blessings' (Sheafe, 1639, 165–66). Sheafe, in placing such a positive emphasis on the correspondence between winter and old age, finds ample justification for his assurance that God furnishes the old with all the necessities for spiritual nourishment before he brings them to an infirm bodily state. Rich mental stores are the basis from which Sheafe elaborates upon the 'priviledges' of old age, chief of which is old age itself, dignified by time and opportunity, wherein 'all priviledges meet' (161). In other words, and remote indeed from notions of old age as indecorous *per se*, old age, in addition to being an acquired perfection, is 'a natural good', bestowed by nature as a just reward for a good life. It is a benefit which confers 'a well framed and well ordered' (Goulart, 1621, 86–87) state of being upon those whose ripeness of judgement has matured over a long period of time. Its slow passage gives old age its value and is man's friend, because nature is perfected only through the long journey to maturity. The older a man is, the more his judgement should be valued, for the older a man is the more respect he receives (93). In their desire to render old age sublime, the treatise writers construct an artifice of oppositional viewpoints whose rhetoric of persuasion seeks to extract truths about aging from their biblical, classical sources and physiological givens. These 'truths', though they have the hollow ring of mere catchphrases to the modern reader, were accepted by early modern apologists for old age, and sometimes even conceded by its detractors. *All's Well* is just one example of a drama that both assumes and interrogates the oppositional slogans of the prescriptive literature.[3]

The play blurs gender as well as intergenerational borders in a manner symptomatic of fictional writing. After his recovery, the King is able to get his 'rich storehouse' in order, and to experience his old age as 'not so neere the end of life, as it is neere the threshold of the dore which opens to an assured happie life' (Goulart, 1621, 97; cf. also fig. 2.2). As a result of Helena's beneficent presence, the King and the Countess are able to pass on to the deserving young of both sexes (Helena and her unborn child, Diana and even Bertram, once he is brought to heel) the gifts nature bestows upon the old. They both 'take vpon' themselves 'the wardship and tuition' not only 'of some young man', but of a young woman also, and 'haue [them] well brought vp, [...] euen as to qualifie strong fuming wines, we doe brewe them with water' (Goulart, 1621, 97–98). Negotiation of difference such as this operates also at the level of prescription; though this tends to be directed primarily to men, occasionally the treatise writers remember to include women in passing (cf. Goulart, 1621, 34, 40; Steele, 1688, 121). They inform their readers that good instruction in youth prevents infection of the mind as well as the body in age as a result of weakness and insufficiency. As one ages, one's mind becomes exercised and more learned through prolonged usage. A man is better equipped to deal with new experiences as they arise, refining his judgement and accumulating knowledge and wisdom through a process of trial and error:

> [n]ever was any man so exact in resolving of the frame and course of his life; whom either new occurrences, or age, or experience did not assist with supply, and adde somewhat for the profiting of his judgement, and resolution, minding him of that whereby he perceived that what he thought he knew, he knew not, and what he held to be his best way, after triall he rejected as not so good. (Sheafe, 1639, 24, elaborating Ecclesiastes 12)

Parenting thus becomes a straightforward process with only two possible outcomes: parents are either happy or miserable in their offspring. If parents 'well season' their children by setting them 'in the right way', they will be happy; miserable if they neglect to do this (198).[4] So that youth is given the care that will benefit future ages, and to prevent misery in later life (201), it should seek the company of the old, be conversant with old men and avoid the fault most common in youth of scorning old age (203). The old in their turn should cast the light of their learning upon the young. Sheafe exhorts old men to

[b]ee not like the tall Cedars that overtop the lowly shrubs. If yee be wise and know much, let others light their candle at your lampes. Know that whatsoever you have or are, you have received it, and not for yourselves alone, but that others may have from you as freely, as you from the great Donor. (206)

At the same time as it stages intergenerational conflict (in Bertram's opposition to the King and the Countess) and contempt for age (in Lafew's exchanges with Parolles), the play explores such close, mutually sustaining relationships as arise between young and old when the young seek out the old and the old nurture the minds and experiences of the young. In these circumstances, the oppositions between young and old melt away. The main characters form a close circuit of mutual aid. Helena basks in the sympathy and goodwill of the older characters, and represents their interests. Her father's influence continues beyond the grave. She might have forgotten what he was like, but his skills live on in her (1.1, 66), and to ensure her safety he has 'bequeathed' (1.1, 29) her to the Countess, whose motherly care extends to approving a socially advantageous marriage; Lafew supports and encourages her bid to the King, and the widow is moved to help her engineer the bed-trick which will win over her husband. The opening scene sketches in this network of relationships and forges protective links between the generations as an integral part of its initial mood of mourning, melancholy and loss, all typically associated with old age (cf. Bright 1586; Laurentius 1599; Wright 1601; Burton 1955). Lafew and the Countess discuss family bereavement specifically in the context of the supportive role of the King in the education of the heir to the Rossillion estate. This scene attempts to keep the dead alive by grafting the memories of the older characters onto the young. The Countess's benediction on her son Bertram is expressed as a desire to see his father alive in him not only in physical resemblance but also in the way he conducts himself at court, where he should be the bearer of his dead father's virtues in order to merit the King's paternal protection. Mention of the King's disease, which has resulted in him 'losing [...] hope by time' (1.1, 12), makes Helena a part of this connective tissue, for it leads to an exchange of recollections between the Countess and Lafew upon the skill and honesty of her recently deceased father, Gerard de Narbon, a physician whose knowledge, ironically, 'could be set up against mortality' (1. 1, 23) had he but lived long enough. Memories of the recent dead bring the young into the orbit of the elders' protection and guidance (1.1, 1–60). For the Countess, Lafew, the King, and the Widow, this means exercising discernment in their self-appointed parental role. Their recognition of Helena's worth regardless of the claims of class involves them in espousing her cause even if it means overriding the wishes of Bertram, the natural male heir.

There are many other instances in the play of the regrouping of the older characters into protective networks around the deserving child which illustrate the breakdown of genre, gender and age categories. The Countess, the Widow, Lafew and the King all perform the generational duties recommended in the prescriptive literature. They perceive Helena's qualities, amply reward them, labour to see justice done on her behalf and feel able to trust her with their honour and their lives. Lafew, for instance, is involved from the start in the complex of restorative affiliations between old and young. His role as commentator is just one illustration of the continuing need for the old to counsel and direct the morals and behaviour of the young. Supposing that Helena's tears are for her father, he sensibly advises moderation in expressing her grief, for in excess, it is 'the enemy to the living' (1.1, 44). He organises Helena's meeting with the King, presenting her as a medical practitioner whose 'sex, her years, profession,/Wisdom, and constancy' have amazed him more even than the acknowledgment of credulity in old age would warrant; he is confident that Helena's 'simple touch' will prove powerful enough to '[q]uicken a rock' and make him 'dance canary/With spritely fire and motion' enough to bring Charlemain and his father Pippen back from their graves (2.1, 70–80). When, just before her audience with the King, Helena seems to suffer from a last-minute crisis in confidence, Lafew chivvies her into making (an initially very timorous) appearance (2.1, 90–94). Later on, he rounds indignantly upon the young lords, misreading their banter as a slight against her (2. 3, 79–80 and 86–87).

In the manuals, the old are the custodians of spiritual strength, but they are told also how to care for the aging body. Following Galen, they provide copious instruction on how to eat, drink and exercise, how to avoid over-exertion or excitement (death is hastened by immoderate passions (cf. Sheafe, 1639, epistle to the reader). The old are advised to live in a temperate climate (cf. Laurentius 1599: 179–81; Newton, 1576, 48–49; Cuffe, 1607, 109; Bacon, 1638, 112–17) and in this at least, there are no gender distinctions; some even remember to include old women, as an afterthought. The regimens, however, are devised exclusively for the aged male body. Goulart, William Vaughan the poet and Andreas Laurentius thus advise their readers that old men must 'content themselves with softer exercises' in order to conserve their depleted store of natural heat. 'They must onely euery morning haue theyr members gently rubd with a linnen cloth; [...] they must be combd, and cherished vp with fine delights' (Vaughan, 1600, 35). This rubbing and chafing needs to be vigorous, and is best done in the morning upon waking up, 'vntill the parts begin to bee red and warme' (Laurentius, 1599, 188–89). Goulart cites the example of Pollio, who lived to be a hundred because he rubbed oil into his joints to keep them supple (cf. Goulart, 1621, 7). Since all human pleasures come from the senses, old men need to be soothed by the sight of beautiful women adorned in rich clothes and precious jewels to flatter and tickle the sight. They also need to hear praise, flattery, and to participate in pleasing and learned discourse (cf. Laurentius, 1599, 192). These gender-specific prescriptions form a discrete category of difference mirrored in *All's Well*; the appearance before the King of a wise and beautiful young virgin is enough in itself to begin a restorative process. In this instance, the play maintains normative gender differences. However, the hard edges of difference are blurred when it comes to the restoration itself.

While the play maintains its own distinct categories of gender in the very act of transformation, it also merges this cultural category with that of science (specifically, medicine) at the same time as it draws upon mythographies of the Fisher King from Chretien de Troyes, Wauchier de Denain, Robert de Boron and other medieval accounts of the Grail by Perlesvaus, for example, or Wolfram von Eschenbach. The King's malady loses its categorical separateness with the arrival of Helena. Until then, his disease has resisted the ministrations of both Galenic and Paracelsan physicians (2. 3, 9–18). However, there are elements of both in the circumstances surrounding the malady and the cure. The merging of the boundaries between cultural formations and medical science is prefigured in Helena's appearance at court and her manner of treating the King. At first glance this seems to be more in the 'empiric' manner of Paracelsus, by healing the spirit through touch and prescription, in contrast to the bloodletting and purges to restore balance to the humours upon which Galenic medicine depended. Paracelsan medicine, in its emphasis upon maintaining the body's balance by chemical rather than herbal means (Solomon, 1993, 141), by its immersion in the occult, and by marking out specific areas of disease in the body, conserves health and prolongs life by harnessing the body's own resources (spiritual and chemical) to fight disease and decay. In this, according to Julie Solomon, the play reflects paradigm shifts in medicine between Galenic and Paracelsan theories, thereby suggesting another thread in the conceptual tangle; the one sees cures of the body as necessarily finite, the other as potentially limitless (138–53). Yet the end result is figured as a Galenic restoration of the balance of humours, and with it the decline of the life-threatening effects of 'melancholy adust' (cf. Laurentius 1599, 107–17; Wright, 1601, 118–45; Bright, 1586, 37). A medical cure is thus achieved by a non-practitioner, with widespread implications for the play's realignment of gender and genre boundaries and kinship patterns, its smudging of class boundaries, its complex rendering of both Protestant and Catholic doctrines of grace, and above all its experimental politics of age.

As an example of the merging of gender and genre, Galenic principles allow the play to exploit the connection between old men and young women. Galen, in expounding the importance of heat in normal and abnormal functioning, explains that the addition of warmth to things already warm makes them bitter; so honey turns to bile in people who are already warm. But where warmth is deficient, as in old people, it turns to useful blood (cf. Galen, 1916, Bk. 2, ch. 6; Ficino, 1989, 201). From this it follows that the physical proximity of young and old warms the blood of the old. Preoccupation with slowing down the process of aging by retaining the body's heat and preserving its 'radical moisture' led writers to recommend such fanciful remedies as sucking blood from a young man's arm (cf. Ficino, 1989, 197). Even more outré is the advice to old men between the ages of sixty-three and seventy, when 'for the first time this human tree must be moistened by a human, youthful liquid in order that it may revive', to 'suck the milk of a young girl who is healthy, beautiful, cheerful, and temperate' when they are hungry, and 'when the Moon is waxing' (197). This given, it is not surprising that the service to which the body's heat and moisture may be put becomes one of the dominant tropes of *All's Well*, suggesting ways in which discourses on age combine to harmonise the wisdom and experience of the old with the warmth and vigour of the young in a mutually reinforcing and life-enhancing continuum. Thus Helena's father passes on to her his knowledge and practical experience, which Helena is able to access to help herself by helping the King.

Recent critics have interpreted the King's recovery as a return to sexual potency, displaced onto Helena's yearning for Bertram and Bertram's lust for Diana (cf. Snyder, 1992, 24–26; Simpson, 1994: 173; Hopkins, 2003, 370–72; Shakespeare, 2003, Introduction, 31–32). Even though the restoration of youthful vitality to an old man through the agency of a young virgin is a cure for men only, and therefore accompanied by an aura of the erotic, and even though *All's Well* suggests this latent eroticism, the fact remains that the King's manifest feelings for Helena are first of all dependent and then paternally beneficent. Those who argue for a latent erotic content do not take into account the King's venerable age and position, nor the play's idealisation of old age. The King's reported '*Lustique*' (2. 3, 36) is an example of the way literary texts accommodate contradictory positions. On one level it plainly refers to robust good health,[5] causing 'useful' blood to course through his veins, though on another, the 'use' to which it will be put could imply the pursuit of venery, a propensity of youth, not age. The play itself does not resolve these paradoxes of youth and age any more than it maintains a binary opposition between these two conditions. Since good judgement, a natural good and privilege of age derived from long years of study and experience, cannot exist without freedom from carnality, only those old men who are no longer at the mercy of their sexual appetites can aspire to good judgement, which for this reason is not normally an attribute of youth. The play enacts this paradox by investing the King with these qualities, and rewarding Helena for possession of the attributes of old age in the same breath as it legitimates her sexual passion.

In company with all the fictional texts looked at so far, *All's Well* considerably complicates the manuals' seemingly straightforward directives at the same time as it keeps intact categories of gender, age and sexuality. Triumph over lusts of the flesh is crucial in the fashioning of the image of content old age and without which the iconic status of elderliness cannot be reached. William Gouge, in his Epistle to the Reader fronting Sheafe's *Vindiciae* reproves those who have spent their time in idle dissipation as ones who do not deserve the honorific title of 'Old-Men'; they are brute beasts. Only he who by gravity has curbed his lusts can count as an 'Old-Man' (Sheafe, 1639, 29–30). A lifetime's character-building ensures the possession of enough strength 'to bridle and restraine' sexual longing (Goulart, 1621, 91). Lust, in its fondness and foolishness, is 'exceedingly hurtfull and most pernittious' to 'Olde and drye bodyes' (Newton, 1576, 55). Old age is hastened by immoderate venery because it 'weakeneth stre[n]gth, hurteth the braine, extinguisheth radicall moisture, & hasteneth on old age and death'. Sperm 'wilfully shed or lost' harms a man more than losing forty times more blood (Vaughan, 1600, 47); indeed, 'Venery' is death's best harbinger (Cuffe, 1600, 105). Though there are many who continue to be 'lusty, mery and well complexioned' well into old age, 'strong of limmes, good footme[n], and in their old dayes as fresh & actiue as many young me[n] be', it is precisely because they have lived continently, 'and spent not their adolescencie in unruly riot and lechery'. Young men are advised to conserve the 'floure and prime of their lusty age' by curbing 'immoderate vse of Venerous daliau[n]ce' (Newton, 1576, 28) and the old themselves are advised to put away all thoughts of sexual activity (cf. 28).

In *All's Well*, the King straddles the two seemingly contradictory positions implied by 'lustique' quite simply through the mechanism of denial. He very effectively curbs venery by not even acknowledging its presence to himself, let alone anybody else, a position reinforced by the text. Though the restoration of youthful vigour to an old man may imply also the restoration of sexual potency, it is the one outcome of robust good health that is denied to old men. The King is restored to the 'lusty age' of youth, but without the annoying symptoms of sexual arousal. As the manuals repeatedly tell their readers, lusts of the flesh may be what old men wish for in their dreams, but what they cannot, indeed should not try or even want to regain. It would be entirely inappropriate for the King to be inflamed by fleshly desires, and, moreover, damaging to his newly-restored health. Perhaps it is for this reason that the only references to restored potency come from Lafew, as a striking image for the King's recovery. If the King's return to health also means a resurgence of libidinous impulses, they are very effectively managed, indeed sublimated, in an act of generosity towards Helena, the new object of his paternal love.

What is true of *All's Well that Ends Well* is also true of the literature of the period which promulgates 'fictions' of old age, as I hope this project has shown. *All's Well*, in company with the other plays exemplified in this study, both exhibits and dismantles the crude binaries of youth–age, good–bad youth, foolish–wise old age. As part of her assimilation into the orbit of the idealised virtues of the old, the text requires both the King and Helena to manage their passion, and achieve its object through the exercise of wit and skill, converting sexual energy into purposeful action. The text projects the qualities of age onto Helena (just as the *Errors* text projects onto Adriana negative aspects of age) of in a series of circuitous motions which serve to illustrate non-linear productions of meaning and investigations into identity and alterity. Accordingly, in ranging medical knowledge against the seemingly certain death of the King, Helena has extended the boundaries of nature (and medicine). An 'earthly actor' in a 'heavenly effect' (2. 3, 22), she has exceeded gender expectations by confounding the doctors who pronounced the King as incurable. The reversal of the King's expectations may contain within its obviously pro-life expression of a return to the robust energy of his youth, a hint of 'lustique' in the '[v]ery hand of heaven' (2. 3, 28). The negotiation between the two genres of prescription and performance in this, as in the book as a whole, can be seen as a fusion of the rhetorical obduracy of the manuals, whose assessment of differences between youth and age discourages play in meaning, and the possibilities of endless play in drama, poetry and performance which can help us understand early modern processes and experiences of old age.

Notes

Prologue

1. Individual essays or chapters in volumes of essays thus usually span from 1500–1700, and works whose aim is more comprehensive have a chapter on aging in the early modern period. Among the best of the wide-spanning historiographical studies are Pat Thane's monograph and two volumes of essays — *Old Age in English History* (2000), *Old Age from Antiquity to Post-modernity*, co-edited with Paul Johnston, and the latest, lushly illustrated coffee-table collection of essays, *The Long History of Age* (2005). The history of elderly women, much more elusive, is nevertheless beginning to emerge in one of the first collections of its kind, *Women and Aging in British Society Since 1500* (2001), co-edited by Lynn Botelho and Pat Thane.

2. This occasionally rises to the level of a minor conflagration, as in the Reith lectures of 2001, 'The End of Age', given by Tom Kirkwood on longevity and aging, and the series of four programmes, 'Life in Old Age' run by BBC Radio 4, 9–30 March 2004.

3. This was published in 1638, though written when he was 62; see Charles Webster, *The Great Instauration* (London: Duckworth, 1975), 246–47.

4. Thomas Newton, *The Worthye Booke of Old Age* (1569). The second, *Fowre Seuerall Treatises of M. Tvllivs Cicero: Conteyninge his most learned and Eloquente Discourses of Friendshippe: Oldage: Paradoxes: and Scipio his Dreame. All turned out of Latine into English, by Thomas Newton* (1577) is a corrected version, and appeared in a compilation dedicated to Lord Francis Russell, Earl of Bedford, eight years later.

5. Printed in English in 1621, though written in the original quite a few years earlier, Goulart's *The Wise Vieillard*, translated from the French by 'an obscure Englishman, a friend and fauourer of all wise Old-Men', predates Sheafe's *Vindiciae Senectutis* (1639) as one of the best examples of this kind of literature. John Smith's *Pourtract of Old Age* (1666) is particularly interesting in that his work constitutes an early example of intertextuality as a tool for interpretation. He interprets the Ecclesiastes verses as a meditation on old age, uncovers their biological basis and proves his point by providing a medical gloss.

6. Bacon's use of the term derives from Aristotle, who stated that the body begins to age when its cooling mechanism breaks down, so that it is consumed by its own heat; in age, little heat remains, so the organs shrivel up. The aged body is thus cold and dry (Aristotle 1984: 1, 760 23(17) 478b–79b). Galen factored in the observation that the body's innate moisture began to dry up soon after adulthood. If the natural heat and moisture of the body could be preserved, human life could be prolonged for ever (Galen 1951: 6–7, 195–204, 216–19; Galen 1997: 233–36).

7. Pierre de la Primaudaye, *The French Academie wherein is discoursed the institution of Maners, and whatsoever els concerneth the good and happie life of all estates and callings, by precepts of doctrine, and example of the lives of ancient Sages and famous men*, transl. Thomas Bowes (1589).

Chapter 1

1. Hereafter referred to as *Dialogue*. Unless otherwise stated, the edition used throughout is the Yale *Complete Works of St. Thomas More*, volume 12.
2. All quotations and citations are from *The Comedy of Errors* (2002) ed. Charles Whitworth, The Oxford Shakespeare, Oxford University Press.
3. In *Maenachmi*, this character appears in one scene only, where he bemoans his age, in the Penguin classics translation of 1965, as 'a bad business, a dead loss. It brings you nothing but troubles, and plenty of them.' Age makes him an unsympathetic witness to his daughter's plight and he advises her to suffer her husband's mistreatment of her because it is he who keeps her in clothes, jewellery, servants and lifestyle (Plautus, 1965, 130–38.) The old man himself is the object of contemptuous mistreatment at the hands of Maenachmus and Sosicles (132–35). Appended to the Arden edition of the play (repr 2001) is a summary of relevant passages Shakespeare took from *Maenachmi*, *Ampitruo* and the Bible (*Errors*, 2001, 109–15).
4. Shakespeare's relocation from Plautus' Epidamnus to St. Paul's Ephesus, at the centre of Eastern and Western trade, amalgamates two polar ancient sources, the Pauline and the Plautine, thereby 'mixing one of antiquity's most spiritual writers with one of its most salacious' (McGuire, 1977, 356). Ephesus, associated with tavern revelling, is both 'actual and visual,' but it is also the locus of spiritual regeneration, as in *Henry IV* 1 & 2, which enacts Paul's metaphor of 'putting off the old man and putting on the new' (Ephesians 5: 16 & 4: 22–24; Maguire, 1997, 36–64).
5. An unfinished play whose plot is constructed around a single theme and one central stock figure, the old miser, Euclio, though there are other elderly personages on the periphery of the action; the old housekeeper, Staphyla whom Euclio abuses, and his contrastingly genial old neighbour Megadorus (Plautus, 1965, 10–41).
6. In a further displacement, the chain her husband has promised her becomes both the emblem of her insecurity and the fetishised gift he is willing to give to another woman.
7. Hair loss is associated with retention of waste products as the body grows older. The same process causes the aging body to fill up with shit as to become bald. While hair is a plentiful 'excrement' in the young it is scant in the old precisely because they are dry by nature but moist in condition. As one ages one 'drain(s) out towards decay' (Newton, 1576, 88) because 'the receyuers and conceptacles of the humours' fill up 'wyth excrements, which thing in Old men is plainly to be discerned & perceyued' (88) and just as hair loss is caused by the drying out of the body, so excremental build-up is caused by the body's heat 'being not able to digest our receiued nourishment; & thence is that corruption and rottennesse which ouertaketh these flowe-backes' (88; see also Cuffe, 1607, 101).
8. 'where nature is offended or grieved, she is cured by that, which is contrary to that, which offends or grieves, as cold by heat, heat by cold, drythe by moisture, moisture by drythe [...] contraries are remedy unto their contraries' (Elyot, 1541, 40).

9. For Joseph Candido, Antipholus of Ephesus's absence from his own dinner table implies a rejection of customary habits surrounding the midday meal which threatens his identity as a respectable married man, and even more so the stability and commitment of his marriage (Candido, 1997, 208–09), but Candido does not go on to make a connection with the mutability of age, or to draw inferences therefrom about gender.

10. The perception that bad habits left uncorrected in youth return to haunt old age is one of the abiding commonplaces of the prescriptive literature on senescence and health, and forms the substratum of all dietary, herbal, medical, moral and spiritual counsel. Chapter two and the Epilogue deal more extensively with this.

11. Documentary evidence shows particular values that attach to the old though living arrangements varied practically from household to household. The1599 census in Ealing, for example, shows inter-generational dependence in households, and in the Norwich census of the poor in 1570, grandchildren live with the elderly in nuclear rather than extended formations. The elderly continued to head their own households (cf. Laslett, 1977, 200; Macfarlane, 1987, 63–86). Contrarily, wills and diaries show that provision for the elderly was in place in both poor and well-to-do households, with the old tending to live with their married children (cf. Howell, 1986, 69; Spufford, 1974, 144, passim). The chapter which follows deals more extensively with inheritance and household formations.

12. As Elyot puts it, regulation 'fares by them as it does by a lamp, the light whereof is almost extinct, which by pouring in of oil little and little is long kept burning: and with much oil poured in at once, it is clean put out.'

13. Levinus Lemnius, for example, advises the old to avoid change of any kind because it depletes their store of energy for their 'iourneyes end' — that is, dying (Newton, 1576, 50v), Sheafe is against travel abroad (Sheafe, 1639, 149) and Steele assumes an old person's travelling days are over (Steele, 1688, 240). For Bacon, however, change of air in travel, exposure to new customs is beneficial, and travellers are long-lived (Bacon, 1638, 117).

14. Subsequently referred to as *della famiglia*.

15. In addition, the *Dialogue*, written in the last few years of More's life, belongs to a tradition of prison literature that includes Plato's *Crito*, Paul's *Epistles*, Boethius' *Consolations of Philosophy*, works whose authors detach themselves from the depressing effects of confinement by concentrating the mind's rational powers upon spiritual contemplation, and as a consequence deal with the problem of suicide only obliquely. Boethius, for example, does so by reference to Seneca and Papinian, both forced to commit suicide (an act of despair) the one by Nero, the other by Caracalla: '[e]ach of them was willing to give up his power. Seneca even tried to give his money to Nero and go into retirement. But like men who lose their footing and are pulled down by their own weight, neither was able to achieve what he wanted' (Boethius, 1995, 3,v,95 Providence provides an instinctive and overriding desire for self-preservation, thereby rendering obsolete impulses towards suicide (3, xii,112).

16. The most recent historical accounts of old age highlight its continuities in the same breath as they identify and analyse the various points at which the stereotypes shifted somewhat. See especially Pat Thane's four publications (1998, 2000, 2001, 2005), the work of Shulamith Shahar (1997, 1998, 2005) and Lynn Botelho (2001, 2005).

17. in *City of God*, Bk. 1 ch. 22 where he discusses whether Cato was justified in killing himself for fear of falling into Caesar's hands (Augustine, 1909, 27–28).

18. His source is Cicero, *De senectute*, from which he goes on to quote directly: 'no man that for all that so old but that he hopeth [yet] that he may lyve one yere more' (Cicero, 2001, 33; *Dialogue*, 4).
19. More himself needed all the stoicism he could muster, for while in prison, all the property the king had given him was taken away, and all his possessions forfeited at the same time as the terms of imprisonment grew even more stringent: he was denied the comfort of visits from his family, and the solace of walks in the garden in the Tower. He wrote to Margaret that he was resigned, and took comfort in knowing that his family were living peacefully together (*Correspondence*, 1947, 543, 540).

Chapter 2

1. Prescriptive literature repeats Cicero's advice; when one is old one is at last free to cultivate the life of the mind, and one can turn one's attention to farming (Cicero, 2001, 73). The best means of cooling the aged body according to Bacon, for example, is to inhale the smell of freshly-dug earth from ploughing, or of fallen leaves from trees and hedgerows (Bacon, 1638, 161–62). Vincent, one of the interlocutors of *Cyuile and vncyuile life* who lives on his father's country estate claims there is nothing so reviving as the roar of hounds, and extols country life for the aged (1579, 55–57)..
2. Interestingly, there is also in this play a parallel safe and hidden place at court where the old flourish, and from which they emerge at the end of the play. The creator of this court retreat, Evander, is also the author and enforcer of the law against the old, which, it turns out, is patriarchy's way of exposing youth's excesses and unseemly impatience to usurp the old. I owe this insight to Tony Bromham.
3. See, for example, George Rowe's discussion of Middleton's tragicomedies as an exploration of the darker more disturbing undertow of Roman comedy so that the Old Law's 'anticomic elements' are 'let loose within a comic framework in order to expose the limitations of that framework' (Rowe, 1979, 156; 153–89) and more recently Mark Hutchings and Tony Bromham's excellent analysis of *The Old Law* as an example of alternating comic and tragic modes in Middleton and Rowley's collaborations (Hutchings and Bromham, 2007, 95–104).
4. All citations and quotations are taken from William Shakespeare, *The Merchant of Venice*, ed. J.L. Halio (1994), World's Classics paperbacks, Oxford: Oxford University Press.
5. Shylock himself draws attention to the contrast in age and religion between himself and Bassanio, Lancelot's new master: 'Well, thou shalt see — thy eyes shall be thy judge —/The difference of old Shylock and Bassanio[...]/[...]Thou shalt not gormandize/As thou hast with me'(2. 5, 1–3). Critics have hitherto made little of Shylock's age, though it is a significant marker of Shakespeare's typecasting.
6. Antonio's request to give one half of Shylock's goods to Lorenzo does not benefit Jessica directly; she loses half of what she is heir to, and control of all of it.
7. Though, to be sure, in youth Googe's Amintas knew the force of love: 'And now, to talke of spring time tales/my heares to hoare,do growe,/Such tales as these, I tolde in tyme,/when youthfull yeares did flowe' (Hallett Smith, 1952, 32).

8. All citations and quotations for *The Old Law* are from Catherine M. Shaw (1982), *The Old Law by Thomas Middleton and* William *Rowley*, Garland English Texts, New York and London: Garland Publishing Inc.

9. The provision of widows was a complex one and varied from family to family. Margaret Spufford, for example, shows how wills varied from village to village in sixteenth- and seventeenth-century Cambridge. Among the wealthy in Chippenham, both widows and sons could inherit, though there were one or two like Robert Gyll who in 1590 'before honeste wynesses saye he wolde geve nothinge of his goodes to ainy of his Children but that his wiefe shoulde have all his goodes' (Spufford, 1974, 88–90). In Orwell, by contrast, widows were left with holdings only till the son reached his majority, after which she was entitled to carefully specified house room (111–19). Inheritance practice differed yet again in Willingham where landed men left tenements in the first instance to widows, and then, as did Henry Graves in 1585, to 'my child, be it man or woman, if it please God she be with any;' and in Willingham only do wills make provision for separate premises for the widow in the event of generational strife (161–64).

10. Jointure, or joint tenancy, involved a tenant giving up part of his holdings on marriage and later taking it back jointly with his wife. This was a way of avoiding accidental alienation of land — that is, land passing out of the control of the person who holds it. Since all land in the sixteenth and seventeenth centuries was ultimately leased by the Crown, it was in the interests of both landlord and tenant for estates to be held intact and in control of one incumbent. In the terms of socage (free tenure in ordinary law) in England and Europe, a widow had a right to one third or a half of her husband's lands, with the remainder going to the firstborn. At villein level, property was more evenly divided; the surviving spouse was entitled to half or more of the other's land (Goody, Thirsk and Thompson, 1976, 30). Despite these reassurances, widows were left feeling vulnerable no matter what their social status. For example, Lady Sarah Cooper expressed concern about her jointure long before her husband died. She asked her lawyer son to scrutinise the jointure papers and later made a copy of the documents in her diary, but these precautions availed her nothing; she was left in straitened circumstances after the death of her husband (Kugler, 2001, 76–77).

11. By refusing to keep on his father's tailor because he will be a laughing-stock if he takes on the garb of an old man 2. 1,, 260–65), Simonides observes dress codes of the early modern period. Clothing was, according to Georges Duby, a means of social discrimination in that it encouraged individuals to appear in a manner befitting their age. Following fashion was a youthful activity, denoting 'a period of flamboyance between the gray of childhood and the paler colors of maturity and old age' (Aries and Duby, 1988–89, 3, 575). Matthus Schwarz in his *Trachtenbuch* sketches contemporary fashions in comparison to those of earlier generations; thus a baby's swaddling clothes are compared to the déshabille of an old man suffering from heart trouble so that he has to hobble around the house in a brown overcoat, stick and bonnet (Aries and Duby, 1988–89, 3, 580).

12. All citations and quotations for *King Lear* are taken from the Arden Shakespeare, edited by R.A. Foakes (2003) Third Series, London: Thompson Learning.

13. Baldwin Maxwell noticed in 1966 that *The Old Law* was a comic counterpart to *Lear* in its treatment of the struggle between the generations and the desire for youth to come into its inheritance when it could enjoy it most (Maxwell, 1966, 138, 141).

14. However, the obligation of children to nurse parents in sickness and old age was accompanied by a whole sheaf of writings which pointed to the discrepancy between the quality of the love of parents to children (natural instinct; grows), and that of children towards parents (from recognition of those who care for them in infancy; wanes). See Shahar, 1997, 92. Some medieval writers sought scientific explanations for the unequal balance of love and care between parents and children: one of the questions in *The Prose Salernitan Questions*, an anonymous collection concerned with science and medicine, written by an Englishman around 1200, asks why parents care for their children more than their children care for them (*quod parentes magis diligunt filios quam filii parentes*). The answer is that offspring inherit from their father and mother (*filii de substantia patris et matris generatur*), but not the other way round (*nichil de essentia filii et filie sit in parentibus* (qu.101, p. 47). The New Testament attributed the difference to selfless giving. Paul's Epistles evoke Christ's sacrifice, and his letter to the Corinthians: 12: 14 insists that 'the parents lay up for the children' though the children ought not to lay up for the parents. Parents care more for their children than children for them because they are the future and live for many more years, thereby ensuring generational continuity.

15. Another version crops up in Perkins's *Christian Oeconomie*, 1609, 149.

16. Evidently things did not turn out well with the young and newly married John at the helm; this account is recorded in a deposition by Walter Webb in the Somerset Record Office for 10 July 1605. John the elder complained to his relative Walter who had been invited to a spread, that 'Yow are like to haue but a shorte feast heere, but I praye if yow haue not good cheere blame my sone John Webbe and not me, for of my troth I haue made him master of all, payinge me x(louis) by the yeare and finding me and my wyfe sufficient meate and drinke and all other maintenance to discharge all rentes and dutyes whatsoever' D/D/Cd 36, 10 Jul 1605, deposition by Walter Webb in Jenkins v.Webb cited in Houlbrooke, 1984, 190).

17. Contrarily, the harsh reality for pre-industrial society for Laslett was that '[n]o parental couple or widowed person seems to have been rejoined by a child, married or unmarried, to help in their care' (Laslett 1972, 207). This applied equally to the well-to-do, who preferred to maintain their own household and their own staff — and to the privileged classes, whose children did not choose to house them (212), and it applies also to Lear's situation, post carve-up of the land.

18. Such stories were part of a literary tradition, informing the medieval versions of Lear and Shakespeare's sixteenth-century sources (Shahar, 1997, 95). For example, there are several versions of a story about an old man who gave away all his property, and was kicked out onto the porch. His grandchild was given a sack to deliver to the grandfather for warmth. The child told his father to cut it in two; one half for his grandfather, and the other for his father, for him to use when his father was old (C'hest de la houce, 1872, 2, 1–7). See also *Liber exemplorum ad usum praedicantium*, 'De filiis malis male se habentibus erga parentes' — 'reqisitus a patre quid inde faceret; 'Servabo,' inquid, 'eas quousque sis qualis est pater tuus. Nec tunc tibi dabo amplius sicut nec tu vis plus modo dare patri tuo, ' (1908, 86) and Robert Mannyng (1901, 41–42). This, along with another, more macabre version appears in *Dives and Pauper* (1, 4: 4, 311–12) a long prose treatise of unknown authorship in dialogue form, written in Middle English as an exposition of the practical meaning of the ten commandments, and in one of Shakespeare's supposed

sourcebooks, *Mery Tales [...] and Quicke Answeres*, readily available in several editions, in which the old man dies of ill-treatment, and his grandchild asks his father for the sackcloth covering the old man in his last days. When asked why, the child replies: 'it shall serue to couer you whan ye be olde, lyke as it did my grandfather,' the moral being that children should reverence their father, help him in his old age, 'and make him not thoughtfull and heuy in his lyfe, and though he dote, forgyue it him. He that honoreth his father, shall lyue the longer, and shall rioyce in his owne chyldren.' (12122; *Dives and Pauper*, 1976, 1, 4:4, 312; *Pasquils Jests*, 1864, 3, 60–61).

19. See also the story of 'the olde man that put him selfe in his sonnes handes' *Mery Tales and quicke answeres* (1567), 121.

20. According to Shahar, Macfarlane, in his two books *The Origins of English Individualism* (New York, 1979), chapter 6, 'English Economy and society in the Thirteenth to Fifteenth Centuries', 131–64 and *Marriage and Love in England 1300–1800* (Oxford 1986), 321–44, formulated his thesis on the basis of warnings and tales such as those found in Rogers. Shahar's objection to the thesis is on the grounds that these were not exclusively English; on the contrary, they were 'virtually universal' and she provides substantial evidence in support for the late medieval period (Shahar, 1997, 95–97, and her chapter on 'Old Age and the Peasantry'). See also Richard Smith, who finds that the old had means other than retirement contracts, which could be met in more than one way (Smith 1991, 43). In an earlier work, Smith looks at provision for fathers-in-law in the event of 'heirship failure' (Smith, 1984, 46–48).

21 Among the Czechs and in parts of Scandinavia it was the custom for the old divided up their land equally and stayed with each heir in turn (Goody et al., 1976, 22–23, 29; Gaunt, 1983, cited in Abendstern et al., 1990, 25). By planning to set himself up in two separate households, in each of which he has entitlement of care, he forms an extended or joint household with the addition of himself and his retainers for half a year. Macfarlane has found such arrangements to be the pattern of residence among the upper gentry in England (Macfarlane, 1986, 96).

22. Elsewhere Smith argues that transferable wealth could be used as a means for the bargaining of relative positions within a family, though subject to external political, legal and economic circumstances, and that this remained a relatively enduring way of organising the disposition of family fortunes and providing for the elderly (Smith, 1991, 45).

23. Old age is unquestioningly treated as a second childhood in early modern writing. Lewes Lewkenor's translation of de la Marche's *The Resolved Gentleman* marvels at the strange descent from vigour to the 'verie extremities of childehood' (1594, 20); Andreas Laurentius likewise (1599, 175); H[umphrey] M[ill]'s melancholy vision was that old men are children, and must die (1639, sig.M8) and Richard Steele's belief that to be old in years was to be a child in understanding (1688, 82) are just but three examples, picked at random.

24. Roger L'Estrange in his *Fables of Aesop and other eminent Mythologists* reflects upon the moral to be drawn: ' for a man to Value himself upon the Reputation of a Popular Favour' is to expose his vanity and affections as 'Violent transports that are carried on by Ignorance and Rage,' leading inevitably into 'Incorrigible Error' (329–30). It invests the old man with the commonplaces of old age; the old man is foolish, eager to please everyone, and easily angered.

25. For evidence of how this worked in seventeenth-century Norfolk and in Essex from 1500 to 1700 see respectively Tim Wales, in Smith ed. 1984, 351–404 and Keith Wrightson, 1984, 'kinship in an English Village', 313–32.

Chapter 3

1. Horace loads the dice against old men, who are 'surrounded by disadvantages' which include dissatisfaction with their lot, miserliness, hesitancy, 'cramped and trembling' administration of their affairs; they are prone to postponing, 'reluctant in expectation', lazy, greedy, difficult, complaining, swamped in nostalgia, and 'ready to punish and criticize the young'. A poet or writer, in order to 'avoid giving to a young man the character of an old man' should as a rule of thumb confine himself to 'what is found in each period of life and is therefore fitting to it' (Horace, 1974, lines 169–74).

2. Falstaff is Shakespeare's comic inversion of this principle. Rejecting all evidence of his own physical decline, he fails to adapt his behaviour to suit his age, and so continues to behave like a giddy youth whilst at the same time figuring himself as the young prince's mentor and guide. As a result, he invests everything in the belief that his influence over the prince will continue once he is crowned. But because he refuses to adapt his behaviour to suit his age, he misreads the signals of rejection. Shakespeare develops this theme of the self-deceptions to which age is prone in his portrayal of Lear, another 'anomalous ager' (Donow, 1992, 736).

3. Burton, living and writing in the age of Shakespeare, probably began to compile the Anatomy after he settled in 1599 for the rest of his life at Christ Church College, Oxford. Though the Anatomy was not published until 1621, Burton draws on earlier treatises on melancholy, written by Agrippa, Timothy Bright, Laurentius, Thomas Wright the Jesuit, Cardan, Levinus Lemnius and Suarez in order to compile his own (Burton, 1955, 219).

4. See Caroline Asp's excellent psychoanalytic account of aging in *King Lear* as a study in the 'dynamics of repression and negation' (Asp, 1986, 197). The steps (from hero to zero, in effect) reduce him to the powerlessness of the outcast because his old age denies him 'maternal solace;' like those in early modern culture who lose respect and status at the onset of old age, he comes instead to 'occupy the place of the female' (193–95).

5. Foakes points to another area in which Lear's actions are unsustainable. In the first place, according to the kingship ideologies of the times, the king is God's anointed representative on earth, and cannot therefore retire. Only God can dispose of him and his estates, and it is God who chooses the moment of handover. The private possession and disposal of land by a monarch was in any case a legal impossibility. Royal ownership of property, no matter how it was acquired — by gift, by inheritance, or by any other means — belonged to the crown and not to the individual. Elizabeth's counsellors explained this by reference to the fact that the king's natural body cannot act independently of the body politic. A monarch can lease, give away, keep or receive land only in the name of the body politic of which his natural body is the lesser part. By this ruling, a monarch cannot hand over land or property to another person directly. Land can only be symbolically transferred, and authorised solely by common law. (Kantorowitz, 1957, 9ff & 405–09; Foakes, 1996, citing *All England Law Reports Reprint*, 1558–1774, 36 vols. (London: Butterworth 1968, vol.1, 148, and his citations from Edmund Plowden's *Law Reports*; Foakes, 1996, 288). So Lear's actions are not only unbefitting to a king; they are in breach of the common law (Foakes, 1996, 277–80).

6. His ripost to Regan's contemptuous 'Oh, Sir you are old' (2.2, 335) is to tell her that 'Age is necessary' (2.2, 344). In this he echoes Laurentius' rationale for writing on old age: 'a man cannot alwaies continue in one state, and that it is necessarie that he should grow old' (Laurentius, 1599, 168).

7. Preparation is all the more necessary, as Henry Cuffe for example, points out, in advanced old age since this results from an evaporation of strength and heat, accompanied by complete debility and the will to remain alive. This final stage resembles 'death itselfe, whose harbinger and fore-runner it is' (Cuffe, 1607, 120). See also above, Prologue, 1.

8. Peacham elevated William Cecil, Lord Burghley into the paradigm of good practice in public speaking '[f]or nothing draws our attention more than good matter eloquently digested and uttered with a graceful, clear, and distinct pronunciation'. Burghley 'to his dying day' carried in his pocket Cicero's *De officio*, a book 'sufficient, as one said of Aristotle's rhetoric, to make both a scholar and an honest man' (Peacham, 1962, 56–57).

9. In the opinion of George Whetstone, English comedies are by their very nature indecorous. They are 'vaine, indiscrete, and out of order', because the playwright 'fyrst groundes his worke on impossibilities; then in three howers ronnes he throwe the worlde, marryes, gets Children, makes Children men, men to conquer kingdomes, murder Monsters, and bringeth Gods from Heauen, and fetcheth Diuels from Hel [...] Manye tymes (to make mirthe) they make a Clowne companion with a Kinge; in their graue Counsels they allow the aduise of fooles; yea, they vse one order of speach for all persons: a grose Indecorum, for a Crowe wyll yll counterfet the Nightingale's sweete voice; euen so affected speeche doth misbecome a Clowne. For, to worke a Comedie kindly, graue olde men should instruct, yonge men should showe the imperfections of youth.' According to this persuasion, indecorum on stage is a national and generic vice (Whetstone, 1578, 1: 59–60).

10. Puttenham, like Aristotle, insists that a good writer can fashion language so that it is not 'vnseemely or misbecoming, but rather decenter and more agreeable to any ciuill eare and vnderstanding' (Puttenham, 1589, 149; Aristotle, 1984, 2: 1404b, 2239). Aristotle had stipulated that 'good' language must be clear and plain; speech which fails to convey a plain meaning falls short of its very function. It must also be appropriate, avoiding both meanness and undue evaluation. Poetical language is certainly free from meanness, but it is not appropriate to prose. To ensure clarity, Aristotle recommends the use of nouns and verbs that are current and ordinary. However, since '[p]eople do not feel towards strangers as they do towards their own countrymen, and the same is true of their feeling for language,' he suggests injecting into everyday speech 'an unfamiliar air' in order to attract an interlocutor's attention. People are struck by what is out of the way. But while such effects are fitting in poetry, it is not quite appropriate for fine language to issue from the mouth of a slave or a very young man, or about very trivial subjects. The rule of thumb should be language which is appropriately muted, natural, and artfully shaped so as to disguise the art that goes into its construction (Aristotle, 1984, Rhetoric, 2: 1404b, 2239).

11. Tony Bromham examines the impact of Justus Lipsius' *de Constantia* in the play's representations of stoicism (Bromham, 1996, 404–21).

12. Bromham perceives a relationship between the ancient Greek derivatives of the names in this play as a means of revealing the significance of their roles in portraying the play's major themes. Thus in selecting the name Creon for one of the old men about to suffer the penalty of the law, Bromham suggests that the playwrights wished to evoke the story of Antigone, Oedipus' daughter, who disobeyed King Creon's edict refusing burial to her two brothers. Antigone, wishing like Cleanthes in *The Old Law* to save a relative, respects divine over human law, and, like Creon in the play, angrily denounces its justice and validity (Bromham 1994, 509–12).

13. Women, according to the physiology of the ancients, aged much more quickly than men; a given adopted without question by early modern manual writers. This was because, pace Hippocrates and Galen, female foetuses grow more slowly in the womb but once born, they mature sooner and age more quickly 'by reason of the weaknes of their bodies and of their manner of living' (Laurentius, 1599, 177). From the point of view of the law, women lived all six ages before they were twenty-one (cf. Cowell, 1607 cited by Dove, 1986, 23). See also Lynn Botelho for cultural conceptions of female aging (Bothelho, 2000, 49–52). Yet even though they aged faster, they still managed to live as long as and sometimes even to outlive men; see Thane, 2000, 21–24.

14. Manuals on health, following the example of Galen, who prescribed a health regime for two very old men, have plenty of recipes for the inner and outer comfort of old men, and to lengthen their days (Galen, 1951, 20–23; cf. Elyot, 1541, 4,3 *passim*; Vaughan, 1600, 65–68; Cuffe, 1607, 99–103; Bacon, 1638, esp. 158–70, 183–91).

15. Bulwer, for example, fulminates against those who attempt to disguise the effects of age: though they are 'a rotten building ready to fall; yet they are willing to deceive themselves, and every body else, (if they could) contrary to all truth and reason, by dying the haires of their beards and heads'. He goes on to ridicule 'these old coxcombs' with hair like a parrot's feathers: 'white at the roots, yellow in the middle, and black at the point' (1654, 212–13).

16. White hair is effeminizing because it results from depletion of body heat, rendering the aged male body in condition like that of a woman, that is, sluggish and cold: 'the horiness, and whitish [...] colour of the haire of the head, is caused by a flamatick quality: and such of nature draw neer to the quality of women, as experience teacheth' (Hill, 1613, 23). The logic of this extends to considerations of baldness, that other indicator of male aging. William Warde, translating *Arcandam* (and repeated in Hill, 1613, 21–23), relegates men whose hair is thinning at the temples to the condition of women, that is, 'cold & without force.' But by implication, men who have a full head of hair in old age are like women, 'who are never bald, for their nature is like the nature of infants or children' (Warde, 1578, sigs.mvii verso; n). So plentiful hair, normally a point of attraction, becomes in the aging male a sign of decay, and gives besides a physiological rationale for figurative displacements of male aging onto young women (see chapter 1, above).

17. All citations and quotations come from *The Broken Heart* in John Ford (1995), *'Tis Pity She's a Whore and Other Plays*, ed. M. Lomax, World's Classics, Oxford: Oxford University Press.

18. Old men were known from the writings of Aristotle onwards to be distrustful and from introspection to be 'peevish' (Aristotle, 1984, 2: Bk.2, ch.13, 2214; Montaigne, 1894, 366; cf. Goulart, 1621, 76; Steele, 1688, 41, 50). Montaigne's self regulation requires him to 'oppose myself to humours' in order to become 'lesse froward and not so testy' (366).

19. Reminiscent of Portia's situation in *The Merchant of Venice*, Ford's main action results from the overturn of Penthea's dead father's betrothal of his daughter to Orgilus. The promise is denied by Penthea's twin, Ithocles, who gives his sister to Bassanes instead, with a hint of incest that recalls the claustrophobic feelings of Ferdinand for his twin sister, *The Duchess of Malfi* (cf. Lomax, Introduction to *The Broken Heart*, in Ford, 1995, xiv).

Chapter 4

1. The marriage of an older man to a young woman is presumably permissible for procreative purposes, whereas older women marrying, 'as the wanton and legerous often doe with wanton young fellowes in these dayes,' receives moral opprobrium. It is a 'staine of their sexe, and reproach to themselues' and leads as often as not 'to their vtter vndoing' (Bernard, 1628, 289–90).
2. And 'the strange woman is a narrow pit', so young men do best to avoid women altogether, (39) and stick to old men as their mentors, because in every well ordered common weal old men are honoured and revered and young men 'frequent their company' (50).
3. All citations and quotations come from *A Critical Edition of Thomas Middleton's The Witch*, ed. E.J. Esche (1993), New York and London: Garland Publishing. The dating of the play remains uncertain, but its reference to the scandal of the day, the Overbury murder and the Frances Howard divorce and trial, connect it to *The Old Law* and suggest a dating after 1613 (Esche (ed)., *Witch*, 1993, Introduction, 16–26).
4. Hecate's longevity bespeaks admiration and respect, and evokes the era's fascination with long livers. John Taylor the Water Poet who published in 1635 an account of *The Olde old very Olde Man or, The Age and long life of of Thomas Par [...] and is now living in the Strand, being aged 152 yeares and odd Monethes*. The accompanying portrait of Parr shows him to be a handsome, healthy man in his late fifties or early sixties. There was evidently some miscalculation going on — possibly the confusion of his dates with his father's (Thane, 2005, 16–17; cf. Botelho, 2005, 128; Gruman, 1666, esp. 21, 74–77).
5. Edward Bever (1982, 175), believes that the condemnation of sexual desires in old women combined with frustration due to lack of opportunities for remarriage is a key component in their persecution as witches while Roper examines representations of the old woman's ravenous sexual appetites in early modern art and literature in Germany (Roper, 2004, 162–70).
6. They receive mention in the manuals only as an afterthought; the authors rarely distinguish between old age in women as opposed to men, despite adverse assumptions about the workings of the post-menopausal female body in Hippocrates, Aristotle and Galen, for an account of which see below. Apart from A.B.'s tract counselling against marriage with an old woman, there is only one old age manual, that of Thomas Brookes, which includes women in its title.
7. Roper, 2004, has a chapter on crones which, among other things, examines German genre woodcuts and paintings in relation to literary representations (160–78).
8. Galen reasons that women are colder than men because they stay at home, idle. The part of the blood which is rich, light, or fine is in hotter bodies consumed as nourishment by the heat, but in cold bodies is preserved, emerges from the veins, and, when it comes into contact with some cold part, such as the membranes, is solidified around them. In contact with naturally hotter bodies, though, such as the fleshy substances, it is consumed and dispersed by the heat — except in cases where there is a lax kind of regime in addition to the coldish mixture, and this encourages the growth of some fat, even in the fleshy parts. This is why women (and hibernating animals) have more fat than men (Galen, 1997, 247). *De sanitate tuenda*, Galen's treatise on gerontology, however, does not concern itself with women at all (Galen, 1951, 195–200).

9. The extent of this is at last beginning to emerge as a result of ground-break-ing studies on the importance of gender and cultural specificity to an under-standing of the complexities of perceptions and representations of old age in the early modern period; Thane, Botelho, Shahar, Pelling, Kugler, Froide, Schen (and Ottaway for the eighteenth century) all build on the work on age begun by the Cambridge team (Smith, Macfarlane, Goody, Spufford, Howell, Wall et al) in the 1970s and 1980s by giving it a new direction and impetus most particularly in their work on older women.

10. This disgust was exploited by artists in the German genre paintings and linked to the practice of witchcraft by old women (cf. Roper, 2004, 162–69).

11. Comedies of manners from mid-sixteenth century onwards adopted this nameless typecasting. See, for example, *Ralph Roister Doister*, Philip Mass-inger's *A New Way to Pay Old Debts*; and there are many references to scan-dalous old women as in John Fletcher's *The Scornful Lady*, *Wit at Several Weapons* and Thomas Killigrew's *The Parson's Wedding*, which contains a character whose name and description, Lady Love-all, An old Stallion Hunt-ing Widow, says it all.

12. Loomis thinks this might be her privy stool (Loomis 1996, 490), though two days and three nights seems a very long time to be crouched upon it.

13. '[H]onest matrons [...] are little given to carnal vices'; the devil tempts them by worldly profit, whereas young girls are 'more given to bodily lusts and pleasures', so the Devil goes to work on their carnal desires (Kramer & Spreuger, *Malleus*, 1971, 97).

14. Much of Bacon's physiology of the old derives from Aristotle, though on the matter of anger Aristotle is less uncompromising: their fits of anger are sud-den but feeble (1984, 2: 1389b–1390a, 2214).

15. All quotations and citations are taken from the Revels Student Edition of William Rowley, Thomas Dekker, and John Ford's *The Witch of Edmonton*, edited by Peter Corbin and Douglas Sedge, 1999.

16. The first witch in *Macbeth* vows to drain the captain of the Tiger 'dry as hay' so that 'Weary sev'n-nights nine times nine,/Shall he dwindle, peak and pine'. The implication seems to be that she will indulge her (sexual) appetite in revenge for his wife's refusal to indulge her greed for chestnuts (1. 3, 3, 23).

17. All quotations and citations are taken from the Globe Quartos edition of Thomas Heywood, *The Wise Woman of Hoxton* (i.e., Hogsdon), Sonia Mas-sai (ed.), 2002.

18. The substantial body of paintings in the 'doctor's visit' genre is examined by Laurinda Dixon in another context. Gabriel Metsu, Jacob Ochtervelt, Franz van Mieris, Jan Steen, Gerard ter Borch, Gerrit Dou and Jacob Toorenvliet, for example, all depict the central role of the old woman in the healing pro-cess, see also fig. 4.2. Usually, she is in a threesome with the doctor and the patient. In Steen's 'Doctor's Visit', ca. 1668–70, the implication is that the older woman is on an equal footing with the doctor; they are both in the background and she is offering him a glass of wine. This parity is even more explicit in his earlier 1666 painting which shows her helping the doctor by handing him something, and in another, it is the doctor who is in the back-ground; the foreground is dominated by the old woman doing the healing. In Gerrit Dou's 'Dropsical Woman', 1663, the doctor is in the foreground, removed from the relationship between patient and healer, who is the old woman; the sick girl is leaning into her. In Gabriel Metsu's 'The Sick Woman,' ca. 1650–60, the old woman is the only healer present, and in Toorenvliet, 1666, in the Wellcome Institute Library, London, the surgeon is doing the practical work while the patient and the old woman are in close conversation (cf. Dixon, 1995, *passim*).

19. If a nettle placed in the fresh urine of the sick person is dry and withered after 24 hours, the person will die; if it remains green, he will live (Simotta, 1631, 30–110). See also The Iudycyall of Uryns (n.d., ?1527); the Key to Unknowne Knowledge (1599). James Hart and Thomas Brian, both writing to convince the doubters, state that it was not possible to diagnose without seeing the person, whose presence was needed for the prognosis (Hart, 1625, 1; Brian, 1637, 3).

20. Like weather-forecasting, fortune-telling is detailed in such works as *Perpetuall and Naturall Prognstications of the Change of Weather*, trans. from Italian by I.F. (1598), whose final section deals also with natural portents of disaster. See also *The Shepheards Legacy: or, John Clearidge his Forty Years experience of the weather* (1670) where the author's age sanctions the work; he shows 'the Antiquity and Honour of Shepheards' (Clearage, 1670, title page).

21. The popularity of this translation caused it to run to seven editions between the years 1632 and 1657. See also Samuel Strangehopes, *A Book of Knowledge* (1664), 44–47; *The True Fortune-Teller* (2nd edn., 1686); Thomas, 1971, 285.

22. John Halle's anecdotes of Maidstone charletans could well be a source for the various actions of the play; Staplehurst's assumed name, his masquerade as a cunning man and his comically uncovered illiteracy (his third wife, when asked by the apothecary why her husband had not written her a list, 'answered that Mayster Wynkfylde was a ryght Latynist, for he coulde wryte no Englishe' all have their counterparts in Chartley's shenanigans, the ignorant Wise Woman and the credulity of her clients. Halle, a surgeon himself and a strenuous seeker-out of bogus practitioners, roundly denounces Staplehurst/Wynkfylde's pretentions: 'By this ye maye perceave he was a well learned manne', cunning only 'to enchaunte women to love, and did for rewardes, dyverse feates insuch cases' (Halle, 1565, 13–14).

23. Aubrey cites Virgil's Eclogues: 'the magick of the Sive and Sheeres, (I thinke) is in Virgil's Ecglogues; The Sheers are stuck in a Sieve, and two maydens hold up ye sive with the top of their fingers by the handle of the Shiers: then say, By St Peter & St Paul He hath not stoln it' (Aubrey, 1686–87, 25).

24. The poor depended not on one job but several based on local economies, which might include day labour, by-employments and casual jobs, loans and begging. The main unit of earning was the family. 'In a society where, in the late seventeenth century, up to one-third of the population was under fifteen, and where under-employment was the norm, all household members rather than the head alone were of necessity earners [...] The welfare of the poor household rested on the employment of as many of its members as possible. (Wales, 1984, 352) The Coton parish officers 'revealingly combined moral, regulative and economic motives' in wanting to withdraw from a (supposedly) 114 year old man his 2s. a week pension because he was abusive, frequented the alehouse and never went to church. They argued that in any case, he did not need money as 'he had a cow and a calf.' (353). Cawston Parish listings of 1601 correlate age with poverty and divide the poor into four groups, the first being 'the names of the pore above the age of three score years and the number in each famylie' (370–71).

25. These statutes exacted penalties for hunting treasure, invoking spirits, inflicting bodily harm, provoking unlawful love (1542 and 1563) and Henry VIII's statute 22 against the legality of fortune telling was reinforced by the Elizabethan and Jacobean statutes 14, 39 and 1, respectively.

26. Rather confusingly, this same statute permits cure of 'outwarde' sores, swellings or 'disease' by herbs or ointments, and 'Stone or Ague' by drink (*Statutes*, 1542, 3, 906).

27. The boundary between what wise women and witches did can be defined as magic — that is, as words and actions that claim efficacy in themselves rather than prayers and incantations that call on the power of God or depend on nature. But in practice of course this boundary was impossible to maintain.

28. 'Wise Woman (to Luce) You would prevent young Chartley's marriage? You shall [...] (to Sencer, in love with Gratiana): You forestall Gratiana's wedding? 'Tis but thus [*Whispers*]. (to Boyster) You would enjoy Luce as your wife, and lie with her to-morrow night? Hark in your ear. [Whispers][...] Away, You shall enjoy her.[to Luce] you are married, Luce; away! [to Sencer] You shall see Chartley discarded from Gratiana; Sencer, begone! And if I fail in any of these or the rest, I lay myself open to all your displeasures.'

29. The second Act is a good example of the continuing involvement of the old in the complicated love lives of the young, and their continuing agency. Having abandoned Second Luce on the wedding-day before the play begins, the gaming, dicing, philandering Young Chartley, at its opening, plans a secret, bogus marriage to Luce. This can only be achieved with the help of the Wise Woman, who will provide the priest. The convoluted main plot is motivated by Wise Woman's desire for revenge upon Young Chartley for his disrespect to her. She decides to adopt Second Luce's plan to pay him back by frustrating his fake marriage plans (2. 1, 156–57). As the action progresses, he plans to woo a third, Gratiana. By the second scene in Act Two, the Wise Woman has begun her revenge upon Young Chartley through the exercise of her matchmaking skills; she plans to dupe Luce into marrying Boyster instead of Young Chartley, who in turn will be duped into marrying Second Luce, who is the real mastermind of the comic confusion, and who is in the employ of the Wise Woman as a cross-dressed youth. The Wise Woman, enthusiastically taking up the plot that Second Luce has set in motion, and characteristically assuming authorship for ideas suggested by others, will have Second Luce 'tired like a woman,' in order 'to have Luce married to this blunt gentleman, she mistaking him for Chartley; and Chartley shall marry thee, being a boy, and take thee for Luce. Wilt not be excellent?'(2. 1, 191–99).

30. Alan Macfarlane, 1986, section 2, and J. Boulton, 1987 examine the kind of job opportunities available to the poor and old. The recent work of Margaret Pelling, 1991, 1996 and 1997 is crucial in determining the kind and extent of the work done by poor old women in the late sixteenth and seventeenth centuries. For the effects of aging and life-cycle on individual social and financial circumstances see Elliott, 1978, 369; Ramsay 1978 in *Economic History Review*, 2nd ser., 31, 526–40, 534–40; Phythian-Adams, 1979, 91–95; Smith 1981b, 595–622, 606–11; Laslett, 1976, 87–116.

31. James Mason, for example, believed that cunning folk sometimes cured people that physicians could not help (Mason, 1612, 69).

32. In art and literature, representations of old age and the experience of debility deformity and death are by no means comic or straightforward. Symbolised by the bleak coldness of the dark winter months, the Grim Reaper, Old Father Time in contrast to youth; the aged female body in addition personified the vices of old age (Shahar, 1997, 47). In the *Secretum Secretorum*, a fifteenth century pseudo-Aristotelian tract, spring is personified in figure of 'a fayre yong man that arrayth hym wel', whereas in old age she is winter, when 'the erthe as an old woman broken with age and nere deed' whose beauty, strength and virtue is despoiled (243–44, 29, 246; fig. 4.1).

Chapter 5

1. Since old age prevented him from drawing clear lines, Michelangelo used Tiberio Calcagni, 'a modest and well-mannered young man', to draw the ground plans for the original foundations of the church of San Giovanni, and to make 'a fair copy' for the Florentine commissioners in Rome, who agreed that Michelangelo should supervise the work but that it should be executed by Tiberio, thereby providing an instance of old and young working in harmony to the exacting standards of the old (Vasari, 1987, 1: 413–14).

2. Castiglione dismisses elderly praise of the courts of the past by 'proving' that in fact the present is far rosier than the past as the writings, paintings, sculpture, architecture 'and everything else' left behind is of an inferior quality to the work being done now. Complaints about the way the young dress and strut about town boil down to the habit the old have of blaming the young for whatever they themselves did not do, good or bad, 'simply because they did not do them' (Castiglione, 1976, 111).

3. The rather flimsy reason as to why 'love is futile' in old men is that 'what women take for agreeable courtesies, pleasantries and elegance in the young are in the old inept and ridiculous follies which will cause some women to detest and everyone to deride whoever indulges in them' (Castiglione, 1976, 323). However, the final section of the book is a neoplatonic hymn to the power of spiritual love to uplift the soul by transcending the carnal. This kind of love is appropriate at all ages (325–45).

4. William Wentworth advises his son to appoint a mature schoolmaster for his own sons 'For I do utterlie dislike of a yonge scolemaister, what faire semblant soeuer be in him' (21).

5. 'whose distrust of the young', according to Keith Thomas, 'went unusually deep' (Thomas, 1976, 228).

6. The Quaker, economist and social reformer John Bellars (1654–1725) adapted Winstanley's recommendation for the foundation of a group of overseers from the over-sixties as a merit reward for the elderly in his employment 'colledge' in place of a pension: 'for Ease and pleasant Life, will equal what the Hoards of a Private Purse can give; and excel, in so much as it hath less care and danger of losing' (Bellars, 1935, 46).

7. 'If authority is legitimised by association with the cosmological system, it is less easy for subjects to reject' (Goody, 1976, 127). See also Eisenstadt (1956), *Generation to Generation: Age Groups and Social Structure.*

8. Goody gives the example of a ruler in Gonja, northern Ghana, who was totally incapacitated by age. He had to be carried into the courtroom, and the pronouncements that he was required to make were 'interpreted' by a spokesman — that is, the words seeming to emanate from the chief in fact came from an adviser. But it was essential that while the chief remained alive, the power of office was totally invested in him (1976, 217).

9. 1596, for example, was the year of the demise of John Puchering, Lord Keeper of the Great Seale; Richard Fletcher Bishop of London; Henry Carey Lord Hunsdon, Lord Chamberlain to the Queen's household, Governor of Barwick and 'Cousin German' to the Queen (he was succeeded as Lord Chamberlain by Lord Cobham, who survived him by only a few months); Sir Francis Knolles, Vice-Chamberlain to the Queen, then Captaine of the Guard, then Treasurer of the Queen's House-hold and Henry Hastings Earle of Huntingdon, President of the Councell in the North (Camden, 1630).

10. Robert Carey, John Chamberlain, John Clapham, John Manningham, Roger Wilraham, Comte de Beaumont, the French Ambassador, and the Venetian ambassador, Giovanni Scaramelli — and Elizabeth Southwell, one of

Elizabeth's maids of honour, all wrote varying accounts of the last few days of the Queen's life, and the circumstances surrounding her death, culminating in rumours of the spontaneous combustion of the Queen's corpse. The contradictions and variations form the basis of a fascinating study by Catherine Loomis (1996, 482–509).

11. On 30 March 1603 he wrote to Dudley Carleton that 'her Majesties sicnes and manner of death [are] diversly related: for even here the papists do tell strange stories, as utterly voyde of truth, as of all civill honestie or humanitie[...]. I [...] find her disease to be nothing but a setled and unremovable melancholie, insomuch that she could not be won or perswaded neither by the counsaile, Divines, phisitians, nor the women about her once to tast or touch any phisicke: though ten or twelve phisitians that were continually about her did assure her with all manner of asseverations of perfect and easie recoverie yf she wold follow theyre advise.' This is reproduced in Nichols, 1823, 604–05 fn 3.

12. In the account of Elizabeth Southwell, one of the (admittedly Catholic) ladies-in-waiting at her bedside, she is 'much offended' by the sight of Canterbury and other prelates and 'cholericklie' sent them all 'packing, saing she was no atheist, but knew full well that they were [...] hedge priests and tok yt for an yndignitie that they should speak to her' (Southwell, *A True Relation* [...] lines 63–66, in Loomis, 1996, 484–87). The privy councillors at the Queen's bedside on March 23, Nottingham, Cecil and an unidentified third, who tried to get her to name her successor, were treated to an angry outburst telling them that she would have none but a king succeed her — that is, all but naming James (Anonymous Manuscript in Nichols, 1823, 3: 607–08).

13. The same is true of her dealings with Essex, Ralegh's contretemps with Popham and Spenser's struggles with Burleigh.

14. As Chamberlain notes, the outcome was that 'the jurisdiction of that court is inlarged out of measure, and so suits become as yt were immortall: this successe is come of my Lord Cookes and some of the judges oppugning the chauncerie so weakely and unseasonablie, that in stead of overthrowing the exorbitant authoritie therof they have more established and confirmed yt'(Chamberlain, 1939, 2, 36).

15. In his work on ancient traditions, Aubrey believes the law in Sardinia, permitting sons to kill their fathers with a club when they became old, and recounted in Pomponius Mela, to have been a widespread practice, surviving until much later around the Baltic. (Aubrey, 1686–87, 19, citing Mela, Pomp. Mela, lib 3, cap.de India. 'Lex erat Sardwae, ut filii patres jam senio confecos fustibus caderent, et interemptos sepelierent'.)

16. The same tradition appears in nineteenth-century Sweden with reports of 'family cliffs' of former times and in the Icelandic Göttrek sagas; see below.

17. See also Grimm's reference to this: 'a cliff in Blekingen is called Valhall, and at two places in Westgotland are hills called Valhall, from which old men weary of life threw themselves into the lake or brook running below' (Grimm, 1888, 4:1542).

18. Bromham's pertinent suggestion is that in the case of Gloucester, the journey and the desire for death take on the significance of a ritual sacrifice originally performed in times when the survival of the tribe was placed above the survival of the individual when food was in short supply or there were not enough resources for the support of the unproductive elderly. The tradition thus places the survival of the community above the survival of the individual (Bromham, 2001, 119–20).

19. As distinct from the Frances Howard/Thomas Overbury scandal.

20. *The Old Law* does not specify Evander's age, so productions might differ in their presentation of him. The question of whether he appears on stage as a young man, a middle-aged one (the 'perfect' age according to Mary Dove, 1986) would affect an audience's reaction to his initial promotion of youth. If he is presented as a young man himself, his reversal and condemnation of the young becomes psychologically unconvincing, whereas a test of youth by an older and graver man would carry more moral weight.

21. Catherine Shaw, in her introduction to the Garland edition of play, perceives the same irony, though in a different context: 'Ironically, the breaking of the law of the land becomes equated with love and compassion and the maintaining of the law with lust and self-interest' (Middleton, 1982, xxxvi).

22. Shaw sees its central motif as a dichotomy between what is '*natural* and *unnatural*', upon the distinction between '*fortune* and *nature*, and upon the subtlety inherent within definitions of *nature* itself' (Middleton, 1982, xliv). To this I add another motif of key significance: that of man-made laws as opposed to the laws of nature.

23. See Bromham, 1996, 401–21 for a discussion of the theories of stoicism underlying this exchange.

24. All citations and quotations are from the New Cambridge Shakespeare: *Coriolanus*, Lee Bliss (ed.), 2000.

25. 'Cato' recommends light exercise and 'just enough food and drink to restore our strength and not to over-burden it' (Cicero, 2001, 45).

26. These are in keeping with Keith Thomas's findings: 'Between 1542 and 1642 the median age of Privy Councillors was never less than 51, never more than 61' (Thomas, 1976, 205–48; 211).

27. Robert Bowyer's *Parliamentary Diary*, 1606–07, quotes here Dudley Carleton's Letter to John Chamberlain, 17 April 1606; *Coriolanus*, 2000, 31.

28. See above, Chapter Four, 104–105, 122; and also Jean Howard and Phyllis Rackin's significant discussion of the changing role of Margaret of Anjou in *Henry VI* part 3 and *Richard III* in *Engendering a Nation* (1997, 83–99; 106, *passim*). See also Spenser's *The Faerie Queene* Bk. 2 where the figure of Occasion (2, iv, 4–12) represents misshapen spite as old and hag-ridden.

29. Sad — Minois, 1989, 43–77; bad — in Greek comedy, cf. Aristophanes, *Ecclesiazusae* (translated as *Women in Parliament*) in *Works*, 1968, 419–62; invisible — Parkin, 1998, 36–37.

30. See chapter 4 above for a discussion of Dutch genre in a related context. Depictions old women in Dutch genre paintings practising medicine at the bedside of a sick young woman casts light on their assumed knowledge and the ways in which it is valorised. See Pelling, 1997. This fascinating and informative essay posits connections between the Netherlands and England by sketching out a 'moral topography' of the role and figure of the old woman in sixteenth- and seventeenth-century Dutch genre painting as the prelude to an examination of 'real' older women practitioners of medicine. These 'real' women were taken to know more and do less harm than regular physicians — a belief galling to the Royal College of Physicians, who took steps to control their practices. Their 'knowingness' is a strong and uniform feature in the paintings (67–68; cf. fig. 4.2).

31. The example of Mrs. Elizabeth Hales, who went against a physician's prescription for blood-letting, yet was able to continue her work, proves the point (Pelling, 1997, 82–83).

32. See also Hilary Marland for the example of Vrouw Schrader, an experienced and wise midwife (Marland, 1996, 271–73).

33. Service to the community and the State, he says, like the love of honour, never grows old, but persists to the end in all forms of life, but women have no role here. No bee becomes a drone upon reaching old age, and settles down to idleness at home. 'Of the many forms of baseness none disgraces an aged man more than idleness, cowardice, and slackness, when he retires from public offices to the domesticity befitting women' (Plutarch, 1998, 81).

34. Continuing independence for the elderly is reinforced by provision in wills. Ralph Josselin, for example, provided for his widow's continuing independence in the early years of the seventeenth century by allowing her a portion of land, furniture, and 'three or four rooms of the mansion house [...] with free ingress, egress and regress out of the same into the yard' from where she could collect as much fuel for her fire as she needed as long as she lived (Macfarlane, 1986, 114). See also *The Diary of Ralph Josselin 1616–1683* (Macfarlane, 1976) for Josselin's observations on his role as father and husband, analysed in Macfarlane 1970, part 2 and Thane, 2000, 129.

35. Adelman, famously, has a different angle on this (Adelman, 1998, 24). It is true that in terms of dramatic impact the tragic end of Coriolanus comes about as a result of the audience's strong awareness of the emotional bond between a mother and her son, so that, in terms of performance, the moment when Coriolanus 'holds her by the hand' and cries 'O mother, mother!/What have you done?' (*Coriolanus*, 5.3, 179–80) depends for its power upon their emotional lives rather than their roles. It is important to note that Shakespeare requires complex responses from his audience with regard to Volumnia; in this scene they are drawn in to an intensely personal and powerful moment between mother and son, yet at the same time they would be aware that her power and influence derives from her seniority and political position.

36. See E. C(hapman), *A Forme of Prayer to be Used in All Christian Families* (1583), The Epistle, sig. C i verso, for a mother's imprint upon her adult children.

37. James Bulman writes interestingly on Volumnia's defence of conventional means of confirming the identity of the heroic warrior through display of wounds as a mark of inner merit (Bulman, 1985, 19–23).

38. Thomas Newton, for example, in his dedicatory epistle to William Paulet, congratulates him on his central position in the family (Newton, 1569, sig.3v), and Thomas Sheafe likewise insists on the importance of the old in household management; grandchildren are the main source of an old man's joy and comfort (Sheafe, 1639, 42–43, 164). See also Ralph Houlbrooke on family structures and the continuing part the old played in the lives of their grandchildren (1984, 192–93).

Epilogue

1. All citations and quotations come from the New Cambridge Shakespeare, *All's Well that Ends Well* (2003), Russell Fraser (ed.), 2003.

2. He resolves the dispute between France and the Florentines by sending troops out there (3.1,1–23), and in the final scenes, as Lafew notes, 'His highness comes post from Marseilles, of as able body as when he numbered thirty' (4. 5, 64–65) in order to resolve the matter of who shall inherit the realm. The Countess, too, is able to exercise mature judgement on Helena's behalf (3. 2, 57–60; 3. 4, 26–29).

3. Such is the premise of a monograph on war as a theatrical and highly theorised and moralised pursuit. See Taunton, 2001, *1590s Drama and Militarism.*

4. Strode, however, sees no way out of the conundrum: 'Hast thou children? Then thou shalt haue sorrow. Hast thou none? Then is thy life vnpleasant'; so 'Iacob saith to his sonnes, If mischiefe befall Beniamin in the way in which yee go, then shall yee bring downe my gray haires with sorrow to the grave' (1618, 20, 27).

5. It is perhaps a mistake to interpret this as a reference to reawakened sexual desire. Lafew explains *'lustique'* as something 'the Dutchman says' (2.3, 36). In recent single editions *'lustique'* is glossed as 'frolicsome', and 'Dutchman', if glossed at all, as 'German'. In fact, Lafew could very well be referring to the health regimens of the eminent Dutch physician, Levinus Lemnius, whose work was translated by Thomas Newton in 1576 as *The Touchstone of Complexions* which was widely circulated and made two more editions in 1591 and 1633 — a likely source hitherto unremarked either by editors of the play, or by those critics who read the King's recovery as a sexual event.

Bibliography

A.B. (1672), *Learn to Lye Warm, or an apology for the proverb, Tis good shel-tring under an old hedge; containing reasons, wherefore a young man should marry an old woman.*

Abendstern, M., Itzin, C., and Thompson, P. (eds.) (1990), *I Don't Feel Old: The Experience of Late Life*, Oxford: Oxford University Press.

Ab Indagine (von Hagen), (1633), *Brief Introductions.*

Acheson, K. O. (1995), *The Diary of Anne Clifford 1616–1619*, New York and London: Garland Publishing.

Adelman, J. (1998), 'Escaping the Matrix: The Construction of Masculinity in *Coriolanus*' in S. Zimmerman (ed.), *Shakespeare's Tragedies*, New Case-books, Basingstoke: Macmillan.

Alberti, L.B. (1969), *I Libri della famiglia. The Family in Renaissance Florence*, R.N. Watkins (trans.), Columbia: University of South Carolina Press.

Anglo, Sydney (ed.) (1977), *Damned Art: Essays in the Literature of Witchcraft*, London: Henley and Boston: Routledge and Kegan Paul.

Arcandam; see Warde, W. (1630).

Archer, R.E. (1984), 'Rich Old Ladies: The Problem of Late Medieval Dowagers', in A.J. Pollard (ed.), *Property and Politics*, Gloucester and New York: Alan Sutton & St. Martin's Press, 15–35.

Aries, P. and Duby, G. (eds.) (1988–89), *History of Private Life*, A. Goldhammer (trans.), Vols. 2 and 3, Cambridge, MA: Belknap, Harvard University Press.

Aristophanes, (1968), *Ecclesiazusae*, translated as *Women in Parliament* in *Works*, Moses Hadas (ed.), New York: Bantam Books.

Aristotle (1981), *The Politics*, T.A. Sinclair (trans.), revised ed., London: Penguin Classics.

—— (1984), *The Complete Works of Aristotle,*. Jonathan Barnes Bollingen (ed.), series 71, Princeton, NJ: Princeton University Press, 2 vols.

Ascham, R. (1904), *English Work*, W. A. Wright (ed.), Cambridge University Press.

Asp, C. (1986), '"The Clamor of Eros": Freud, Aging, and King Lear' in K. Woodward and M.M. Schwartz (eds.), *Memory and Desire: Aging, Literature, Psychoanalysis*, Bloomington: Indiana State University Press, 192–204.

Aubrey, J. (1686-7), *Remaines of Judaisme and Gentilisme*, James Britten (ed.) (1881), London: W. Satchell, Peyton and Co.

Augustine (1909), *The City of God (De Civiate Dei) ... a translation into English by John Healey, first published in 1610*, Edinburgh: John Grant.

Autobiography of Thomas Raymond and Memoirs of the Family of Guise of Elmore, Gloucestershire (1917), G. Davies (ed.), London: Camden Third Series vol. 28.

The Autobiography of Mrs. Alice Thornton, of East Newton, Co. York (1875), Charles Jackson (ed.), Durham: Surtees Society, vol. 62.

Bacon, F. (1638), *The Historie of Life and Death. With Observations Naturall and Experimentall for the Prolonging of Life*.

Barrough, P. (1591), *Method of Phisick*.

Batman vppon Bartholome (1582).

Bayne, P. (1647), *An Entire Commentary upon the whole Epistle … to the Ephesians*.

Beam, A.C.L. (2006). '"Should I as Yet Call You Old?" Testing the Boundaries of Female Old Age in Early Modern England' in E. Campbell (ed.), *Growing Old in Early Modern Europe: Cultural Representations*, Aldershot: Ashgate.

Beauregard, D.N. (1999), '"Inspired Merit": Shakespeare's Theology of grace in *All's Well That Ends Well*', *Renascence*, 51: 4, 219–39.

Becon, T. (1564), *The worckes of Thomas Becon*.

——— (1830) *Writings of the Rev. Thomas Becon*, The Religious Tract Society.

Bellars, J. (1935), *John Bellars 1654–1725, Quaker, Economist and Social Reformer* (ed.), A.R. Fry, London: Cassell.

Bernard, R. (1628), *Ruths Recompence*.

Bett, H. (1952), *English Myths and Traditions* London: B.T. Batsford Ltd.

Bever, E. (1982), 'Old Age and Witchcraft in Early Modern Europe' in *Old Age in Pre-industrial Society*, P.N. Stearns (ed.), New York: London: Holmes and Meier.

Bevington, D. (1989), '"Is this the Promised End?" Death and Dying in *King Lear*', *Proceedings of the American Philological Society*, 404–15.

Birch, T. (1754), *Memoirs of the Reign of Queen Elizabeth*, 2 vols. London: Millar.

Boaistuau, P. (1574), *Theatrum Mundi* .

Boethius (1998), *The Consolations of Philosophy*, London: the Folio Society .

Botelho, L. and Thane, P. (eds) (2001), *Women and Aging in British Society Since 1500*, Harlow, England; London; New York: Longman.

——— (2001), 'Old age and the menopause in rural women of early modern Suffolk in L. Botelho and P. Thane (eds.), *Women and Aging in British Society Since 1500*, ed., Harlow, England; London; New York: Longman.

——— (2005), 'the Seventeenth Century' in P. Thane (ed.), *The Long History of Old Age*, London: Thams and Hudson.

Boulton, J. (1987), *Neighbourhood and Society: a London Suburb in the Seventeenth Century*, Cambridge: Cambridge University Press.

Bowyer, R. (1931), *The Parliamentary Diary of Robert Bowyer*, 1606–1607, D.H. Willson (ed.), Minneapolis: University of Minnesota Press.

Bradshaw, W. (1621), *A Meditation of Mans Mortalitie*.

Brian, T. (1637), *The pisse-prophet, or, Certaine pisse-pot lectures*.

Bright, T. (1613), *A Treatise of Melancholy*, first published 1586.

Brock, A.J. (1929), *Greek Medicine, Being Extracts Illustrative of Medical Writers from Hipporcates to Galen*, London: Library of Greek Thought.

Bromham, A.A. (1984), 'The Contemporary Significance of The Old Law', *Studies in English Literature*, 24: 327–39.

——— (December 1994), 'The Significance of Names in Middleton and Rowley's *The Old Law*', *Notes and Queries*, New Series Vol. 41, No. 4, 509–12.

——— (1996), '"Have you read Lipsius?": Thomas Middleton and Stoicism', *English Studies*, 77: 401–21.

——— (June 1996), 'A Suggestive Source for a Scene in The Old Law', *Notes and Queries*, New Series Vol. 23, No. 2.

——— (2001), '"Is the Law Firm?" Rewriting Middleton and Rowley's *The Old Law* for the 1990s', *European Studies: A Journal of European Culture, History and Politics*, 17: 117–27.

Brookes, T. (1659), *Apples of Gold for Young Men and Women and A Crown of Glory for Old Men and Women or, The happiness of being good betimes, And the honor of being an Old Disciple. Clearly and fully discovered, and closely and faithfully applyed. Also The Young Mans Objections answered, And the Old Mans doubts resolved.*

Bufford, S. (1696), *A Discourse against Unequal Mariages.*

Bullinger, H. (1541), Miles Coverdale (trans.), *The Christen State of Matrimony* .

Bulman, J. (1985), *The Heroic Idiom of Shakespearean Tragedy*, Newark: University of Delaware Press.

Bulwer, J. (1654), *Anthropometamorphosis.*

Burton, R. (1955), *Anatomy of Melancholy*, F. Dell and P. Jordan-Smith (eds.), New York: Tudor Publishing Company.

Calver, E. (1641), *Passion and Discretion, in Youth and Age.*

Candido, J. (1997), 'Dining Out in Ephesus: Food in *The Comedy of Errors'* in *The Comedy of Errors: Critical Essays*, R.S. Miola (ed.), London: Routledge.

Camden, W. (1630), *The Historie of the Most Renowned and Victorious Princesse Elizabeth, Late Queene of England....Composed by Way of Annals.*

Campbell, E. (ed.) (2006), *Growing Old in Early Modern Europe: Cultural Representations*, Aldershot: Ashgate.

—— (2002), 'The Art of Aging Gracefully', *Sixteenth Century Journal*, 33: 321–31.

Carew, R. (1953), *The Survey of Cornwall*, F.E. Halliday (ed.), London: Andrew Melrose.

Carey, Sir R. (1972), *The Memoirs of Robert Carey*, F.H. Mares (ed.), Oxford: Clarendon Press.

Carpenter, J. (1597), *A Preparatiue to Contentation.*

Carpenter, P. (1991), '*King Lear, Macbeth* and the use of memory', *Critical Survey*, 3: 194–207

Castiglione, B. (1976), *The Book of the Courtier*, G. Bull (trans.), London: Penguin Classics

Chamberlain, J. (1939), The *Letters of John Chamberlain*, N.E. McClure (ed.), vols. 1 and 2, Philadelphia: Memoirs of the American Philosophical Society, 12 vols.

Charlton, K. (1988), '"Not publike onely but also private and domesticall": Mothers and familial education in pre-industrial England', *History of Education*, 17: 1–20.

—— (1994), 'Mothers as educative agents in pre-industrial England', *History of Education*, 23: 129–56.

—— (1999). *Women, Religion and Education* London: Routledge.

C'hest de la houce (1872), in *Recuil general des Fabliaux*, A. Montaiglin and G. Raynaud (eds.), Paris: Librairie des Bibliophiles, Vol. 2.

Christopherson, J. (1554), *An Exhortation to all menne to take hede and beware rebellion ....*

Cicero (1923; repr.2001), *De Senectute*, W.A. Falconer (trans.), Loeb Classical Library, Cambridge, Mass.: Harvard University Press, Vol. XX.

—— (1577), *Fower Seuerall Treatises of M. Tullius Cicero: Conteyninge his most learned and Eloquente Discourses of Frienshippe: Old age: Paradoxes: and Scipio his Dreame. All turned out of Latine into English, by Thomas Newton.*

Clapham, J. (1951), *Elizabeth of England: Certain Observations Concerning the Life and Reign of Queen Elizabeth* by John Clapham, E.P. Read and C. Read (eds.), Philadelphia: University of Pennsylvania Press.

Clearidge, J. (1670), *Shepheards Legacy: or, John Clearidge, his Forty Years experience of the weather*, London.

Clifford, Lady Anne (1916), *Lives of Lady Anne Clifford Countess of Dorset, Pembroke and Montgomery (1590–1676) and of her Parents Summarized by Herself*, introduction by J.P. Gilson, London: The Roxburghe Club.

Clifford, D.J.H. (ed.) (1992), *The Diaries of Anne Clifford*, Phoenix Mill: Alan Sutton Publishing.

Cobbett, W. (1806–12), *Parliamentary History of England*, 36 vols. London: Longmans & Co., Vol. 1.

Coeffeteau, F.N. (1621), *A Table of Humane Passions With their Causes and Effects*, E. Grimeston (trans.).

Collins, A. (ed.) (1746), *Letters and Memorials of State*, 2 Vols., London: Osborne.

Collomp, A. (1989), 'Families: habitations and Cohabitations' in Aries and Duby (eds.), *History of Private Life*, A. Goldhammer (trans.), vol 3, Cambridge, MA: Belknap, Harvard University Press.

Combe, K and Schmader, K. (1996), 'Shakespeare Teaching Geriatrics: Case Studies in Aged Heterogeneity', *Journal of Aging and Identity*, Vol. 1: 2 June, 99–116.

Commons Debates, 1621, W. Notestein, F.H. Relf and H. Simpson, H. (ed.) (1935), New Haven: Yale University Press.

Cornwallis, W. (1601), *A Second part of Essayes*.

Correspondence of Lady Katherine Paston, The (1603–1627), R. Hughey (ed.) (1941), London: Norfolk Record Society, Vol. 14.

Cotta, J. (1612), *A Short Discoverie of the unobserved Dangers of severall sorts of ignorant and unconsiderate Pracisers of Physicke in England*.

Covey, H.C. (1989), 'Old Age Portrayed by the Ages-of-Life Models From the Middle Ages to the 16th Century', *The Gerontologist*, 29, 692–98.

Cuddon, J.A. (1982), *A Dictionary of Literary Terms*, London: Penguin Reference.

Cuffe, H. (1607), *The Different Ages of Man's Life*.

Cyuile and Vncyuile Life (1579), in *Inedited Tracts*, W. Hazlitt (ed.) (1868), The Roxburghe Library, London.

Dariot, C. (1598), *A Briefe and most easie Introduction to the Astrologicall Iudgement of the starres*, F.W. Gent (trans.).

Danti, V. (1960), 'Trattato delle Perfette Proporzioni (1567)', in *Trattati d'Arte del Cinquecento fra Manierismo e Controriforma*, Paola Barocchi (ed.), Bari: G. Laterza & Figli.

Davis, L. (2003), '"Sick Desires": All's Well That Ends Well and the Civilizing Process' in L. Davis (ed.) *Shakespeare Matters: History, Teaching, Performance*, London: Associated University Presses, 89–102.

Dean-Jones, L.A. (1994), *Women's Bodies in Classical Greek Science*, Oxford: Oxford University Press.

D'Ewes, S. (1682), *The Journals of all the Parliaments during the Reign of Queen Elizabeth, Both for the House of Lords and House of Commons*

Dictionary of National Biography (DNB).

Dives and Pauper (1976), P.H. Barnum (ed.), 2 vols., published for the Early English Text Society, Oxford: Oxford University Press, Vol. 1

Dixon, L. (1995), *Perilous Chastity: Women and Illness in Pre-Enlightenment Art and Medicine*, Ithaca, NY: Cornell University Press.

Dobson, M. and Watson, N. (2002), *England's Elizabeth: an Afterlife in Fame and Fantasy*, Oxford: Oxford University Press.

Donaldson, I. (1970), *The World Upside-Down* Oxford: Clarendon Press.

Donow, H.S. (1992), '"To Everything There Is a Season": Some Shakespearean Models of Normal and Anomalous Aging', *The Gerontologist*, 32, 2 parts; part 2, 733–38.

Dove, M. (1986), *The Perfect Age of Man's Life*, Cambridge: Cambridge University Press.

Draper, J. (1940), 'The Old Age of King Lear,' *Journal of English and Germanic Philology*, 39: 527–40.

E.C(hapman) (1583), *A Forme of Prayer to be Used in All Christian Families*.

Eisenstadt, S.N. (1956), *Generation to Generation: Age Groups and Social Structure*, London: Routledge & Kegan Paul.

Elton, C. (1882), *Origins of English History*, London: Bernard Quaritch.

Elyot, T. (1534; repr. 1541), *The Castel of Helth*.

Erasmus (1529), *De pueris instituendis*.

——— (1978), *In Praise of Folly*, B. Radice (ed.), London: Penguin.

Essex, Robert Devereux, Earl of (1600), *An apologie of the Earle of Essex*.

Evans, A. (1659), *A Rule from Heaven*.

Evans, R. (2000), '"New" Poems by Early Modern Women: 'A Maid under 13'. Elizabeth With, Elizbeth Collett, and 'A Lady of Honour': Literary Context in the Age of Elizabeth, James and Charles,' *Ben Jonson Journal*, 7: 447–515.

Evans, J.X. (1990), 'Erasmian Folly and Shakespeare's *King Lear*: A Study in Humanist Intertextuality', Moreana, 27: 103 (September), 3–23.

Falconer, J. (1618), *A briefe refutation of Iohn Traskes iudaical and nouel fancyes*.

Ficino, M. (1989), *Three Books on Life*, C.V. Kaske and J.R. Clark (trans. and ed.): Medieval and Renaissance Texts and Studies in conjunction with the Renaissance Society of America, Binghamton, New York.

Florio, J. (1591), *Perpetuall and naturall prognostications of the change of weather Gathered out of diuers ancient and late writers, and placed in order for the common good of all men*. Newly translated from Italian into English by I.F.

Foakes, R.N. (1996), 'King Lear: Monarch or Senior Citizen?' in R.B. Parker and S.P. Zitner (eds.), *Essays in Honour of S. Schoenbaum*, New York, London: University of Delaware Press, 271–89.

——— (ed.) (2003), *King Lear*, London: The Arden Shakespeare.

Ford, J. (1995), *The Broken Heart* in John Ford, *'Tis Pity She's a Whore and Other Plays*, ed. M. Lomax, World's Classics, Oxford: Oxford University Press.

Freud, S. (1985, repr. 990), *Sigmund Freud: Art and Literature*, vol. 14, J. Strachey (trans.), The Penguin Freud Library, London: Penguin.

Froide, A.M. (2001), 'Old maids: the lifecycle of single women in early modern England' in L. Botelho and P. Thane (eds.), *Women and Aging in British Society Since 1500*, Harlow, England: Longman.

Fry, A.R. (1935), *John Bellars, 1654–1725*, London: Cassell.

Gale, T. (1586), *Certaine vvorkes of Galens, called Methodus medendi with a briefe declaration of the worthie art of medicine, the office of a chirurgion, and an epitome of the third booke of Galen, of naturall faculties: all translated into English, by Thomas Gale Maister in Chirurgerie*.

Galen (1916), *On the Natural Faculties*, A.J. Brock (trans.), London and New York, Loeb: Classical Library.

——— (1929), *On the Utility of Parts*, in A.J. Brock (1929), *Greek Medicine, Being Extracts Illustrative of Medical Writers from Hipporcates to Galen*, London: Library of Greek Thought.

——— (1951), *Galen's Hygiene: De sanitate tuenda*, Robert Montraville Green (trans.), Springfield, IL: Charles C. Thomas.

——— (1997), *Selected Works*, P.N. Singer (trans.), Oxford World's Classics, Oxford University Press, 233–36.

Gaunt, D. (1983), *Familjelivi i Norden*, Gilunds.

George, E.V. (1992), 'Rhetoric in Vives' in *Opera Omnia*, A. Mestre (ed.), Valencia: Universitat de Valencia, 163–65.

Gifford, G. (1587), *A Discourse of the Subtill Practises of Devilles by Witches and Astrologers*.

God and the King: Or a Dialogue shewing that our Soueraigne Lord King Iames, being immediate vnder God within his Dominions, Doth rightfully claime whasoeveuer is required by the Oath of Allegiance (1616).

Goodcole, H. (1621), *The wonderful discovery of Elizabeth Sawyer, a Witch, late of Edmonton, her conviction, condemnation and death,* appendiced to Rowley, Dekker and Ford, *The Witch of Edmonton,* eds. P. Corbin and D. Sedge, 1999, Revels Student Editions, Manchester: Manchester University Press, 135–49.

Goody, J. (1976), 'Aging in Nonindustrial Societies', R.H. Binstock and E. Shanas (eds.), *Handbook of Aging and the Social Sciences,* New York and London: Van Nostrand Reinhold, 117–128.

—— (1983), *The Development of the Family and Marriage in Europe,* Cambridge: Cambridge University Press.

Goody, J., Thirsk, J. and Thompson, E.P. (eds.) (1976), *Production and Reproduction: A Comparative Study of the Domestic Domain,* Cambridge: Cambridge University Press.

Googe, B. (1563), *Eglogs, Epytaphes & Sonnettes,* E.A. Arber (ed.) (1871), London: English Reprints.

Goulart, S. (1621), *The Wise Vieillard, or Old Man, translated out of French into English by an obscure Englishman, a friend and fauourer of all wise Old-Men.* 'TW'

Grantley, D. and Taunton, N. (eds.) (2000), *The Body in Late Medieval and Early Modern Culture,* Aldershot: Ashgate.

Green, R.M. (1951), *A Translation of Galen's Hygiene (de sanitate tuenda),* Springfield, Illinois: Charles C. Thomas.

Greenham, R. (1599), 'On the good education of children', *Works.*

Grimm, J. (1888), *Teutonic Mythology,* 4 vols.; London: George Bell & Sons.

Gruman, G.J. (1961), 'The rise and Fall of Prolongevity Hygiene', *Bulletin of the History of Medicine,* 35: 221–29.

—— (1966), 'A History of Ideas about the Prolongation of Life', *Transactions of the American Philosophical Society,* New Series, 5: 56 (9), 1–97.

Guazzo, S. (1581), *The Civil Conversation,*George Pettie (trans.).

Gutmann, D. (1977), 'The Cross-Cultural Perspective: Notes Toward a Comparative Psychology of Aging' in J. Birren, J. and W. Schaie (eds.), *Handbook of the Psychology of Aging,* New York: Van Bostrand Reinhold.

Hajnal, J. (1983), 'Two kinds of pre-industrial household formation system' in R. Wall, J. Robin and P. Laslett (eds.), *Family Forms in Historic Europe,* Cambridge: Cambridge University Press, 65–104.

Hall, J (1863), *The Works of the Right Reverend Joseph Hall, D.D. Bishop of Exeter and Afterwards of Norwich,* P. Wynter (ed.), 10 vols.; Oxford; Oxford University Press.

Halle, J. (1565), *An Historiall Expostulation against The Beastlye Ausers, Both of Chyrurgerie and Physyke, in Oure Tyme: with A goodley Doctrine and Instruction necessarye to be marked and folowed, of all true chirurgiens,* T. J. Pettigrew (ed.) (1844), The Percy Society, London: T. Richards.

Hammond, N.G.L (1967), *A History of Greece to 322 B.C,* Oxford: Clarendon Press.

Hampson, E.M. (1934), *The Treatment of Poverty in Cambridgeshire, 1597–1834,* containing the Linton list of 1693, Cambridge University Press.

Harrington, J. *Oceana and his other Works* (1737), J. Toland, Dublin (ed.).

Hart, J. (1625), *The Anatomie of Vrines.*

Heinemann, M. (1980), *Puritanism and Theatre: Thomas Middleton and Opposition Drama under the Early Stuarts,* Cambridge: Cambridge University Press.

Herrero, J. (1984), 'Celestina: The Aging Prostitute as Witch' in Porter, L. and L.M. (eds.), *Aging in Literature*, Michigan: International Book Publishers, 31–47.

Heywood, O. (1882), *Rev. Oliver Heywood, B.A. 1630–1702; His Autobiography, Diaries, Anecdonte and Event Books*, ed. J. Horsfall Turner Brighouse: Bingley: T. Harrison, 4 vols.

Hilder, T. (1653), *Conjugal Counsell.*

Heywood, T. (1638), *The Wise Woman of Hoxton*, ed. S. Masai (2002) Globe Quartos, London: Nick Hern Books.

Hill, C. (1972), *The World Turned Upside Down* London: Maurice Temple Smith.

Hill, T. (1613), *A Pleasant History: Declaring the whole Art of Phisiognomy.*

Hippocrates (1923–1931), *Nature of Man* in W.H.S. Jones and E.T. Withington (trans) *Hippocrates*, 4 vols., London and New York: Loeb Classical Library.

Holderness, G. (1995), *M. Shakespeare: HIS True Chronicle Historie of the life and death of King LEAR and his three Daughters* (1608) Hemel Hempstead: Harvester Wheatsheaf.

Holderness, G. and Carter, N. (1996), 'The King's Two Bodies: Text and Genre in *King Lear, Journal of the English Association*, 45: 1–31.

Holdsworth, W.S. (1903), *A History of English Law* (rev. 1956), 14 vols, London: Methuen, Vol.1.

Holstein, M. (1994), 'Taking Steps: Gerontological Education, Research, and the Literary Imagination', *The Gerontologist*, 34:6, 822–27.

Hopkins, L. (2003), 'Paris Is Worth a Mass: *All's Well That Ends Well* and the Wars of Religion' in D.Taylor and D.N. Beauregard (eds.), *Shakespeare and the Culture of Christianity in Early Modern England*, New York: Fordham University Press, 369–81.

Horace (1974), *The Art of Poetry, A Verse and Prose Translation with the Original*, B. Raffel (ed.), New York, State University of New York Press.

Howard, J. and Rackin, P. (1997), *Engendering a Nation*, London: Routledge.

Howell, C. (1983), *Land, Family and Inheritance in Transition: Kibworth Harcourt 1280–1700*, Cambridge: Cambridge University Press.

Houlbrooke, R.A. (1984), *The English Family 150–1700*, London and New York: Longman.

Hunt, M. (2003), 'Helena and the Reformation Problem of Merit in *All's Well That Ends Well*' in D, Taylor and D.N. Beauregard (eds.), *Shakespeare and the Culture of Christianity in Early Modern England*, New York: Fordham University Press, 335–67.

Hutchings, M. and Bromham, A.A. (2007), *Middleton and His Collaborators*, Writers and their Work Series, Tavistock: Northcote House Publishers.

Jacquart, J. and Thomasset, C. (1988), *Sexuality and Medicine in the Middle Ages*, M. Adamson (trans.), Cambridge: Polity Press.

Janssen, A. (2005), 'The Iconography of Old Age in Rembrandt's Early Work' in C. Vogelaar and G. Korevaar (eds.), exh. Cat. *Rembrandt's Mother: Myth and Reality*, Leiden: Woanders Publishers.

Jardine, L. and Stewart, A. (1998), *Hostage to Fortune: The Troubled Life of Francis Bacon*, New York: Hill and Wang.

James I (2000), *Demonology*, in L. Normand and G. Roberts (eds.), *Witchcraft in Early Modern Scotland*, Exeter: University of Exeter Press.

Janowitz, M.D. (2001), 'Helena's Medicine in *All's Well That Ends Well*: Is it Paracelsian or Hermetical in Origin?' *Cauda Pavonis: Studies in Hermeticism*, 20: 1, 20–22.

Johnson, P. and Thane, P. (eds.) (1998), *Old Age from Antiquity to Post-Modernity*, London: Routledge.

Josselin, R. (1976), *The Diary of Ralph Josselin 1616–1683* A. Macfarlane (ed.), London: Published for The British Academy by the Oxford University Press.

Juvenal (1983), *Sixteen Satires upon The Ancient Harlot*, trans. Steven Robinson, Manchester: Carcanet.

Kahn, C. (1981), *Man's Estate*, Berkeley: California University Press.

Kantorowitz, E. (1957), *The King's Two Bodies: a Study in Mediaeval Political Theology*, Princeton: Princeton University Press.

Kempe, W. (1588), *The Education of Children in Learning*.

Kenny, A. (ed.) (1994), *The Oxford Illustrated History of Western Philosophy*, London: Quality Paperbacks Direct.

Killigrew, T. (1921), *The Parson's Wedding*, in *Restoration Comedies* ed. M. Summers, London: Jonathan Cape.

Kirsch, A. (1988), 'The Emotional Landscape of King Lear', *Shakespeare Quarterly*, 39, 154–70.

Knappen, M.M. (ed.), (1933), *Two Elizabethan Puritan Diaries by Richard Rogers and Samuel Ward*, Chicago: The American Society of Church History.

Kramer, H and Sprenger, J. (1928, repr. 1971), *Malleus Maleficarum*, M. Summers (trans.), New York: Dover and London: Arrow.

Kugler, A. (2001), ' "I feel myself decay apace": Old age in the diary of Lady Sarah Cowper' (1644–1720) in L. Botelho and P. Thane (eds.), *Women and Ageing in British Society Since 1500*, Essex: Longman.

Larkin, J.F. and Hughes, P.L. (1973), *Stuart Royal Proclamations. Volume 1: Royal Proclamations of King James I, 1603–1625*, Oxford: Clarendon Press.

Laslett, P. and Wall, R. (eds.) (1972), *Household and Family in Past Time* Cambridge: Cambridge University Press.

——— (1977), *Family Life and Illicit Love*, Cambridge: Cambridge University Press.

Laurentius, (Laurens, du A.) (1599), *A Discourse of the Preservation of the Sight: of Melancholike Diseases; of Rheumes, and of Old Age*, S.V. Larkey (ed.) (1938), Shakespeare Association Facsimile No.15, Oxford: Oxford University Press.

Lea, H.C. (1939), *Materials Toward a History of Witchcraft*, Arthur Howland (ed.), 3 vols., Philadelphia: University of Pennsylvania Press.

L'Estrange, R. (1692), *Fables of Aesop and other eminent Mythologists*.

Lesthaeghe, R. (1980), 'Population and Development of Human Reproduction', *Population and Development Review* 6, 527–48.

Levinson, D.J. (1979), *The Seasons of Man's Life*, New York: Ballantine Books.

Liber exemplorum ad usum praedicantium (1908), G.G. Little (ed.), Aberdeen: British Society of Franciscan Studies.

Lincoln Diocese Documents 1450–1544 (1914), A. Clark (ed.), Early English Text Society, London: Kegan Paul, Trench, Trübner & Co.

Livy (1919), *History of Rome*, B.O. Foster (trans.), Loeb Classical Library, (13 vols.), London: Heinemann, New York: G.P. Putnam's Sons.

Loomis, C. (1996), 'Elizabeth Southwell: Manuscript Account of the Death of Queen Elizabeth,' *English Literary Renaissance (ELR)* 26: 3, 482–509.

MacCaffrey, W.T. (1992), *Elizabeth I War and Politics 1588–1603*, New Jersey: Princeton University Press.

Macfarlane, A. (1986), *Marriage and Love in England 1300–1840*, Oxford: Basil Blackwell.

——— (1978), *The Origins of English Individualism: The Family, Property and Social Transition*, Oxford: Basil Blackwell.

—— (ed.) (1976), *The Diary of Ralph Josselin 1616–1683*, Cambridge: Cambridge University Press.

—— (1970), *Family Life of Ralph Josselin; A Seventeenth-Century Clergyman*, Cambridge: Cambridge University Press.

Magnan, R. (1984), 'Sex and Senescence in Medieval Literature,' in L. and L.M. Porter (eds.), *Aging in Literature*, Michigan: International Book Publishers, 13–30.

Maguire, L. (1997), 'The Girls from Ephesus' in *The Comedy of Errors: Critical Essays* R. S Miola (ed.), London: Routledge.

Mancini, G. (1956–57), *Considerazioni Sulla Pittura*, A. Marucchi and L. Salerno (eds.), Rome: Accademia nazionale dei Lincei.

Manningham, J. (1868), *Diary of John Manningham of the Middle Temple 1602–1603*, J. Bruce (ed।)., London: Camden Society, No. 99, J.B. Nichols and Sons.

Mannyng, R. (1901), *"Handlyng Synne,"A.D. 1303*, F. Furnivall (ed.), London: Early English Text Society.

Marius, R. (1986), *Thomas More*, London: Fount Paperbacks.

Marland, H. (1996), 'Stately and dignified, kindly and God-fearing': midwives, age and status in the Netherlands in the eighteenth century' in Marland, H. and M. Pelling, (eds.), *The Task of Healing: Medicine, Religion and Gender in England and the Netherlands 1450–1800*, Rotterdam: Erasmus Publishing, 271–305.

Marland, H. and Pelling, M. (eds.) (1996), *The Task of Healing: Medicine, Religion and Gender in England and the Netherlands 1450–1800*, Rotterdam: Erasmus Publishing.

Marshall, J.D., (ed.) (1967), *The Autobiography of William Stout of Lancaster*, Mancherster; Manchester University Press.

Marx, S. (1985a), '"Fortunate Senex": The Pastoral of Old Age', *Studies in English Literature*, 25: 21–44.

—— (1985b), *Youth Against Age: Generational Strife in Renaissance Poetry*, New York: Peter Lang.

Mason, J. (1612), *The Anatomie of Sorcerie*.

Maxwell, B. (1966), *Studies in Beaumont, Fletcher and Massinger*, London: North Carolina Press.

Mela, Pomponius (1997), *De Situ Orbis*, P. Berry (trans.), Lewiston: Edwin Mellen Press.

Mery tales and quicke answeres (1567) in Shakespeare Jest-Books; Reprints of the Early and Very Rare Jest-Bookes supposed to have been used by Shakespeare; ed. N.C. Hazlitt (1880), Vol. 2, London: Henry Southeran & Co.

Mery tales, wittie questions and quicke answere, very pleasant to readde) in Shakespeare's jest book, (1814).

Memoirs of the Family of Guise of Elmore, Gloucestershire (1917), G. Davies (ed.), London: Camden Third Series, vol. 28.

Middleton, T. and Rowley, W. (1982), *The Old Law*, C.M. Shaw (ed.), Garland English Texts 4, New York and London: Garland Publishing Inc.

—— (1993), *A Critical Edition of Thomas Middleton's The Witch*, E.J. Esche (ed.), New York & London: Garland Publishing.

M[ill], H. (1639), *Poems*.

Minois, G. (1989), *History of Old Age: from Antiquity to the Renaissance* Cambridge: Polity Press.

Miola, R. (ed.) (2001) *The Comedy of Errors: Critical Essays*, London: Routledge.

Montaigne, M. de (1894), *The Essayes of Michael Lord of Montaigne*, John Florio (trans.), H. Morley (ed.), London: George Routledge and Sons.

More, T. *A Dialogue of Comfort Against Tribulation* in L. Martz and F. Manley, (eds.), (1976), *The Complete Works of St. Thomas More*, Vol. 12, New Haven and London: Yale University Press.

——— (1953), *Dialoge of comfort against tribulacion, made by Syr Thomas More ... not before this time imprinted.*

——— (1947), *The Correspondence of Sir Thomas More*, E. Rogers (ed.), Princeton: Princeton University Press.

Mornay, P.de (1592), *Discourse of Life and Death. Antonius, A Tragoedie written also in French by ro. Garnier. Both done in English by the Countess of Pembroke.*

Munson-Deats, S. (1996), 'The Problem of Aging in King Lear and The Tempest', *Journal of Aging and Identity* Vol. I, No. 2 (June), 87–99.

Newton, T. (1569), *The Worthye Booke of Old Age.*

——— (1576), *The Touchstone of Complexions* ... first written in latine, by Leuine Lemnie, i.e., Levinus Lemnius.

——— (trans.) (1577), *Fower Seuerall Treatises of M. Tullius Cicero: Conteyninge his most learned and Eloquente Discourses of Frienshippe: Old age: Paradoxes: and Scipio his Dreame. All turned out of Latine into English, by Thomas Newton.*

News from Scotland (?1591), in Normand, L. and Roberts, G. (eds.) (2000), *Witchcraft in Early Modern Scotland*, Exeter: University of Exeter Press.

Nichols, J. (1823), *The Progresses and Public Processions of Queen Elizabeth to which are subjoined some of the early Progresses of King James.* 3 vols.

Normand, L. and Roberts, G. (eds.) (2000), *Witchcraft in Early Modern Scotland*, Exeter: University of Exeter Press.

Norwich Census of the Poor (1570), J.F. Pound (ed.), Norfolk Rec. Soc., 1971, Vol. XVI. 3 parts: Index of Wills Proved at Norwich, 1370–1550.

Oglander, Sir J. (1936), *A Royalist's Notebook: The Commonplace Book of Sir John Oglander, Kt. of Nunwell (1585–1655)*, F. Bamford (ed.), London: Constable & Co. Ltd.

Ovid (1931), *Fasti*, James George Frazer (trans.), T.E. Page (ed.), Loeb Classical Library, London and New York: William Heinemann.

Parkin, T. (2005), 'The Ancient Greek and Roman Worlds' in P. Thane (ed.), *The Long History of Old Age*, London: Thames & Hudson, 31–69.

——— (1998), 'Aging in Antiquity' in Johnson, P. and Thane, P. (eds.), *Old Age from Antiquity to Post-modernity* London: Routledge, 20–41.

Parkinson, R. (1852), *Newcome's Autobiography*, 2 vols., Manchester: The Chetham Society.

Pasquils Jests (1604), in *Shakespeare Jest-Books*, W.C. Hazlitt (ed.) (1864), 3 vols, London: Willis & Sotheran, vol. 3.

Paston Letters and Papers (up to 1479), N. Davis (ed.), 1971, Oxford: Clarendon Press.

Peacham, H. (1622), *The Compleat Gentleman.*

——— (1634), *The Compleat Gentleman*, V.B. Heltzel and H.H. Hudson (eds.), 1962, Ithaca, NY: Folger Shakespeare Library, Cornell University Press.

——— (1638), *The Truth of our Times.*

Pelling, M. (2001), 'Who most needs to marry? Ageing and inequality among women and men in early modern Norwich' in L. Botelho and P. Thane (eds.), *Women and Aging in British Society Since 1500*, Harlow, England; London; New York: Longman.

——— (1997), 'Thoroughly Resented? Older Women and the Medical Role in Early Modern London' in Lynette Hunter and Sarah Hutton (eds.), *Women, Science and Medicine 1500–1700*, Stroud: Sutton Publishing.

—— (1996), 'Compromised by gender: the role of the male medical practitioner in early modern England' in Marland, H. and Pelling, M. (eds.), (1996) *The Task of Healing: Medicine, Religion and Gender in England and the Netherlands 1450–1800*, Rotterdam: Erasmus Publishing, 101–33.

—— (1991), 'Old Age, Poverty and Disability in Early Modern Norwich' in M. Pelling and Smith, R. (eds.) (1991), *Life Death and the Elderly* London: Routledge, 74–101.

Pelling M. and Smith R. M. (eds.) (1991), *Life Death and the Elderly* London: Routledge.

The Petty Papers (1927), Marquis of Lansdowne (ed.), London: Constable & Co., 2 vols.

Perkins, W. (1600), *A Golden Chaine*, Cambridge.

—— (1608), *A discourse of the damned art of witchcraft*.

—— (1609), *Christian Oeconomie: Or, a Short Svrvey of the Right Manner of erecting and ordering a Familie, according to the Scriptures*, translated from the Latin by T. Pickering.

Pilkington, J. (1842), *The Works of James Pilkington*, James Scholefield (ed.), Cambridge: The Parker Society, Cambridge University Press.

Plautus (1964), *Amphitruo*, E.F. Watling (trans.), Penguin Classics, London: Penguin.

—— (1965), *Aulularia, Menaechmi*, E.F. Watling (trans.), Penguin Classics, London: Penguin.

Plato (1995), *Phaedrus*, A. Nehamas & P. Woodruff, (trans.), Indianapolis/Cambridge: Hackett Publishing.

—— *The Laws*, Benjamin Jowett (trans.). http://www.constitution.org/pla/laws.html

—— (1962), *The Republic*, H.D.P. Lee (trans.), Penguin Classics: Harmondsworth Penguin.

—— (1926), *Crito*, H. Cary (trans.), Paris: The Pleiad.

Plumpton, Sir R. (1839), *Plumpton Correspondence*, T. Stapleton (ed.), Camden Society

Plutarch (1936; repr. 1998), *Moralia*, H.N. Fowler (trans.), Loeb Classical Library, London: Harvard University Press, vol. 10.

—— (1595), *Lives of the Noble Grecians and Romanes ... translated out of Greeke by J. Amyot ... and out of French into Englishe by T. North*.

—— *Lives*, J. Dryden (trans.), http://classics.mit.edu/Plutarch/lysander.html.

Pollock, L. (1993), *With Faith and Physic: The Life of a Tudor Gentlewoman, Lady Grace Mildmay 1552–1620*, London: Collins and Brown.

Porritt, E. (1903), *Unreformed House of Commons*, Cambridge University Press.

Porter, L. and L.M. (eds.) (1984), *Aging in Literature*, Michigan: International Book Publishers.

Porter, L. (1984), 'King Lear and the Crisis of Retirement' in Porter, L. and L.M. (eds.) (1984), *Aging in Literature*, Troy, Mich.: International Book Publishers, 59–72.

Porter, L.M. (1984), 'Montaigne's Final Revisions: An Eriksonian Assessment' in Porter, L. and L.M. (eds.), *Aging in Literature*, Troy, Mich: International Book Publishers, 49–58.

Prest, W.R. (1972), *The Inns of Court under Elizabeth I and the early Stuarts, 1590–1640*, London: Longman.

Price, S. (1624), *Two Twins of Birth and Death: A sermon preached in Christs Church in London, the 5. of September. 1624. By Samson Price, Doctor of Diuinitie, one of his Majesties chapleins in ordinarie. Vpon the occasion of the funeralls of Sir William Byrde Knight. Doctor of the Law, deane of the Arches, and iudge of the Prerogatiue Court of the Archbishop of Canterburie.*

Primaudaye, P. de la (1589), *The French Academie, wherein is discoursed the institution of Maners*, T. Bowes (trans.).

Prose Salernitan Questions, The (1979), B. Lawn (ed.), London: Oxford University Press.

Purkiss, D. (repr. 1997), *The Witch in History*, London: Routledge.

Puttenham, G. (1589), *The Arte of English Poesie*, Facsimile 1971, Amsterdam & New York: Da Capo Press.

Resolved Gentleman, The (1594), written by O. de La Marche, tranlated by L. Lewkenor.

Rebhorn, W. (2000), 'Outlandish fears: Defining decorum in renaissance rhetoric', *Intertexts* 3/22/2000; http://www.highbeam.com/doc/1G1-80849923.html.

Recueil Général des Fabliaux (1872), A. Montaiglon and G. Raynaud (eds.), 6 vols., Paris: Librairie des Bibliophiles , vol. 2.

Rhodes, N., Richards, J., Marshall, J. (eds.) (2003), *King James VI and I Selected Writings*, Aldershot: Ashgate.

Robartes, F. (1613), *The Revenue of the Gospel is Tythes*, Cambridge.

Roberts, Gareth (1976), 'A Re-examination of the magical material in Middleton's *The Witch*', *Notes and Queries*, 221 New series 23, 216–19.

———— (2000), 'the Bodies of Demons' in D. Grantley and N. Taunton (eds.), *The Body in Late Medieval and Early Modern Culture*, Aldershot: Ashgate.

Robinson, J.V. (1999), 'Helena's Living Mother: *All's Well That Ends Well*' 5. 3, 314', *English Studies*, 80, 423–27.

Rochester Wilmot J., Earl of, (1968), 'A Song of a Young Lady to her Ancient Lover' in *Complete Poems*, D.M. Vieth (ed.), New Haven and London: Yale University Press.

Rogers, D. (1642), *Matrimoniall Honour*.

Roper, L. (1994), *Oedipus & the Devil: Witchcraft, sexuality and religion in early modern Europe*, London: Routledge.

———— (2004), *Witch Craze*, New Haven and London: Yale University Press.

Ross, W.O. (ed.) (1940), *Early English Sermons*, edited from British Museum Ms. Royal 18 B.xxiii, London, Oxford: Oxford University Press.

Rowe, G. Jr. (1979), *Thomas Middleton and the New Comedy Tradition*, Lincoln and London: University of Nebraska Press.

Rowley, W., Dekker, T. and Ford, J. (1999), *The Witch of Edmonton*,. P. Corbin and D. Sedge (eds.), Revels Student Editions, Manchester: Manchester University Press.

Sanderson, R. (1854), *The Works of Robert Sanderson, D.D. Sometime Bishop of Lincoln*, W. Jacobson (ed.), 6 vols., Oxford: Oxford University Press, vol. 3.

Secretum Secretorum (1898), R. Steele (ed.), *Three Prose Versions of the Secretum Secretorum* E.E.T.S., London: Kegan Paul.

Schen, C.S. (2001), 'Strategies of poor aged women and widows in sixteenth-century London' in L. Botelho and P. Thane (eds.), *Women and Aging in British Society Since 1500*, London; New York: Longman.

Scot, R. (1584), *Discoverie of Witchcraft*.

Shahar, S. (2005), 'The Middle Ages and Renaissance' in P. Thane (ed.), *The Long History of Old Age*, London: Thames & Hudson, 71–111.

———— (1998), 'Old age in the high and late Middle Ages: Image, expectation and status', in P. Johnson and P. Thane (eds.), *Old Age from Antiquity to Post-Modernity*, London: Routledge, 43–63.

———— (1997), *Growing Old in the Middle Ages* London: Routledge.

Shakespeare, W. (2003), *All's Well That Ends Well*, Russell Fraser (ed.) with an Introduction by Alexander Leggatt, The New Cambridge Shakespeare, Cambridge: Cambridge University Press.

—— (2002), *The Comedy of Errors*, C. Whitworth (ed.), The Oxford Shakespeare: Oxford University Press.

—— (repr.2003), *King Lear*, R.N. Foakes (ed.), The Arden Shakespeare, London: Thompson Learning.

—— (2000), *Coriolanus*, L. Bliss (ed.), The New Cambridge Shakespeare: Cambridge University Press.

—— (1994), *The Merchant of Venice*, J.L. Halio (ed.), The Oxford Shakespeare: Oxford University Press.

—— (1981), *Henry VI Parts One, Two and Three*, N. Sanders (ed.), Harmondsworth, New Penguin.

—— (1988), Twelfth Night, J.M. Lothian and T.W. Craik (eds.), London: Routledge

—— (1961), *The Complete Works*, P. Alexander (ed.), 2 vols., London and Glasgow: Collins.

Sheafe, T.(1639), *Vindiciae Senectutis, or, a plea for Old-Age*.

Shower, J. (1698), *Of Long Life and Old Age*.

Simotta, G. (1631), *A theater of the planetary houres for all dayes of the yeare*.

Simpson, L.M. (1994), 'The Failure to Mourn in *All's Well That Ends Well*', *Shakespeare Studies*, 22, 172–88.

Smith, H. (1952), *Elizabethan Poetry: A Study in Cconventions, Meaning and Expression*, Cambridge, MA: Harvard University Press.

—— 1976), 'Bare Ruined Choirs: Shakespearean Variations on the Theme of ld Age', *Huntington Library Quarterly*, 39: 233–49.

Smith, J. (1666), *The Pourtract of Old Age*, second edition.

Smith, R.M. (ed.) (1984), *Land, Kinship and Life-Cycle*, Cambridge: Cambridge University Press.

—— (1984), 'Some Issues Concerning Families and their Properties in Rural England', in R.M. Smith (ed.), *Land, Kinship and the Life-Cycle*, Cambridge: Cambridge University Press, 1–86.

—— (1991), 'The Manorial Court and the Elderly Tenant in Late Medieval England' in R.M. Smith and M. Pelling (eds.), *Life, Death and the Elderly*, London: Routledge, 39–61.

Smith, S. R. (1976), 'Growing Old in Early Stuart England', *Albion*, 8/2: 125–41.

Snyder, S. (1982), 'King Lear and the Psychology of Dying', *Shakespeare Quarterly*, 33, 449–60.

—— (1992), '"The King's not here": Displacement and Deferral in All's Well That Ends Well', *Shakespeare Quarterly*, 43, 20–32.

Solomon, J.R. (1993), 'Mortrality as Matter of Mind: Toward a Politics of Problems in *All's Well That Ends Well*', *English Literary Renaissance*, 23, 134–69.

Southwell, Lady E. (1996), *A True Relation of what succeeded at the sicness and death of Queen Elizabeth*, transcribed in C. Loomis, 'Elizabeth Southwell: Manuscript Account of the Death of Queen Elizabeth', *English Literary Renaissance* 26: 3, 482–509.

Southwell, R. (1973), *Two Letters and Short Rules of a Good Life*, N.P. Brown (ed.), Charlottesville, VA: University Press of Virginia.

Spenser, E. (1579), *The Shepheardes Calender* in *Poetical Works*, J.C. Smith and E. de Selincourt (eds.) (repr. 1985), Oxford: Oxford University Press.

—— (1590), *The Faerie Queene*, A.C. Hamilton (ed.) (1977), London and New York: Longman.

Spottiswoode, J. (1668), *History of the Church of Scotland*, third edition.

Sprengnether, M. (1986), 'Annihilating Intimacy in Coriolanus' in M. B. Rose (ed.), *Women in the Middle Ages and the Renaissance*, New York: Syracuse University Press.

Spufford, M. (1971), 'The Scribes of Villagers' Wills in the Sixteenth and Seven-teenth Centuries and Their Influence', *Local Population Studies*, 7 (1971), 28–43.

—— (1974), *Contrasting Communities: English Villagers in the Sixteenth and Seventeenth Centuries*, Cambridge: Cambridge University Press.

St. Helen's Association for Research into Local History (1999), 'Angells to yarwin-dels. The wills and inventories of twenty-six Elizabethan and Jacbean women living in the area now called St. Helens', *Wills and Inventories*, Surtees Soci-ety, 1860, vol. 2.

Statutes of the Realm from Magna Carta to the end of the Reign of Queen Anne, 9 vols., Public Record Office, vols. 3–6.

Stearnes, P. (1977), *Old Age in European Society, the Case of France*, London: Croom Helm.

Steele, R. (1688), *Discourse concerning Old-Age*.

Strabo's Geography H.C. Hamilton (trans.) (1854), 3 vols., London Henry G. Bohn, vol. 1.

Strangehopes, S. (1664), *A Book of Knowledge*.

Strode, G. (1618), *The Anatomy of Mortality*.

Taunton, N. and Hart, V. (2003), '*King Lear*, King James and the Gunpowder Treason of 1605,' *Renaissance Studies*, 17: 4 (December).

—— (2001), *1590s Drama and Militarism: Portrayals of War in Marlowe, Chap-man and Shakespeare's Henry V*, Aldershot: Ashgate.

Taylor, J. (1635), *The Olde old very Olde Man or, The Age and Long life of Thomas Par*.

Thane, P. (ed.) (2005), *The Long History of Old Age*, London: Thames & Hudson.

—— (2000), *Old Age in English History: Past Experiences, Present Issues*, Oxford: Oxford University Press.

Thomas, K., (1971), *Religion and the Decline of Magic*, London: Penguin.

—— (1976), 'Age and Authority in Early Modern England', *Proceedings of the British Academy*, 62, 205–48.

Thompson, P., Itzin, C. and Abendstern, M. (eds.) (1990), *I Don't Feel Old: The Experience of Later Life*, Oxford: Oxford University Press.

Thurloe, J. (1742), *A Collection of State Papers of John Thurloe*, T. Birch (ed.), vol. 7.

Tilley, M.P (1966), *A Dictionary of the Proverbs in England in the Sixteenth and Seventeenth Centuries*, Ann Arbor: The University of Michigan Press.

Tilney, E. (1568), *Flower of Friendship*, V. Wayne (ed.) (1992), Ithaca, NY: Cornell University Press.

Trevisa, John (1975), *On the Properties of Things: John Trevisa's Translation of Bartholomaeus Anglicus' De Proprietatibus Rerum*, M.C. Seymour (ed.), 2 vols, Oxford: Clarendon Press, vol. 2.

The True Fortune-Teller (1686).

Vasari, G. (1966–), *Le vitae de'piu eccellenti pittori e architettori nelle redazione di 1550 e di 1568*, R. Bettarini and P. Barocchi (eds.), Florence: Sansoni.

—— (1962), *La Vita di Michelangelo nelle redazioni del 1550 e del 1568*, P. Barocchi (ed.), Milan: R. Ricciardi.

Vaughan, W. (1600), *Naturall and artificial directions for health*.

Virgil, Aeneid, John Dryden (trans.), http://classics.mit.edu/virgil/aeneid.8.viii.html.

—— (2000), *Eclogues*, J. Michie (trans.), London: The Folio Society.

Virgoew, R. (1992) 'The Earlier Knyvetts: The Rise of a Norfolk Gentry Family, Part II', *Norfolk Archaeology*, Vol. 41, No. 3, 249–278.

Vives (1532), *De ratione dicendi* in *Opera Omnia*, G. Majansio (ed.) (1782), 3 vols., Valencia, Monfort.

W[alkington] , T. (1639), *Optic Glasse of Hvmors.*

Wales, T. (1984), 'Poverty, poor relief and the life-cycle: some evidence from seventeenth-century Norfolk' in R.M. Smith (ed.), *Land, Kinship and Life-Cycle*, Cambridge: Cambridge University Press, 351–404.

Wall, R., Robin, J. and Laslett, P. (eds.) (1983), *Family Forms in Historic Europe*, Cambridge: Cambridge University Press.

Ward, W. (trans.) (1578), *Arcandam: The Most Excellent Profitable, and pleasaunt Booke of the famous Doctor and expert Astrologican Arcandam, tourned out of the French into our vulgar tongue by William Warde.*

Warde, W. (trans.) (1630), *The most excellent, profitable and pleasant, booke of the famous doctor and expert astrologian, Arcandam, or Alcandrin to finde the fatall destiny, constellation, complection, and naturall inclination of euery man and child, by his birth: with an addition of phisiognomie, very pleasant to reade.*

Waterhous, E. (1663), *Fortescutus Illustratus.*

Webb, J. (ed.) (1966), *Poor Relief in Elizabethan Ipswich*, Vol. 9, Ipswich: Suffolk Record Society.

Webster, C. (1976), *The Great Instauration*, London: Duckworth.

—— (2001), *The Great Instauration*, Oxford: Peter Lang.

Wentworth Papers 1597–1628, J.P. Cooper (ed.) (1973), 4th series, vol. 12, London: Camden.

Westwood, J. (1985), *Albion: A Guide to Legendary Britain* London: Granada.

Weyer, J. (1563), *De Prestigiis Daemonum*, trans. excerpts in *European Witchcraft*, E. William Monter (ed.) (1969), New York: Wiley & Sons.

—— (1583), *De Praestigiis Daemonum*, trans. J. Shea, in *Witches, Devils, and Doctors in the Renaissance: 'De Praestigiis Daemonum'*, Binghamton, NY, Medieval and Renaissance Texts and Studies.

Whately, W. (1619), *A Bride-Bush: or, a Direction for Married Persons.*

—— (1624), *A Care-Cloth or a Treatise of the Cumbers and Troubles of Marriage.*

Wheeler, R. (1981), *Shakespeare's Development and the Problem Comedies*, Berkeley: California University Press.

—— (1986), and C.L. Barber (eds.), *The Whole Journey: Shakespeare's Power of Development*, Berkeley: University of California Press.

Whetstone, G (1578), 'The Dedication to Promos and Cassandra' in *Elizabethan Critical Essays*, G. Gregory Smith (ed.) (1904), 2 vol., Oxford: Clarendon Press.

Whitelocke, B. (1855), *A Journal of the Swedish Embassy, 1653–1654*, C. Morton (ed.), London: Longman.

Whitforde, R. (1537), *A Werke for Householders.*

Wilbraham, R. (1902), *The Journal of Sir Roger Wilbraham, Solicitor-General in Ireland and Master of Requests for the Years 1593–1616*, Harold Spencer Scott (ed.), London: Royal Historical Society, 1902.

Willis, D. (1995), *Malevolent Nurture: Witch Hunting and Maternal Power*, Ithaca, NY: Cornell University Press.

Wills and Inventories (1860), Surtees Society, vol. 2.

Wilson, T. (1560), *The Art of Rhetorique*, G. H.Mair (ed.) (1909), Oxford: Clarendon Press.

Winstanley, G. (1941), *The Works of Gerrard Winstanley*, George H. Sabine (ed.), Ithaca, NY: Cornell University Press.

With, E. (1659), *Elizabeth Fools Warning*, transcribed in R. Evans (2000), '"New" Poems by Early Modern Women: 'A Maid under 14, Elizabeth With, Elizabeth Collett, and 'A Lady of Honour': Literary Contexts in the Age of Elizabeth, James and Charles', *Ben Johnson Journal*, 7, 447–515.

Woodall, J. (1617), *The Surgions Mate*.

Wright, L. B. (1935), *Middle-Class Culture in Elizabethan England*, Chapel Hill: University of North Carolina Press.

Wright, T. (1601), *The passions of the minde*, Shakespeare Association Facsimile No. 15.

Wrightson, K. (1984), 'Kinship in an English Village' in R.M. Smith (ed.), *Land, Kinship and Life-Cycle*, Cambridge: Cambridge University Press, 313–32.

Young, B.W. (1992), 'Ritual as an Instrument of Grace: Parental Blessings in *Richard III*, *All's Well That Ends Well*, and *The Winter's Tale*' in L. Woodbridge and E. Berry (eds.) *True Rites and Maimed Rites: Ritual and Anti-Ritual in Shakespeare and His Age*, Urbana and Chicago: University of Illinois Press, 169–200.

Index